Managerial Issues in Productivity Analysis

Studies in Productivity Analysis

Ali Dogramaci, Editor
Rutgers, The State University of New Jersey

Titles in the Series:
Adam, Dogramaci; Productivity Analysis at the Organizational Level
Dogramaci, Adam; Aggregate and Industry-Level Productivity Analysis
Dogramaci; Productivity Analysis: A Range of Perspectives
Dogramaci; Developments in Econometric Analyses of Productivity: Measurement and Modelling Issues
Färe, Grosskopf, Lovell; The Measurement of Efficiency of Production
Sudit; Productivity Based Management

Managerial Issues in Productivity Analysis

Edited By

Ali Dogramaci and Nabil R. Adam
Rutgers, The State University of New Jersey

Kluwer-Nijhoff Publishing
a member of the Kluwer Academic Publishers Group
Boston-Dordrecht-Lancaster

Distributors for North America:
Kluwer Academic Publishers
190 Old Derby Street
Hingham, MA 02043, U.S.A.

Distributors outside North America:
Kluwer Academic Publishers Group
Distribution Centre
P.O. Box 322
3300 AH Dordrecht
The Netherlands

Library of Congress Cataloging in Publication Data
Main entry under title:

Managerial issues in productivity analysis.

(Studies in productivity analysis)
Includes bibliographies and index.
1. Industrial productivity-Addresses, essays, lectures. 2. Industrial productivity—Measurement—Addresses, essays, lectures. I. Dogramaci, Ali. II. Adam, Nabil R. III. Series.
HD56.M35 1984 658.5′036 84-12574
ISBN 0-89838-162-2

Printed in the United States of America

Contents

Contributing Authors ix

Acknowledgment to Referees x

1
Introduction 1
Ali Dogramaci and *Nabil R. Adam*

Part One

2
Corporate Tax Policy and Economic Growth: An Analysis 1981 and 1982 Tax Acts 5
Charles R. Hulten and *James R. Robertson*
2.1 Introduction 5
2.2 The Estimation of Effective Tax Rates 8
2.3 Effective Tax Rates on Income from Capital: 1952–1980 17
2.4 The Tax Acts of 1981 and 1982 22
2.5 User Costs and the Demand for Capital 25
Notes 30
References 33
Appendix to Chapter 2 37

3
Inflation and Productivity Growth 49
Peter K. Clark
3.1 Introduction 49
3.2 Measurement Problems 51
3.3 Real Efficiency Losses 57
3.4 Energy Price Effects 61
3.5 Conclusions 63
Notes 64
References 65

Appendix 1 to Chapter 3 69
Appendix 2 to Chapter 3 73

Part Two

4
NIPA: A Model for Net Income and Productivity Analysis 81
M. Ali Chaudry, Malcolm Burnside, and *Dan Eldor*
4.1 Introduction 81
4.2 The Model 84
4.3 The Data 92
4.4 The Results 96
4.5 Uses of NIPA 104
Notes 107
References 108

5
Productivity Measures: Descriptive Averages Versus Analytical Needs 109
Bela Gold
5.1 Introduction 109
5.2 On the Vulnerability of Aggregate Measures of Productivity 110
5.3 On the Vulnerability of Analyses and Interpretations of Industry-Level Changes in Productivity 114
5.4 Elements of a More Effective Approach to the Diagnosis and Improvement of Productivity Performance 119
5.5 Some Concluding Observations 128
Notes 130
References 130

6
Analyzing the Effects of Computed-Aided Manufacturing Systems on Productivity and Competitiveness 133
Bela Gold
6.1 Introduction 133
6.2 Study Objectives 134
6.3 Some Common Elements in Evaluations of Major Equipment Acquisitions 135
6.4 On the Distinctive Capabilities of Computer-Aided Manufacturing 136
6.5 Improving Management's Approach to Exploring CAM Potentials 138
6.6 Improving Managerial Evaluations of CAM Proposals 141
6.7 Some Problems of Implementation 149
6.8 Conclusions 158
Notes 159
References 160

7
Productivity Analysis Using Subjective Output Measures: A Perceptual Mapping Approach for "Knowledge Work" Organizations 161
Michael B. Packer
7.1 Introduction 161
7.2 Present Approaches for Measuring Knowledge Work Effectiveness 163
7.3 An Integrated Approach to Measuring Effectiveness in Knowledge Work Organizations 165
7.4 Conclusions 178
Notes 179
References 181

Part Three

8
Measuring Efficiency in Production: With an Application to Electric Utilities 185
Rolf Färe, Shawna Grosskopf, James Logan, and *C.A. Knox Lovell*
8.1 Introduction 185
8.2 The Production Technology 186
8.3 Measures of Technical Efficiency 189
8.4 Calculating the Efficiency Measures 197
8.5 An Application to Electric Utilities 200
8.6 Summary and Conclusions 204
Notes 212
References 213

9
Alternatives for Productivity-Based Pricing in Public Utility Regulation—The Case of Telecommunications 215
M. Ali Chaudry and *Ephraim F. Sudit*
9.1 Introduction 215
9.2 Rate of Return Regulation: A Behavioral Model 217
9.3 Costs, Rates, and Productivity 218
9.4 A Comprehensive Interim Productivity-Based Rate Adjustment Clause 221
9.5 Productivity Incentives 223
9.6 Built-In Cost Efficiency Incentives 224
9.7 Built-In Rate of Return Incentives 225
9.8 Pricing Efficiency 226
9.9 Uncertainties and Efficiency in Planning and Control 227
9.10 Key Issues in Choosing Productivity and Cost Standards 228
9.11 Adjustment Clauses in Telecommunications: Historical Perspective and Current Practice 232
9.12 Simulation Results 236

9.13 Concluding Remarks 238
Notes 239
References 239

Author Index 242
Subject Index 244

Contributing Authors

Malcolm Burnside, A.T.&.T. Company

M. Ali Chaudry, A.T.&.T. Company

Peter K. Clark, Yale University

Dan Eldor, University of Haifa

Rolf Färe, Southern Illinois University at Carbondale

Bela Gold, Claremont Graduate School

Shawna Grosskopf, Southern Illinois University at Carbondale

Charles R. Hulten, The Urban Institute

James Logan. Southern Illinois University at Carbondale

C.A. Knox Lovell, University of Pennsylvania and University of North Carolina

Michael B. Packer, Management Analysis Center and Massachusetts Institute of Technology

James R. Robertson, The Urban Institute

Ephraim F. Sudit, Rutgers The State University of New Jersey

Acknowledgment to Referees

Anonymous refereeing is a process that accompanies every paper that appears in the series Studies in Productivity Analysis. The list below includes the names of reviewers who contributed to the refereeing of at least one paper considered for this volume. To ensure anonymity, the list also includes names of some additional referees who evaluated papers for other volumes of Studies in Productivity Analysis.

We would like to express our deep appreciation for the expert counsel and guidance they provided.

Robert W. Crandall	The Brookings Institution
Nelson M. Fraiman	International Paper Co. and Columbia University
Barbara Fraumeni	Northeastern University
Arthur W. Harrigan	New York University
Georg Hasenkamp	University of Hamburg
Henry M. Levin	Stanford University
Alex Orden	University of Chicago
Celik Parkan	The University of Calgary
James M. Poterba	Oxford University and M.I.T.
C.F. Pratten	Cambridge University
Eduardo Rhodes	State University of New York at Buffalo
Dan Usher	Queens' University
Leonard Waverman	University of Toronto

1 INTRODUCTION

A. Dogramaci and N.R. Adam

Productivity of a firm is influenced both by economic forces which act at the macro level and impose themselves on the individual firm as well as internal factors that result from decisions and processes which take place within the boundaries of the firm. Efforts towards increasing the productivity level of firms need to be based on a sound understanding of how the above processes take place.

Our objective in this volume is to present some of the recent research work in this field. The volume consists of three parts. In part I, two macro issues are addressed (taxation and inflation) and their relation to productivity is analyzed. The second part of the volume focuses on methods for productivity analysis within the firm. Finally, the third part of the book deals with two additional productivity analysis techniques and their applications to public utilities. The objective of the volume is not to present a unified point of view, but rather to cover a sample of different methodologies and perspectives through original, scholarly papers.

The volume begins with Hulten and Robertson's in depth analysis of corporate tax policy in the United States and its implications on economic growth. This paper is followed by Peter Clark's study of the relation between inflation and productivity. Both Hulten and Robertson's paper as well as Peter Clark's carry important messages to policymakers at the government level as well as to managers and economists who focus on individual firms.

The second part of the volume begins with a chapter by Chaudry, Burnside, and Eldor which is specifically oriented toward business management. The chapter develops a model for establishing links between productivity measures and financial measures that business managers are familiar with. The application of the model to measure productivity of a hypothetical company in the United States is presented together with a detailed discussion on the model's input data and their sources. The next two chapters are both authored by Bela Gold. The first one is entitled "Productivity Measures: Descriptive Averages versus Analytical Needs." In this chapter Gold discusses his views on aggregate versus disaggregate approachs. He follows with a second chapter discussing the potentials of computer aided manufacturing (CAM) systems for providing advances in productivity. Also in this paper he recommends an effective approach for evaluating CAM systems. Part II ends with a paper by Michael Packer who addresses knowledge work organizations and provides an approach that uses graphical means of depicting effectiveness of work units measured through cluster analysis.

The first paper included in the third part of the book is co-authored by Färe, Grosskopf, Logan and Lovell. In this paper measures of overall technical efficiency and its components (purely technical efficiency, congestion, and scale efficiency) are studied using mathematical programming models. The application of the methodology is illustrated using data from electric utility plants. The final paper of the volume also deals with utilities, but from a different perspective. It makes use of total factor productivity measures rather than the frontier based approach of the previous chapter and uses it to develop a productivity based price adjustment method. Thus in the last two papers of this volume, the reader not only gets a picture of some of the models for accounting for productive efficiency, but also an appreciation of their relation to prices we pay as consumers.

We hope that the diverse set of perspectives and methods included in this volume will help stimulating further research ideas in productivity analysis.

PART ONE

2 CORPORATE TAX POLICY AND ECONOMIC GROWTH: AN ANALYSIS OF THE 1981 AND 1982 TAX ACTS

Charles R. Hulten and James W. Robertson

2.1. Introduction

While there is considerable dispute over the contribution of inadequate capital formation to the recent U.S. productivity slowdown, there is a much wider consensus that increased capital formation is a major part of the solution to the productivity problem.[1] During the post-World War II period, the desire to promote capital investment has been translated into a

This paper is a product of the *Changing Domestic Priorities* project which is examining the shifts that are occurring in the nation's economic and social policies under the Reagan administration. Funding for this multi-year study was provided by a consortium of foundations and corporations, principally The Ford Foundation and the John D. and Catherine T. MacArthur Foundation.

Opinions expressed are those of the authors and do not necessarily represent the view of The Urban Institute or its sponsors.

We would like to acknowledge the considerable assistance of Sally Davies on an earlier study on effective tax rates. This paper builds on that previous study, which was funded by the Office of Community Development, U.S. Department of Housing and Urban Development, and by the Office of Tax Analysis, U.S. Department of the Treasury. We would also like to thank Larry Dildine, George Peterson and Robert Schwab, and participants at the Conference on Current Issues in Productivity, Cornell University, for comments on earlier drafts.

series of tax reductions on income generated by business plant and equipment. These reductions were not generally brought about through changes in the nominal tax rate, but were instead effected by liberalizing tax depreciation methods or through the granting of the investment tax credit, (ITC). Following this trend, the response to the slow growth of the late-1970s has been the Economic Recovery Tax Act of 1981 (ERTA), which reduced the tax lives for most assets and increased the rate of the ITC.

This paper analyzes the historical setting of ERTA by calculating the marginal effective tax rates on new corporate plant and equipment for the 1952–1980 period and by comparing them to those which will prevail under ERTA, as modified by the Tax Equity and Fiscal Responsibility Act of 1982 (TEFRA). Following recent trends in the literature, we define the marginal effective rate of tax as the difference between the before and after-tax rates of return to capital, expressed as a percentage of the before-tax rate of return. Measured in this way, the marginal effective tax rate reflects the impact of accelerated depreciated deductions and investment tax credits as well as the tax liabilities imposed by the nominal tax rate. Since marginal effective tax rates are potentially important determinants of investment flows, this approach will permit us to link variations in depreciation policy, the investment tax credits, and nominal tax rates to variations in the rate of capital formation.

Our principal findings may be summarized briefly: During the period 1952–1980, there has been a significant secular decline in marginal effective corporate tax rates on new structures and equipment (see Figure 2–1). This decline was, however, far from smooth with the major tax cuts of 1954, 1962–1964, and 1971, followed by subsequent (but somewhat smaller) tax increases. Each of these tax reductions was preceded by a recession, with the ensuing increases occurring during the subsequent recovery. Overall, the marginal effective tax rate for the total nonresidential business sector fell by almost half, from 61.2 percent in 1952 to 33.1 percent in 1980, while the average effective tax rate fell from 51.5 percent to 38.7 percent.

The business tax reduction embodied in ERTA was far deeper than any of the cuts during the 1952–1980 period. At moderate future rates of inflation (i.e., 6 percent), the marginal effective tax rate under ERTA would have been −11.6 percent when the system was fully phased in in 1986. ERTA thus represented a 44.7 percentage point reduction in the marginal effective tax rates, compared to a 25.5 percentage point reduction in effective tax rates during the Kennedy-Johnson era. However, the size of the ERTA cut, along with a mounting federal budget deficit, combined to produce the major tax increase in 1982. This increase—the "TEFRA

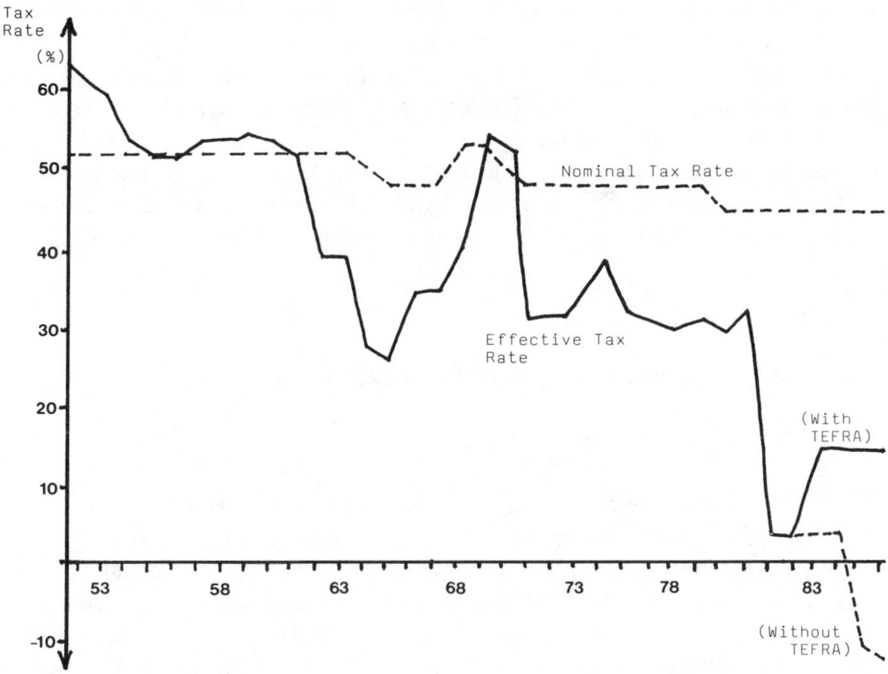

Figure 2-1. Marginal Effective and Nominal Corporate Tax Rates for Total Nonresidential Business

Source: Table 2.1.

takeback"—will lead to a marginal effective corporate tax rate on plant and equipment of 15.8 percent in 1983 and beyond (with 6 percent inflation) and therefore rescinds 60 percent of the original ERTA tax cut.

It is important to emphasize that these estimates depend crucially on the assumed rate of inflation prevailing in future years. If expected inflation rises from 6 percent to 12 percent, the corresponding marginal corporate tax rates under TEFRA would rise from 15.8 percent to 31.9 percent. On the other hand, if the current anti-inflationary monetary policy is successful and the expected rate of inflation falls to 3 percent, the marginal effective corporate tax rate would fall to 1.0 percent. In this case, the corporate tax on plant and equipment would be effectively repealed.

The remaining sections of this paper have the following organization: Section 2.2 provides a description of the theoretical model used in calculations and contains a critique of the framework. Section 2.3 describes the evolution of the tax code and the marginal effective tax rates for 1952–1980. Section 2.4 examines the marginal effective tax rates associated with the 1981 and 1982 Tax Acts. Section 2.5 examines the trends in user costs and the demand for capital. A final section sums up our results and considers implications for future growth in output and capital. A description of the data used and estimates of marginal tax rates based on alternative assumptions and from other studies is contained in an Appendix.

2.2. The Estimation of Effective Tax Rates

Definitions and the Model.

The effective tax rate on capital income is intended to provide a summary measure of the tax burden, net of all provisions in the tax code. It thus measures the combined impact of various deductions, credits, exclusions, as well as the rate structure on the underlying tax base.[2] In principle, the combined effect of all of these provisions is reflected in the wedge between the rate of return on an investment to society (gross of taxes) and the rate of return received by the investor (after taxes).

The concept of an effective tax rate can be made explicit using the following notation: Let K denote the stock of capital, h denote the social return to capital (i.e., the marginal product of capital gross of taxes, but net of economic depreciation), and $\bar{r}$ denote the after tax return to the investor. The effective tax rate u^* can be expressed as:

$$u^* = \frac{h - \bar{r}}{h}. \tag{2-1}$$

The numerator, $h - \bar{r}$, is the tax "wedge." Since before-tax (social) income is equal to hK and the income received by the investor is $\bar{r}K$, the total tax burden is equal to $(h - \bar{r})K$.

The measurement of effective tax rates would appear to be a straightforward application of equation (2–1). If both numerator and denominator are multiplied by K, the numerator can be approximated by the observed taxes paid, and the denominator by observed gross profits. This approach, which yields estimates of average effective tax rates and has been termed the "flow of funds" approach by Bradford and Fullerton [1981] has been taken in a number of studies, (see, for example, Harberger [1966], Shoven [1976], and Hulten and Robertson [1983]). Unfortunately, while the flow of funds approach measures the average effective rate of taxation, it does not yield estimates of the marginal incentives implied by any one tax law. This follows because the observed ratio of taxes paid to gross profit income depends on the time path of past investment spending, and abnormally large expenditures will tend to lower the ratio because of the investment tax credit and accelerated depreciation allowances in the early years of an asset's life. The ratio of taxes to gross income will thus tend to vary even though the tax code remains unchanged, and effective tax rates defined by this ratio will therefore not be uniquely related to the tax code, nor to marginal tax incentives.[3]

The Cost of Capital Approach.

An alternative approach to defining and measuring effective tax rates has recently appeared in the literature, (e.g., Auerbach and Jorgenson [1980], Bradford and Fullerton [1981], Hall [1981], Hulten, Robertson, and Davies [1981], Hulten and Wykoff [1981b], Jorgenson and Sullivan [1981], Fullerton and Henderson [1983], Gravelle [1980, 1982], King and Fullerton [1984], and Hulten [1983]). This approach—termed the *cost of capital* approach by Bradford and Fullerton [1981]—uses the cost of capital framework developed by Hall and Jorgenson [1967, 1971] to impute an effective tax rate to a marginal investment. Under the main variant of this approach, a real after-tax rate of return, $\bar{r}$, is imposed on the cost of capital model, and used to infer a before-tax rate of return, h. Equation (2–1) is then used to determine a marginal effective tax rate, u^*. Since the calculations presented in this paper are based on the cost of capital framework, it is useful to provide a detailed description of this approach.

The General Framework.

The starting point of the analysis is the concept of the rental price, or equivalently, the user cost of an asset. This is the implicit cost associated with using the services of capital for a given period of time. Letting q denote the asset purchase price, c the rental price, $\bar{r}$ the real private rate of return, and δ the rate of economic depreciation, the simplest form of the equilibrium relationship is given by:[4]

$$q_t = \int_0^{\infty} e^{-\delta s} e^{-\bar{r} s} c_t \, ds. \tag{2-2}$$

Note that this formulation assumes a constant rate of economic depreciation, and no taxation.[5] It also assumes that prospective investors forecast a path of user costs equal to $e^{-\delta s}c_t$ over the future time period, and take the present value of these costs to be the value of owning the asset. Equation (2-2) is thus an equilibrium condition, in which the value of owning the asset is equal to the cost of its acquisition, q_t.

The user cost, c_t, represents a cost from the standpoint of the user of the capital services, and a source of revenue from the standpoint of the owner of the capital stock. (The owner and user are frequently the same, in which case the distinction is implicit.) But what determines c_t? The answer is provided by the traditional theory of the firm: If profits are maximized subject to the firm's technology, the user cost is equal to the value of the marginal product of capital. This follows because c_t is the cost of using the capital for one period, and is thus the cost which enters the firm's profit function. If $Q = F(K, L)$ denotes the technological relationship between output, capital, and labor, the value of marginal product is:

$$p_t \frac{\partial Q}{\partial K} = p_t F_k(K_t, L_t) = c_t, \tag{2–3}$$

where p_t is the price of output.[6] Equation (2–3) relates the cost of capital services to the corresponding value, and (2–3) can in fact be combined with (2–2) to eliminate the user cost entirely.

For current purposes, however, this elimination is not convenient. We will use c_t to generate effective tax rates, and therefore make the determination of c_t explicit by solving the integral (2–2) to yield:

$$c_t = (\bar{r} + \delta)q_t. \tag{2–4}$$

This states that the user cost of capital must be sufficient to cover the opportunity cost of tying-up funds in the investment for one year ($\bar{r}q_t$), plus the depreciation costs (δq_t). Economic equilibrium requires that the user cost simultaneously satisfy (2–3) and (2–4).

Tax Policy in the Cost of Capital Framework.

Given the focus of this paper, the cost of capital framework must be modified to include parameters which capture the essential features of the tax code. This may be accomplished by recognizing that the value of asset ownership (the right-hand side of (2–2)) is reduced by a factor $1 - u$, if the marginal tax rate u is applied to income, $e^{-\delta s}c_t$. Tax depreciation deductions are also allowed on the original cost of the asset, and an investment tax credit is granted for equipment and some types of structures. Letting $D(s)$ denote the tax depreciation on one dollar's investment s years in the future, T the life over which the investment is written-off, and k the investment tax credit; (2–2) becomes:

$$q_t = \int_0^\infty e^{-(\delta+\bar{r})s}(1-u)c_t\,ds + \int_0^T e^{-(\bar{r}+\rho)s}D(s)q_t\,ds + k\,q_t. \quad (2\text{–}5)$$

Because tax depreciation allowances are based on the original cost of the asset, q_t, a nominal rate of return is used in discounting $D(s)$. The nominal after-tax discount rate is the real after tax rate plus the expected rate of inflation, ρ. As inflation increases the value of ρ, the expected present value of the depreciation allowances falls. This is the principal way in which inflation enters the analysis.

Equation (2–5) may be solved for the user cost, in the same way that (2–2) was solved to yield (2–4). The result is the well-known Hall-Jorgenson formula:

$$c_t = \frac{1-uz-k}{1-u}(\bar{r}+\delta)q_t, \quad (2\text{–}6)$$

where z is the present value of tax depreciation deductions on one dollar's worth of asset:

$$z = \int_0^T e^{-(\bar{r}+\rho)s}D(s)\,ds. \quad (2\text{–}7)$$

Equation (2–6) is the fundamental equation of the user cost approach.[7] It captures the effect of the investment tax credit through the parameter k, the effect of tax depreciation policy and inflation through the parameter z, and the impact of marginal tax rate changes through the parameter u.

The implications of the present value of depreciation deductions, the z function in (2–7), can be made clearer by considering two special cases. First, under immediate expensing, the value of the investment (q_t) is written off when the asset is purchased. In this case, $D(0) = 1$ and $D(s) = 0$ for s greater than 0. The corresponding z is equal to one. Second, if the tax depreciation deductions are based on economic depreciation, $D(s) = \delta(1-\delta)^s$ when the rate of economic depreciation is constant (as is assumed in this paper). In this case, $z = \delta/(\bar{r}+\delta)$. In general, tax depreciation formulas like straight-line, declining balance, and sum-of-years' digits can be expressed in terms of z functions and embedded in the user cost formula (2–6). For example, the z function corresponding to the double declining balance form of depreciation (with the half-year convention and the optimal switch to straight-line) is given by:

$$z^{DDB} = \left[\frac{(2/T)}{r + (2/T)}\right]\left[1 - e^{-[r+(2/T)](T/2)}\right] + \left[\frac{e^{-1}}{r(T - (T/2))}\right] x \tag{2-8}$$

$$\left[e^{-r(T/2)} - e^{-rT}\right]\left[1 + \frac{r}{2}\right]$$

Note, in this formula, r is the nominal rate of discount, (i.e., $\bar{r} + p$). Similar expressions exist for the sum-of-years' digits and straight-line depreciation methods. By selecting the relevant formula for z and the appropriate tax life T, the depreciation provisions of the tax code can be built into the cost of capital model.

Marginal Effective Tax Rates.

The tax adjusted user cost framework (2–6) is the basis for calculating the marginal effective rate of tax, which captures the combined effects of u, z, and k. The marginal effective tax rate is defined, as before, as the wedge between the after-tax return $\bar{r}$ and the social return h, expressed as a proportion of h. The difference in this approach lies in the way in which of the before-tax (social) return, h, is defined and calculated.

Economic equilibrium requires that the value of the marginal product (2–3) satisfy the tax adjusted user cost (2–6):

$$p_t F_k(\bar{K}_t, \bar{L}_t) = c_t = \frac{1 - uz - k}{1 - u}(\bar{r} + \delta)q_t. \tag{2-9}$$

The bars over K and L denote that these are the profit maximizing quantities of capital and labor. From society's standpoint, however, $p_t F_k (\bar{K}_t, \bar{L}_t)$ is the value of output produced by the marginal unit of capital. Thus, the return to capital from the social point of view (h) is defined by:

$$p_t F_k(\bar{K}_t, \bar{L}_t) = (h + \delta)q_t. \tag{2-10}$$

In other words, given the profit maximizing production plan $(\bar{K}_t, \bar{L}_t)$, the return to society on a dollar's worth of investment is:

$$h_t = p_t F_k(\bar{K}_t, \bar{L}_t) - \delta. \tag{2-11}$$

This is also the return to the taxpaying investor before taxes are paid. But, since h is a before-tax return, and $\bar{r}$ is an after-tax return, the wedge $(h_t - \bar{r}_t)$ measures the effective tax paid on one dollar's worth of investment, and the rate $u_t^* = (h_t - \overline{r}_t)/h_t$ is the marginal effective rate of taxation as defined previously.

An explicit form for the marginal effective tax rate can be obtained by combining (2–9) and (2–10). This yields;

$$h = \frac{1 - uz - k}{1 - u}(\overline{r} + \delta) - \delta, \qquad (2\text{–}12)$$

which, in view of (2–1), implies,

$$u^* = \frac{-(1 - u)\overline{r}}{(1 - uz - k)(\overline{r} + \delta) - (1 - u)\delta} + 1. \qquad (2\text{–}13)$$

This last equation expresses the marginal effective tax rate as a function of the nominal marginal tax rate, u, depreciation policy, z, and the rate of the investment tax credit k. u^* also depends on the after-tax real marginal rate of return, $\overline{r}$, and rate of economic depreciation, δ, and given estimates of these parameters, the effective tax rate associated with any tax policy (u, z, k) can be calculated. Note also that when investments are immediately expensed (i.e., $z = 1$), then $h = \overline{r}$ and $u^* = 0$. On the other hand, when tax and economic depreciation are equal, (i.e., $z = \delta/(\overline{r} + \delta)$), then $u^* = u$, the nominal and effective tax rates are equal.[8]

The cost of capital framework developed in the preceding sections nominally refers to a single type of capital asset. In practice, many types of capital are introduced into the analysis, since different assets tend to have different tax depreciation schedules and different rates of economic depreciation. In principle, one ought to allow for as many different classes of assets as there are economic and tax depreciation rates, but this is computationally impractical and exceeds the limits of available data. As a result, 21 types of equipment and 10 types of structures are typically included in the analysis.

An example.

To see how the model actually produces effective tax rates for individual assets, consider the case of a piece of equipment written off over three years using the current ACRS depreciation system. In the first year of asset ownership, current tax law allows 25 percent of the cost of the asset to be taken as a deduction against income. In the second and third years, 38 and 37 percent of the original cost may be written off. Assuming that the firm in question has sufficient income to absorb the tax deductions, an important assumption implicit in the cost-of-capital model, the present value of the tax depreciation deductions per dollar of asset cost is given by

$$z = .25 + \frac{.38}{1 + r} + \frac{.37}{(1 + r)^2} \, . \qquad (2\text{–}14)$$

This is the z function of equation (2–7); the discount rate r is the nominal after-tax rate of return, reflecting the fact that tax depreciation deductions are denominated in nominal dollars (unadjusted for inflation). Note also that the first year's deduction is not discounted, reflecting the convention that quarterly tax payments are immediately adjusted to reflect the increased depreciation allowances.

Explicit values for z in (2–14) require an estimate of the discount rate r. We shall assume that the real after-tax rate of return is 4 percent, and that the expected rate of inflation is 6 percent. These assumptions imply that the nominal after-tax rate r is 10 percent, and therefore that $z = .901$. Thus, the present value of tax depreciation allowances is 90 cents per dollar invested.

Three further pieces of information are needed to complete the analysis. We assume that the appreciable tax rate u is the maximum marginal corporate tax rate of 46 percent. We also assume that the rate of economic depreciation, δ, is 30 percent per year, and that the 6 percent ITC available to the three year ACRS recovery class is fully used (i.e., $k = .06$). Under these assumptions, (2–6) becomes

$$c_t = \frac{1 - (.46 \times .901) - .06}{1 - .46} (.04 + .30) = 0.331. \qquad (2\text{–}15)$$

Thus, the before tax rate h_t is 0.031, and

$$u^* = \frac{.031 - .04}{.031} = -.295. \qquad (2\text{–}16)$$

The effective marginal corporate tax rate on this type of equipment is thus a negative 29.5 percent. This implies that the deductions and credits accorded this asset can be used to shelter income from other sources.

Implementation of This Framework.

The procedures shown in the preceding example have been implemented in this paper for (1) 31 different types of assets, (2) 8 sectoral divisions, and (3) for the tax code provisions relating to (u, z, k) prevailing in the U.S. since 1952. The following general assumptions have been employed: for δ, we have used estimates of economic rates of depreciation from the Hulten-Wykoff [1981a, 1981c] studies; for u, the maximum marginal nominal corporate tax prevailing in each year since 1952 have been used; for z, we have used data on the amount of investment in each tax depreciation class in each sector to compute a z using the appropriate form of (2–7) and the appropriate discount rate r;[9] for k, the maximum rate of the ITC available to each depreciable asset has been used;[10] for $\bar{r}$, we have used a baseline assumption of 4 percent (based on Fraumeni and Jorgenson [1980] and Holland and Myers [1980]), but present results based on other values of $\bar{r}$ in the Appendix; and finally, for the expected rate of inflation ρ, the estimates of Schwab [1981] have been used, although we also consider other possibilities.[11]

These assumptions yield an effective tax rate for the various types of assets under consideration in each industry. We then aggregate the z and k parameters across assets in each industry to an all-structures and all-equipment total. This aggregation is accomplished using investment share weights derived from the *Capital Transaction Matrix* published by the Bureau of Economic Analysis. The rates of economic depreciation are also aggregated across assets with each industry to obtain the required aggregated industry δ for structures and equipment separately. Given (u, z, k, δ, $\bar{r}$, r) for aggregate structures and equipment in each industry, the computation of marginal effective tax rates is straightforward.

Some Caveats and Comments.

The model presented in the preceding section is subject to a number of qualifications. First, our analysis focuses only on federal corporate tax policy and does not include the additional burden on corporate income implied by the U.S. personal income tax or by state and local government taxes. Our choice was dictated by the following considerations. First, variations in the effective rate of the *corporate* tax have been the primary vehicle used by Congress to stimulate investment, and we wish to trace the history of such efforts. Second, while the combined burden of all taxes is of great policy interest, it is also extremely difficult to measure. The total tax burden on corporate income depends on how the income is distributed (i.e., through dividends, interest, capital gains, pensions, insurance) and on how much financial intermediation takes place. There are, in fact, a multitude of possible total marginal tax rates, and it is therefore not surprising that the various studies of the total tax rate have arrived at very different conclusions.[12]

The second general qualification is that we restrict our attention to the tax treatment of structures and equipment. This choice was, as above, dictated by the fact that Congress has implemented its corporate tax cuts primarily by reducing the tax burden on structures and equipment in order to stimulate investment in these assets. Our choice was also dictated by our aggregation weights (see below), which limited our ability to incorporate the marginal corporate tax on land and inventories. However, even if land and inventories are added into the overall marginal tax rate, corporate income from other assets (e.g., financial income, income accruing to investment in technology, etc.) would still be unaccounted for. However, the results of this paper must be understood as referring only to business fixed investment. It can be shown, however, that the marginal rates of structures and equipment move over time, very closely with the average tax rate on *all* corporate income.

This third qualification concerns our use of investment weights in obtaining aggregate effective tax rates. Gravelle and Esenwein [1983] (among others) have recently advocated the use of capital stock weights instead of investment weights, noting that the latter approach gives more weight to shorter-lived assets than does the former. The use of capital stock weights yields results which indicate the marginal effective tax rate occurring if the entire capital stock is increased proportionately, while the use of investment weights yields results that indicate the marginal tax rate on the investment that actually takes place. While we have chosen the latter, it should be noted that our results based on investment shares differ from the capital stock weighted results of Jorgenson and Sullivan [1981] as to level, but the time trends are quite close.[13]

The fourth qualification to the cost-of-capital model is that it does not explicitly allow for the effect of debt finance. Hall [1981] and Hulten [1983] demonstrate the effective corporate marginal tax rate does indeed change when leverage is introduced. The model as presented above is, however, consistent with leveraged finance when borrowers and lenders are in the same marginal income tax bracket. This special case, which Feldstein and Summers [1979] argue is empirically valid, is in fact an equilibrium condition for the case in which taxpayers in all brackets have the same after-tax real rate of return (Hulten [1983]). Although space does not permit a full discussion of this issue, the basic mechanism through which equation (2–6) comes to hold involves the Cordes-Sheffrin [1981] effect in which increased leverage bids up the cost of borrowing until the debt-equity terms drop out of the cost of capital equation.

As a final comment, we stress that the U.S. Tax Code is an exceeding complex entity that is impossible to summarize in a few simple equations.

Yet it is important for the conduct of economic and tax policy that some insight into the overall trend in corporate tax rates be developed. The cost of capital effective tax rate provides a summary measure which, however imperfect, does indicate the general impact of the periodic changes in accelerated depreciation and in the investment tax credit.

2.3. Effective Tax Rates on Income From Capital: 1952–1980

In section 2, it was shown that effective tax rates can be expressed as a function of the nominal tax rate, the rate of economic depreciation, the investment tax credit, the present value of tax depreciation deductions, and implicitly, the rate of expected inflation. In this section, we present the estimates of effective corporate tax rates on plant and equipment for the total non-residential business and manufacturing sectors, and explain their movement between 1952 and 1980 in terms of changes in the tax code and in the expected rate of inflation.

Effective tax rates based upon our assumption of a 4 percent real after-tax rate of return are presented in Table 2–1.[14] Before 1954, we find that effective tax rates were above the nominal tax rate (i.e., 52 percent) and since we have shown that nominal and effective tax rates are equal when tax and economic depreciation are equal, this would suggest that in 1952–1953, tax depreciation was slower (more decelerated) than economic depreciation. During this period, taxpayers generally used the straight line formula for calculating depreciation deductions. The tax lives of assets were based upon guidelines published by the Treasury in *Bulletin F*, although different lives, based on "facts and circumstances" could be used.[15]

In 1954, there was a major shift in corporate tax policy as accelerated methods of depreciation (i.e., the double declining balance and sum-of-years'-digits methods) were made available to taxpayers.[16] These methods allowed relatively larger deductions in the early years of an assets life, increasing the present value of capital consumption allowances for taxpayers with sufficient income to absorb the deductions. As is shown in equation (2–13), it is the present value of depreciation deductions (z) which is used in calculating effective tax rates. The introduction of accelerated methods of depreciation had the effect of reducing effective tax rates so that they were approximately equal to the nominal rate (i.e., 52 percent). This suggests that the switch from straight-line to the double-declining balance method brought tax depreciation practices roughly in line with economic depreciation.[17] This is consistent with the finding by Hulten and Wykoff

Table 2-1. Marginal Effective Corporate Tax Rates on Plant and Equipment* (Percentages)

		Total Nonresidental Business			*Manufacturing*		
Year	*Statutory Tax Rate*	*Total*	*Equipment*	*Plant*	*Total*	*Equipment*	*Plant*
1952	52.0	61.2	63.4	57.4	62.8	64.1	59.9
1953	52.0	59.2	61.1	56.1	60.9	61.8	58.6
1954	52.0	53.9	54.9	52.1	55.1	55.5	54.2
1955	52.0	51.8	52.5	50.6	52.9	53.1	52.7
1956	52.0	51.4	52.1	50.2	52.5	52.6	52.4
1957	52.0	53.1	54.0	51.5	54.3	54.5	53.6
1958	52.0	53.2	54.2	51.6	54.4	54.7	53.7
1959	52.0	54.0	55.1	52.2	55.2	55.6	54.3
1960	52.0	53.4	54.4	51.8	54.6	55.0	53.9
1961	52.0	51.8	52.5	50.6	52.9	53.1	52.7
1962	52.0	39.6	35.0	47.1	39.2	34.2	50.5
1963	52.0	39.3	34.8	46.8	38.9	34.0	50.0
1964	50.0	27.5	17.8	43.9	25.1	16.0	47.6
1965	48.0	26.3	16.8	42.1	25.7	15.1	45.8
1966	48.0	34.5	29.0	43.8	24.5	28.3	47.1
1967	48.0	34.1	28.1	44.0	33.4	27.3	47.3
1968	52.8	40.7	35.7	50.3	40.1	34.2	53.5
1969	52.8	54.8	55.1	54.2	56.2	55.7	57.2
1970	49.2	52.3	52.9	51.3	53.7	53.6	54.2
1971	48.0	31.3	21.3	48.0	28.5	17.8	52.8
1972	48.0	31.3	21.3	48.0	28.5	17.8	52.8
1973	48.0	34.1	25.1	49.1	31.6	21.8	53.8
1974	48.0	39.3	32.2	51.2	37.5	29.5	55.5
1975	48.0	32.1	21.2	50.2	29.3	17.6	55.8
1976	48.0	31.4	20.3	50.0	28.5	16.5	55.7
1977	48.0	30.6	19.2	49.8	27.7	15.4	55.5
1978	48.0	31.4	20.3	50.0	28.5	16.6	55.7
1979	46.0	30.0	19.1	48.3	27.3	15.5	54.1
1980	46.0	33.1	23.5	49.2	30.8	20.3	54.8

*Assumes 4 percent real after-tax rate of return.

[1981a, 1981c] that economic depreciation appears to follow a declining balance form. It should be noted that during this period the effective tax rates for both plant and equipment remained in the 50 percent to 55 percent range, with the rates for equipment generally about 3 percentage points higher than those for plant.

The Kennedy tax cut of 1962 introduced the investment tax credit (ITC) for investment in new equipment and shortened the tax lives used in calculating depreciation allowances for both plant and equipment. Originally, the ITC amounted to a credit against tax liability of up to 7 percent of the amount of the investment on equipment with tax lives of eight years, or more.[18] Two-thirds of the credit was available for investment in new equipment with tax lives of six to eight years, while one-third of the credit was available for equipment with lives of four to six years.[19] The ITC was introduced in an attempt to promote increased investment in equipment, by significantly increasing the after-tax rate of return. The Kennedy tax cut also introduced Revenue Procedure 62-21, which reduced write-off periods by 30 percent to 40 percent and which also grouped assets by industry and applied a common useful life to all assets in the group, regardless of actual durability.[20] This revision represented an important conceptual shift in depreciation policy, moving away from the treatment of individual assets towards the evaluation of the broader practices of firms and industries.[21]

The impact of the shorter write-off periods and of the ITC was to lower overall marginal effective corporate tax rates from 51.8 percent to 39.6 percent. Furthermore, because the ITC did not generally apply to investment in buildings and structures, these measures led to a considerable divergence between the rates for plant and equipment, (see Figure 2–2).[22]

Another factor contributing to the decline in effective tax rates during this period was the fall in the expected rate of inflation. Using Schwab's [1981] estimates of expected inflation, the rate had reached a peak in 1959 of 1.74 percent and fell steadily to 0.63 percent in 1964. The lower rates of expected inflation resulted in higher present values of depreciation deductions, and thus in lower effective tax rates. This downward pressure on effective tax rates was reinforced by still another component of the Kennedy tax cut: the lowering of the nominal corporate tax rate.[23] The nominal tax rate, which had remained constant from 1952 to 1964, was reduced to 50 percent, in 1964, and was further reduced to 48 percent in 1965.

The period after 1965 was characterized by rising effective tax rates. The ITC was eliminated twice during this period, from October 10, 1966 to March 9, 1967 and from April 19, 1969 until August 15, 1971. This explains, in part, the sharp increases in effective tax rates on equipment

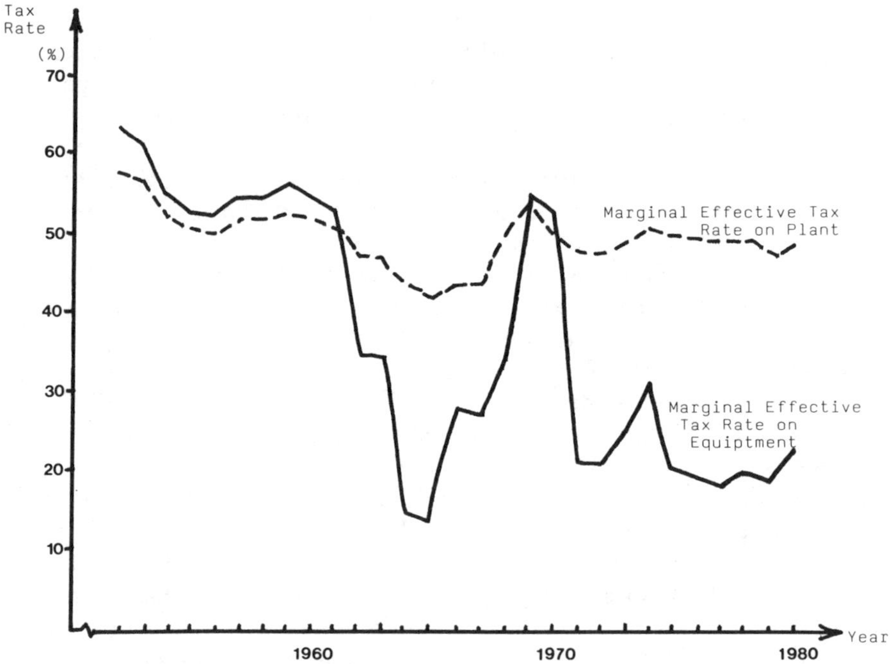

Figure 2-2. Marginal Effective Corporate Tax Rates: Total Nonresidential Business

Source: Table 2-1.

after 1965. However, the rise in effective tax rates after 1965 can only be partly attributed to the repeal of the ITC. Other factors that contributed to this increase included the increase in the nominal tax rate, the limiting of depreciation methods for structures to 150 declining balance, and increases in the expected rate of inflation.[24] Together, these factors, with the repeal of the ITC, resulted in an increase in the effective tax rates for total nonresidential business from 26.3 percent in 1965 to 54.8 percent in 1969. It is interesting to note that the bulk of this increase fell on equipment. During this period, the effective tax rates for equipment rose from 16.8 percent to 55.1 percent, while the corresponding structure rates only rose from 42.1 percent to 54.2 percent.

After 1970, there was yet another shift in tax policy. First, the ITC was reinstated in 1971 and liberalized. The full credit was granted for new equipment with tax lives of seven or more years, two-thirds for equipment with lives of five to seven years, and one-third was available for equipment with lives of three to five years. Second, the year 1971 saw the introduction of the Asset Depreciation Range (ADR) system.[25] Write-off periods were shortened by 20 percent under ADR and the number of asset clauses was increased (to 130). Greater flexibility was built into the system as taxpayers were allowed to use tax lives which were up to 20 percent longer or shorter than the guidelines lives.[26] These changes had the greatest impact on the effective tax rates for equipment, which fell from 52.9 percent in 1970 to 21.3 percent in 1971 for total non-residential business. The effective tax rate on structures also declined, but by much less, from 51.3 percent to 48.0 percent for total non-residential business. These changes reintroduced the differential treatment between plant and equipment which was evident during the mid-1970s.

After 1971, effective tax rates began to move upwards due to increases in the expected rate of inflation. According to Schwab's [1981] estimates, expected inflation increased from 4.00 percent in 1972 to 6.85 percent in 1974, resulting in a rise in the effective tax rate for non-residential business from 31.3 percent to 39.3 percent. The response to this increase was an increase in the amount of the full ITC in 1975 from 7 percent to 10 percent. This reduced the effective tax rates for equipment from 32.2 percent to 21.2 percent for the total non-residential business sector but had no effect on the effective tax rates for plant.

During the latter half of the 1970s, there was relatively little change in effective tax rates. Expected inflation fell somewhat between 1975 and 1978, but began to increase again in 1979 (7.63 percent) and 1980 (8.83 percent), leading to increases in effective tax rates. This was offset to some extent by a reduction in the nominal tax rate in 1979, from 48.0 percent to 46.0 percent.

Overall, the period from 1952 to 1980 was characterized by a series of major tax reductions, each followed by a period of rising effective tax rates. It is interesting to note that recessions occurred before each major tax reduction (i.e., in 1954, 1961, and 1970) and that the tax cuts were motivated in large part by the desire to stimulate economic recovery.[27] The subsequent expansions typically saw a reaction to the tax cuts, during which much of the initial stimulus was taken back. The takeback was explicit in the 1965–1969 period, and was implicit, due to inflationary pressures, during the 1955–1961 and 1972–1980 periods.

This pattern of tax cuts and tax increases reflect the Keynesian policy of demand management in effect over this period. Countercyclical policy does not, however, explain the secular trend in marginal effective corporate tax rates during the 1952–1980 period. The trend rate fell at an average annual rate of 1.0 percent, and, correspondingly, corporate tax revenues, as a percentage of GNP, fell from 5.3 percent to 2.7 percent. The widespread view that the double taxation of corporate income impedes economic growth and economic efficiency was doubtless a factor behind the secular decline of the corporate income tax.

2.4. The Tax acts of 1981 and 1982

The Economic Recovery Tax Act of 1981 followed the pattern of its predecessors. The slow growth of the 1970s culminated in the recession of 1980, and the Reagan Administration took office at the beginning of 1981 with the objective of stimulating economic growth. The centerpiece of the Administration's Program for Economic Recovery was the estimated $750 billion cut in tax liabilities, of which approximately 20 percent was targeted to business tax reductions.

The Asset Cost Recovery System (ACRS) was the principal component of the business tax reduction under ERTA, and included an increase in the effective rate of the ITC, and a considerable shortening of write-off periods for most assets.[28] Where ADR had grouped equipment into 130 categories, ACRS groups all equipment, including public utility structures, into four asset categories, each with a common tax life and depreciation method:[29] three-year assets, which includes autos, light tracks, equipment used in research and experimentation as well as other short-lived assets; five-year assets, which covers virtually all other types of machinery and equipment as well as several types of structures, (i.e., petroleum storage facilities and some agricultural structures); ten-year assets, which includes railroad tank cars, burners and boilers converted to coal from gas and oil, theme and amusement parks and public utility assets with an ADR midpoint life of 18 to 25 years; and fifteen-year assets, which includes public utility assets with an ADR mid-point life greater than 25 years and other buildings and structures. Assets in the three-year class are allowed an ITC of 6 percent, while the five-, ten-, and fifteen-year equipment classes receive the full 10 percent tax credit. Structures (other than those treated as equipment) are assigned a fifteen-year class and are not eligible for the ITC.

The ACRS took effect in 1981 and the equipment component was to be phased in over six years. While the precise percentage deductions for each type of equipment are contained in the legislation, for the equipment and public utility asset classes, they can be approximated by 150-percent-declining balance with a switch to straight-line for 1981–1984, 175-percent-declining balance with a switch to sum-of-years' digits for 1985, and double-declining balance with a switch to sum-of-years' digits for 1986. The fifteen-year structures class is allowed a 175-percent-declining balance form with switch to straight-line and is not subject to the phase-in.

Most types of assets do better under ACRS when fully phased-in than under ADR. Shorter-lived assets, such as autos, do not receive an advantage from the shorter write-off period, but receive added benefits through the increased ITC. Long-lived equipment, on the other hand, does not generally gain through an increase in the ITC, but does receive an advantage from a significantly reduced write-off period.

Effective tax rates under the ACRS are presented in Table 2–3 for three assumed rates of inflation: 3 percent, 6 percent, and 12 percent. From these estimates, it can be seen that even for the moderate levels of inflation that are currently anticipated (i.e., 6 percent), the ACRS constitutes another significant downward plunge in effective tax rates, comparable with the Kennedy-Johnson tax cuts of 1962–1964, (see Figures 2–1 and 2–2). Note that although the tax lives for buildings and structures are significantly

Table 2-3. Marginal Effective Corporate Tax Rates Under ACRS*
(Percentages)

	Total Nonresidential Business			*Manufacturing*		
Year	*Total*	*Equipment*	*Plant*	*Total*	*Equipment*	*Plant*
		3% Annual Inflation				
1981–1984	−16.9	−45.2	30.5	−22.6	−47.6	34.1
1985	−34.8	−73.1	29.3	−39.8	−72.4	34.1
1986	−36.6	−76.0	29.2	−41.6	−74.9	34.1
		6% Annual Inflation				
1981–1984	4.7	−14.2	36.3	−0.8	−18.5	39.6
1985	−10.0	−36.9	35.1	−15.6	−39.9	39.6
1986	−11.6	−39.4	35.0	−17.2	−42.2	39.6
		12% Annual Inflation				
1981–1984	26.2	16.1	43.0	22.0	11.5	46.0
1985	15.4	−0.5	42.0	10.4	−5.2	46.0
1986	14.1	−2.5	41.9	9.1	−7.2	46.0

*Based upon a 4% after-tax real rate of return. See the text and the appendix for further details.

reduced under the ACRs, the considerable differential in effective tax rates between equipment and structures persists, and is further increased by 1986 when fully phased-in.

It can be seen from the estimates in Table 2–3 that the assumed rate of future inflation has a considerable impact on effective tax rates. Even under higher than anticipated inflation (i.e., 12 percent), there is a decline in rates from those in 1980, but with 3 percent annual inflation, the decline in effective tax rates is more dramatic, (particularly for equipment). This makes it clear that the stimulative impact of ERTA, at least with respect to business taxation, will depend to a large extent upon the success of the current anti-inflation policies.

Because federal expenditures proved much more difficult to cut than federal taxes, the most immediate effect of the ERTA was to greatly increase the projected size of the federal budget deficit. In response to those projected deficits, the Tax Equity and Fiscal Responsibility Act of 1982 (TEFRA) was enacted in order to rescind part of the tax cut provided in ERTA. With respect to business taxation, TEFRA cancels the additional depreciation deductions for equipment which were to be phased-in during 1985 and 1986, and introduces a "basis step-down" provision, which reduces the depreciable basis of equipment by half of the amount of the ITC. Because the depreciation provisions for buildings and structures were fully implemented in 1981 and because most buildings and structures are not eligible for the ITC, the TEFRA provisions will have their main impact on effective tax rates for equipment.[30]

Estimates of effective tax rates under the ACRS and TEFRA for 3 percent, 6 percent, and 12 percent rates of inflation are presented in Table 2–4. Under moderate expected rates of inflation (i.e., 6 percent), these provisions will leave effective tax rates below those which prevailed in 1980, but will result in significant increases above those which would have resulted under the ACRS. At a 6 percent rate of inflation, ACRS cut the effective tax rate by 44.7 percentage points. Approximately two-thirds of the reduction was due to the 1981–1984 part of the phase-in, with the rest attributed to the 1985 and 1986 components of the phase-in. Thus, by rescinding the latter, TEFRA takes back nearly one-third of the ACRS tax cut. The basis step-down aspect of TEFRA also has a significant impact. This provision raises effective tax rates from 4.7 to 15.8 percent, and thus takes back another one-fourth of the original tax cut. Overall, nearly 60 percent of the original ACRS cuts are rescinded by TEFRA.[31]

Another important aspect of TEFRA must be noted. Because the TEFRA provisions result in increases in effective tax rates for equipment relative to plant, it will largely eliminate the increase in the differential

Table 2-4. Marginal Effective Corporate Tax Rates Under ACRS and TEFRA* (Percentages)

	Total Nonresidential Business			*Manufacturing*		
Year	*Total*	*Equipment*	*Plant*	*Total*	*Equipment*	*Plant*
	------------ *3% Annual Inflation* ------------					
1981–1982	−16.9	−45.2	30.5	−22.6	−47.6	34.1
1983+	1.0	−16.5	30.5	−3.2	−19.6	34.1
	------------ *6% Annual Inflation* ---------					
1981–1982	4.7	−14.2	36.3	−0.8	−18.5	39.6
1983+	15.8	3.5	36.3	11.7	−0.6	39.6
	------ *12% Annual Inflation* ---------					
1981–1982	26.2	16.1	43.0	22.0	11.5	46.0
1983+	31.9	25.2	43.0	28.6	21.0	46.0

*Based upon a 4% after-tax rate of return. See the text and the appendix for further details.

between plant and equipment which would have taken place under ACRS.

2.5 User Costs and the Demand for Capital

Our analysis has thus far concentrated on the effective tax rates on corporate structures and equipment. These tax rates indicate the extent to which marginal tax burdens have changed in response to changes in the tax code and variations in the rate of inflation. Effective tax rates do not, however, indicate the impact that inflation and tax code changes will have on the demand for capital. Rather, it is the user cost of capital which determines, *ceteris paribus*, the optimal stock of capital.

Recall from equation (2–3) that the value of the marginal product (VMP) of each type of capital is equal to the corresponding user cost c_t. These relationships, along with the VMP equation for other non-capital inputs, determines the derived demand for each input. For the ith type of capital, the derived demand has the form

$$K_{i,t} = \phi^i(\overline{c}_t, \overline{w}_t, Q_t),$$

where $\overline{c}_t$ is a vector containing the individual user costs for each type of capital, and $\overline{w}_t$ is a vector of non-capital input prices. Given the usual concavity conditions on the technology $F(\cdot)$, a tax-induced reduction in the user cost will lead, other variables held constant, to a larger desired flow of capital services. Furthermore, when the production function has two types of capital, structures S and equipment E, and can be written in separable form

$$Q_t = F(L_t, K(E_t, S_t), A_t).$$

the ratio of desired equipment to structures is determined by the ratio of the user cost of structures c_S to the user cost of equipment c_E. Tax-induced changes in the ratio c_S/c_E will lead to changes in the ratio S/E, and thus to the relative demand for structures and equipment.

The user cost, rather than the effective tax rate, is therefore the appropriate variable to analyze when considering the demand for capital. Fortunately, the same framework generating the effective tax rates u^* also generates estimates of the user costs (via equation (2–6)). Such estimates are presented in Table 2–5, which parallels the effective tax rates of Table 2–2.[32]

The user costs of both structures and equipment were at their highest levels during the 1950s, as were the corresponding effective tax rates. The Kennedy-Johnson tax cut in the early 1960s lowered the user cost of both types of capital, with equipment benefiting more than structures (as indicated in the c_S/c_E ratios of columns (3) and (6)). This, too, parallels the experience of the effective tax rates. The user costs rose again in the 1966–1971 period, as did effective tax rates, and were brought down again in 1971. The user cost of both structures and equipment were relatively constant throughout the 1970s with the c_S/c_E ratio more favorable to equipment than any time since 1952.

The user costs associated with ERTA and TEFRA are also shown in Table 2–5. ERTA is seen to have reduced the equipment user cost in total nonresidential business by 8.2 percent, and the structure user cost by 14.4 percent. This pattern is rather surprising in light of the preceding discussion in which ERTA was shown to have lowered the effective tax rate of equipment to a much greater extent than it lowered the effective tax rate on structures (see Table 2–3). The reason for this apparent paradox is that the average rate of economic depreciation is much higher for equipment (approximately 15 percent) than for structures (approximately 3 percent). Since the user cost includes the cost of economic depreciation, a much greater effective tax cut is required to change the user cost of equipment by

Table 2-5. User Costs for Plant and Equipment

	Total Nonresidential Business			*Manufacturing*		
	Equipment[a] (1)	*Structures*[a] (2)	*Ratio of (2) to (1)* (3)	*Equipment*[a] (4)	*Structures*[a] (5)	*Ratio of (5) to (4)* (6)
1952	26.5	12.6	.475	25.2	13.7	.543
1953	25.9	12.3	.476	24.5	13.4	.546
1954	24.5	11.6	.473	23.0	12.4	.541
1955	24.0	11.3	.471	22.5	12.2	.539
1956	23.9	11.3	.471	22.5	12.1	.539
1957	24.3	11.5	.473	22.8	12.3	.540
1958	24.3	11.5	.473	22.9	12.3	.540
1959	24.5	11.6	.474	23.0	12.5	.541
1960	24.4	11.5	.473	22.9	12.4	.540
1961	24.0	11.3	.471	22.5	12.2	.539
1962	21.8	10.8	.496	20.1	11.8	.586
1963	21.7	10.7	.494	20.1	11.7	.583
1964	20.5	10.4	.506	18.8	11.3	.603
1965	20.4	10.1	.497	18.7	11.1	.592
1966	21.2	10.3	.487	19.6	11.3	.574
1967	21.2	10.4	.490	19.5	11.3	.578
1968	21.7	11.3	.519	20.1	12.3	.612
1969	24.5	12.0	.488	23.0	13.0	.566
1970	24.1	11.4	.475	22.6	12.4	.549
1971	20.7	10.9	.528	18.9	12.2	.645
1972	20.7	10.9	.528	18.9	12.2	.645
1973	20.9	11.1	.530	19.1	12.4	.646

(continued)

Table 2-5. *(continued)*

	Total Nonresidential Business			*Manufacturing*		
	Equipment[a] (1)	*Structures*[a] (2)	*Ratio of (2) to (1)* (3)	*Equipment*[a] (4)	*Structures*[a] (5)	*Ratio of (5) to (4)* (6)
1974	21.5	11.4	.531	19.7	12.7	.645
1975	20.7	11.3	.544	18.9	12.8	.676
1976	20.6	11.2	.545	18.8	12.7	.677
1977	20.5	11.2	.545	18.7	12.7	.677
1978	20.6	11.2	.545	18.8	12.7	.677
1979	20.5	11.0	.534	18.8	12.4	.662
1980	20.8	11.1	.533	19.0	12.5	.659
1981	19.1	9.5	.498	17.4	10.3	.594
1982	19.1	9.5	.498	17.4	10.3	.594
1983+	19.7	9.5	.482	18.0	10.3	.572
Detail: User Costs if TEFRA had not been enacted:						
1983	19.1	9.5	.498	17.4	10.3	.594
1984	19.1	9.5	.498	17.4	10.3	.594
1985	18.5	9.4	.508	16.9	10.3	.612
1986+	18.5	9.4	.509	16.9	10.3	.613

[a]Cents per dollar of asset cost.

1 percent than is required to change the user cost of structures by the same percentage.

Thus, while ERTA reduced the effective tax rate of equipment by 160 percent and the effective tax rate on structures by 26 percent (at a 6 percent expected rate of inflation) the resulting change in the hurdle rates of return, h_t, was only 32.7 percent for equipment and 20.2 percent for structures. Since $c = h + \delta$, the percentage change in c is

$$\frac{dc}{c} = \frac{h}{h + \delta} \frac{dh}{h}.$$

The resulting change in user cost is therefore only a fraction of the change in the hurdle rate, and this fraction is much smaller for equipment (around 20 percent) than for structures (around 70 percent). The result is a larger change in the structure's users costs.

Another implication of this line of argument is that rather large changes in tax policy do not seem to produce large changes in user costs. For example, the 160 percent change in the effective tax rate on equipment produces only an 8 percent change in the user cost. This seems to suggest that tax policy operating through the user cost does not have a very strong effect on the demand for capital. This inference is, however, not correct. According to Bureau of Labor Statistics estimates, the 1980 stock of equipment in the business sector was \$727 billion. Assuming own price elasticity of demand of one (i.e., a Cobb-Douglas production function), the 8 percent changes in the user cost implies a \$58 billion change in the desired level of equipment. Since net investment in equipment averaged \$38 billion per year in the preceding three years, the \$58 billion increase, if phased in over three years, represents a 50 percent increase in the net investment required to attain the new desired level of the equipment stock.

The preceding example raises the question of how potent has tax policy actually been in stimulating investment spending. This question has been debated for years with no resolution and is beyond the scope of this paper (for a sense of the disarray of the relevant literature, see Clark [1979], Chirenko and Eisner [1981], and Feldstein [1982]). It is, however, interesting to note that the introduction of the ITC in 1962, and the consequent twist in the c_S/c_E ratios of columns (3) and (6), were associated with a relative boom in equipment investment. In 1961, the BEA equipment stock (in constant dollars) stood at \$233 billion, and the non-residential structures stock at \$326 billion.[33] By 1979, the corresponding figures were \$577 billion and \$597 billion. This shift in favor of equipment accords well the theory of section 2.2 and with the converse shift in the c_S/c_E ratio from

.47 to .53 (that is, as structures became relatively more expensive, substitution in favor of equipment took place).

The composition of capital is thus apparently influenced by tax policy. Whether or not the *level* of investment spending is also influenced is more controversial. The Kennedy-Johnson tax cut was indeed followed by an investment boom, but the 1971 tax cut failed to result in a major expansion. This reflects the fact that investment demand is also strongly influenced by expected output demand, interest rates, and inflation. These variables were generally more favorable to investment in the mid 1960s than in the 1970s.

High interest rates and recession have thus far dominated economic events in the 1980s. It is thus difficult to forecast on the ultimate success of ERTA/TEFRA in stimulating productivity and growth. TEFRA provides for a reduction of approximately 10 percent in the average user cost of structures and equipment and this could ultimately trigger a correspondingly large increase in capital formation.[34] On the other hand, the impact of other variables—particularly of high real interest rates—could offset the progrowth effects of ERTA/TEFRA.

Notes

1. Norsworthy, Harper, and Kunze [1979] found that over half of the productivity slowdown can be explained by a decline in the growth rate of the capital-labor ratio, while Denison [1979] assigned a very minor role to capital. The Bureau of Labor Statistics [1983] also assigns a relatively small role to capital formation.

2. It is important to note that only in highly restrictive cases will the effective tax (so defined) be equal to the corresponding nominal tax rate (as stipulated by the tax code). Thus, nominal tax rates are not, in general, accurate indicators of tax burdens.

3. Average effective tax rates are, nonetheless, of considerable interest, since they indicate the burden of the tax system as it is actually experienced by taxpayers.

4. Note that this is not inconsistent to the previous definition of $\bar{r}$ as a *real* rate of return, and that $e^{-\delta s}c_t$ is the real path of the user costs. This convention corresponds to discounting nominal magnitudes with nominal rates of return, and real magnitudes with real rates of return. The distinction between real and nominal magnitudes is important for the discussion of the effects of inflation.

5. The assumption of a constant rate of economic depreciation is not essential to the theory (as Jorgenson [1973] has shown). It does, however, seem to have empirical support (see Hulten and Wykoff [1981a, 1981c]), and will therefore be used in this paper.

Note, also, that the rate of economic depreciation is expressed as a weight $e^{-\delta s}$ associated with the rental, c_t. This convention indicates that the asset loses income-producing capacity at a rate so that the asset earns c_t when new, $e^{-\delta}c_t$ when it is one year old, $e^{-2\delta}c_t$ when two years old, etc.

6. This follows from the maximization of profit, $\pi = pQ - wL = cK$, subject to $Q = F(K, L)$. Note that cK is the relevant total capital cost concept, since it represents the cost of using

the stock of capital for one year. For simplicity of exposition, we assume that the technology uses only one type of capital, K. In practice, we distinguish between many types of assets.

7. Under TEFRA and during certain periods in the past, the tax code has stipulated that the depreciable basis of the asset be reduced by the same proportion of the asset. Under TEFRA, the basis is reduced by one-half of the ITC. This is equivalent to (2–7) to replacing z with $z(1 - (k/2))$.

8. In both of these cases, we assume $k = 0$.

9. The link between assets classified according to their tax treatment and assets classified by industry is based on unpublished data made available by the Office of Tax Analysis, U.S. Treasury. Development of this link was unquestionably the most difficult and time-consuming component of the entire research project.

10. For the years 1974–1980, the available ITC depended on the write-off period selected. The parameters k and z were thus not determined independently. We selected those allowable (k, z) combinations which maximized the total present value of deductions and credits.

11. Schwab's [1981] estimates of expected inflation have been derived by re-estimating the Modigliani-Shiller [1973] model.

12. Feldstein and Summers [1979], and Feldstein, Poterba, and Dicks-Mireaux [1981] find a very high combined tax rate, while Gravelle [1980] argues it is much lower, and King and Fullerton [1984] report a still lower rate.

13. See Appendix Table 2.11.

14. The sensitivity of our results to the assumed after-tax real rate of return, as well as to other assumptions embodied in our estimates, is discussed in an appendix.

15. When *Bulletin F* was originally published in 1931, the burden of proof in determining whether the useful lives claimed by taxpayers was unreasonable lay with the Treasury. Three years later, with Treasury Decision 4422, the burden of proof in determining the reasonableness of asset lives shifted to the taxpayer. Because the *Bulletin F* lives did not necessarily reflect the actual economic lives of assets, disputes arose which, with other changes in tax policy, led to revisions in *Bulletin F* in 1945. As Jorgenson and Sullivan [1981] point out, these revised guideline lives were generally longer than those published in 1931. In addition, in 1953, the Internal Revenue Service announced that "revenue employees shall propose adjustments in the depreciation deduction only when there is clear and convincing basis for change," thereby shifting the burden of proof of reasonableness back to the Treasury.

16. It should be noted that accelerated methods of depreciation (e.g., 150 declining balance) had been available prior to 1954 for certain types of assets, but that the straight-line method was used for a large proportion of investment.

17. Although the sum-of-years' digits method may yield a higher present value of depreciation deductions, according to the Office of Tax Analysis, Department of the Treasury, the great majority of taxpayers used the double-declining balance method, with the optimal switch to straight-line, during this period. When the sum-of-years' digits method is adopted, an initial adjustment for the asset's scrap value must be made, which makes this method more difficult to use and can result in a lower present value of depreciation deductions.

18. One provision in the 1962 legislation, the Long Amendment, required firms to reduce the depreciable basis of assets by the amount of the ITC. This "basis step-down," which was repealed in 1964, reduced the effective rate of the ITC to the taxpayer.

19. An ITC of 3 percent for some public utility structures was granted, which explains, in part, why the effective tax rates for total non-residential plant declined somewhat more than did the rates for manufacturing plant. Public utilities accounted for approximately 20 percent of total non-residential business investment, but are not included in the estimates for the manufacturing section.

20. Rev. Proc. 62-21 lives were 30 percent to 40 percent shorter than the stated *Bulletin F* lives, but only 15 percent shorter than the effective *Bulletin F* lives. A press release from the Department of the Treasury (July 1962) noted that in practice, taxpayers had previously claimed asset lives which were about 21 percent shorter than the stated *Bulletin F* lives. Note that we have used the effective *Bulletin F* lives in our analysis.

21. Rev. Proc. 62-21 also established the Reserve Ratio Test, which was intended to serve as a basis for checking the reasonableness of individual firm's depreciation practices. The Reserve Ratio Test, which proved to be cumbersome and difficult to administer, was never fully implemented because of the long transition period.

22. To consider the value of the ITC and the impact of the Long Amendment, note that for a qualifying asset with a useful life of 10 years, the present value of depreciation deductions on one dollar of investment would be $0.8655. With the repeal of the Long Amendment, the present value of tax benefits would be $0.9253, 8.2% greater than the present value of depreciation in deductions without the ITC.

23. It should be noted that lower nominal tax rates apply to lower levels of corporate income and that when we refer to the nominal tax rates, it is to the maximum rate. See appendix Table 2–7.

24. In 1968, the Vietnam War tax surcharge increased the nominal rate to 52.8 percent, although by 1970, the surcharge had been reduced by 75 percent, leaving the nominal tax rates at 48.2 percent. The expected rate of inflation rose steadi'v between 1964 and 1970, from 0.63 percent to 3.9 percent, reducing the present value of depreciation deductions and thereby increasing the effective tax rate. Finally, beginning in 1969, the depreciation of buildings and structures was restricted to the 150-declining balance method, where the double-declining balance method had been previously available.

25. Like Revenue Procedures 62-21, the ADR system was originally designed to be a self-enforcing system, requiring taxpayers who adopted tax lives shorter than the ADR mid-point life to report the retirement of assets identified by year of acquisition. Like the Reserve Ratio Test, the information required was found to be excessive and this aspect of ADR was abandoned, although the provisions permitting tax payers to vary tax lives by 20% from the guideline lives was maintained.

26. Since taxpayers were given the option under ADR of choosing lives within a range, and since the allowable rate of the ITC depended on the write-off period, it is plausible that taxpayers selected tax lives that maximized the present value of depreciation deductions plus the after-tax value of the tax credit (i.e., $z + k/u$). The optimal tax life was therefore greater in some cases than the shortest allowable life.

27. The troughs of the three recessions in question were: May 1954, February 1961, and November 1970.

28. There were other important aspects of the tax bill, such as the establishment of the "safe harbor" leasing regulations (which are not considered here since our model presumes sufficient income to absorb all credits and deductions).

29. For a more detailed treatment of these and other provisions in the ACRS, the reader is referred to the legislation or to Deloitte, Haskins, and Sells [1981].

30. The depreciation provisions for fifteen-year public utility structures were to be phased-in and are therefore affected by TEFRA.

31. Other studies of the 1981 and 1982 Tax Acts reach essentially the same conclusions, although differences in methodology and assumptions result in somewhat different estimates of the marginal effective tax rates. Several of these studies are summarized in Appendix Table 2–12.

32. The units in which the user costs are measured are cents per dollar invested. In 1952, for example, one dollar invested in equipment implied a user cost of 26.5 cents.

33. BEA [1982].

34. If the elasticity of substitution between capital and labor is approximately one, a 10 percent reduction would ultimately increase the demand for capital by 10 percent (but only if other factors affecting the demand for capital stay constant). Furthermore, a 10 percent increase in the demand for capital will not be translated into a 10 percent increase in stock unless the supply of capital is elastic.

References

Auerbach, Alan J. and Dale W. Jorgenson [1980], "Inflation-Proof Depreciation of Assets," *Harvard Business Review*, September-October.

Bradford, David F. [1981], "Issues in the Design of Savings and Investment Incentives" in Charles R. Hulten (ed.), *Depreciation, Inflation, and the Taxation of Income From Capital*, The Urban Institute, Washington, D.C., 1981

Bradford, David F. and Don Fullerton [1981], "Pitfalls in the Construction and Use of Effective Tax Rates," in Charles R. Hulten (ed.), *Depreciation Inflation, and the Taxation of Income From Capital*, The Urban Institute, Washington, D.C. 1981.

Chirinko, R. and Robert Eisner [1981], "The Effects of Tax Parameters on the Investment Equations in Macroeconomic Econometric Models," Office of Tax Analysis, U.S. Treasury; Washington, D.C.

Clark, Peter [1979], "Investment in the 1970's: Theory, Performance, and Prediction," *Brookings Papers on Economic Activity*, No. 1.

Commerce Clearing House, Inc. [1981], *Economic Recovery Tax Act of 1981: Law and Explanation*, Chicago.

Cordes, Joseph J. and Stephen M. Sheffrin [1981], "Taxation and The Sectoral Allocation of Capital," *National Tax Journal*, 34(4), December.

Deloitte, Haskins, and Sells [1981], *Accelerated Cost Recovery System*, New York.

Denison, Edward F. [1979], *Accounting For Slower Economic Growth: The United States in the 1970s*, The Brookings Institution, Washington, D.C.

Feldstein, Martin F. [1976], "Inflation, Income Taxes, and the Rate of Interest: A Theoretical Analysis," *American Economic Review*, 66, December.

Feldstein, Martin F. [1982], "Inflation, Tax Rules and Investment: Some Econometric Evidence," *Econometrica*, 50(4), July.

Feldstein, Martin F., James Poterba, and Louis Dicks-Mireaux [1981], "The Effective Tax Rate and the Pretax Rate of Return", N.B.E.R. Working Paper No. 740, August.

Feldstein, Martin F. and Lawrence H. Summers [1979], "Inflation and the Taxation of Capital Income in the Corporate Sector," *National Tax Journal*, December.

Fraumeni, Barbara M. and Dale W. Jorgenson [1980], "The Role of Capital in U.S. Economic Growth, 1948–76", in George M. Von Furstenberg (ed.), *Capital, Efficiency, and Growth*, Ballinger, Cambridge, Mass.

Fullerton, Don and Yolanda Kodnzycki Henderson [1981], "Long Run Effects of the Accelerated Cost Recovery System", Discussion Paper #20R, Woodrow Wilson School, Princeton University, Princeton, New Jersey (revised February 1983).

Gravelle, Jane G. [1980], "Inflation and the Taxation of Capital Income in the Corporate Sector: A Comment," *National Tax Journal*, 33(4), December.

Gravelle, Jane G. [1982], "The Effects of the 1981 Depreciation Revisions on the Taxation of Income from Business Capital," *National Tax Journal*, December.

Gravelle, Jane G. and Gregg A. Esenwein [1983], "The Measurement and Interpretation of Effective Corporate Tax Rates: A Comment," *Tax Notes*, June 6.

Hall, Robert E. and Dale W. Jorgenson [1967], "Tax Policy and Investment Behavior," *American Economic Review*, 57, June.

Hall, Robert E. [1981], "Tax Treatment of Depreciation, Capital Gains, and Interest in an Inflationary Economy," in Charles R. Hulten (ed.), *Depreciation, Inflation, and the Taxation of Income from Capital,* The Urban Institute, Washington, D.C.

Hall, Robert E. and Dale W. Jorgenson [1971], "Application of the Theory of Optimal Capital Accumulation," in Gary Fromm (ed.), *Tax Incentives and Capital Spending*, The Brookings Institution, Washington, D.C.

Harberger, Arnold C. [1966], "Efficiency Effects of Taxes on Income from Capital," in M. Kruzyzaniak (ed.), *Effects of the Corporation Income Tax*, Wayne State University Press, Detroit.

Holland, Daniel M. and Stewart C. Myers [1980], "Profitability and Capital Costs for Manufacturing Corporations and All Nonfinancial Corporations", *American Economic Review*, 70, May.

Hulten, Charles R. [1983], "An Analysis of the 167(k) Accelerated Depreciation Program," Working Paper, The Urban Institute, Washington, D.C.

Hulten, Charles R. and James W. Robertson [1983], "The Taxation of High Technology Industries," The Urban Institute, Washington, D.C. Unpublished.

Hulten, Charles R., James W. Robertson, and Sally M. Davies [1981], "A History of Effective Tax Rates on Income From Capital: 1952–1980," The Urban Institute, Washington, D.C.

Hulten, Charles R. and Frank C. Wykoff [1981a], "The Estimation of Economic Depreciation Using Vintage Asset Prices: An Application of the Box-Cox Power Transformation," *The Journal of Econometrics*, No. 15.

Hulten, Charles R. and Frank C. Wykoff [1981b], "Economic Depreciation and Accelerated Depreciation: An Evaluation of the Conable-Jones 10-5-3 Proposal," *National Tax Journal*, 34, March 1981.

Hulten, Charles R. and Frank C. Wykoff [1981c], "The Measurement of Economic Depreciation," in Charles R. Hulten (ed.), *Depreciation, Inflation, and the Taxation of Income from Capital*, The Urban Institute, Washington, D.C. 1981.

Jorgenson, Dale W. [1973], "The Economic Theory of Replacement and Depreciation," in W. Sallykaerts (ed.), *Essays in Honor of Jan Tinbergen.*

Jorgenson, Dale W. and Martin A. Sullivan [1981], "Inflation and Capital Recovery in the United States," in Charles R. Hulten (ed.), *Depreciation, Inflation, and the Taxation of Income From Capital*, The Urban Institute, Washington, D.C.

King, Mervyn A. and Don Fullerton [1984], *The Taxation of Income from Capital: A Comparative Study of the U.S., U.K., Sweden, and West Germany*, N.B.E.R., forthcoming.

Modigliani, Franco and Robert Shiller [1973], "Inflation, Rational Expectations and the Term Structure of Interest Rates," *Economica.*

Norsworthy, J.R., and Michael J. Harper, and Kent Kunze [1979], "The Slowdown in Productivity Growth: Analysis of Some Contributing Factors," *Brookings Papers on Economic Activity*, No. 2.

Pechman, Joseph A. [1976], *Federal Tax Policy*, The Brookings Institution, Washington, D.C.

Schwab, Robert M. [1981], "Effective Rates of Taxation on Income Producing Non-Residential Structures," University of Maryland, College Park.

Shoven, John B. [1976], "Incidence and Efficiency Effects of Taxes on Income from Capital," *The Journal of Political Economy*, 84, December.

Stiglitz, Joseph E. [1973], "Taxation, Corporate financial Policy and the Cost of Capital," *Journal of Public Economies*, No. 2.

Summers, Lawrence H. [1981], "Tax Policy and Corporate Investment," in Laurence H. Meyer (ed.), *The Supply-Side Effects of Economic Policy*, Kluwer Nijhoff Publishing, Boston, Massachusetts.

U.S. Department of Commerce [1982], Bureau of Economic Analysis, *Fixed Reproducible Tangible Wealth in The United States, 1925–79.* Government Printing Office, Washington, D.C., March.

U.S. Department of the Treasury [1982], "Treasury Interprets Its Effective Tax Rate Tables," *Tax Notes*, December 6.

APPENDIX TO CHAPTER 2 THE ASSUMPTIONS AND DATA USED IN THE MODEL

The estimates presented in the text reflect our basic set of assumptions; a 4 percent real after-tax rate of return, tax depreciation which embodies the half-year convention, and the nominal rate of return equal to the real after-tax plus expected inflation. In this appendix, we examine the sensitivity of our estimates to these assumptions, explain a number of the other assumptions and the data which were used, and finally, contrast our results with those which have been presented elsewhere.

We have relied extensively on three data sources to generate the estimates presented in this paper; a capital transactions matrix (CTM) created by averaging the 1963 and 1967 CTM's developed by the U.S. Department of Commerce, the estimates of economic depreciation developed by Hulten and Wykoff [1981a, 1981c], and data made available by the Office of Tax Analysis, U.S. Department of the Treasury, which was used to develop weights for investment in industry specific machinery and equipment. The average CTM was used to develop detailed investment weights for 32 asset classes (22 for equipment and 10 for plant), for 76 activities.[1] The estimates for total non-residential business are based on all non-residential activities while estimates for the manufacturing sector are based on 52 activities, (i.e., CTM input-output categories 13 through 64). The weights based on the averaged CTM were then used with the 1967

CTM investment totals to yield the matrix used in our structures. They were to be phased-in and are therefore affected by TEFRA.

The tax lives and the methods used to calculate the present value of tax depreciation depended upon the tax code in effect at that time. Between 1952 and 1954, the straight-line method was used for all assets and tax lives were based on the effective *Bulletin F* lives.[2] With the introduction of accelerated depreciation in 1954, the double-declining balance method, with a switch to straight-line at the mid-point of the tax life, was used. As was noted in the text, this assumption reflects the position of the Office of Tax Analysis that the great majority of taxpayers used this method at that time. When tax lives were shortened under Revenue Procedure 62-21 and the ITC introduced, taxpayers were permitted to tax lives up to 20 percent longer than the guidelines lives without being challenged. (Taxpayers were still assumed to be using the double-declining balance methods with the switch to straight-line.) For each asset class, it was assumed that the optimal life, that is, the life which maximized $z + k/u$, was chosen, within the 20 percent range. When the ADR system was introduced in 1971, the permissible range was broadened to include lives 20 percent shorter than the ADR lives. It was again assumed that the optimal lives for each were adopted. Furthermore, according to the Office of Tax Analysis, taxpayers adopted the double-declining balance method, with a switch to sum-of-years' digits.

All of the estimates in this paper embody the half-year convention, which assumes that assets are put in place in the mid-point of their first year of service. Taxpayers are able to deduct one-half year's depreciation and receive the full ITC (if available) during the first half-year. Since assets are generally put in place throughout the year, this is intended to represent average practice. Note that the estimates of economic depreciation have also been adjusted accordingly.

While expressions for the present value of depreciation deductions have been developed (see Hall and Jorgenson [1967, 1971] and equation (2–8) in section 2.2), these are approximations. Rather than rely on these expressions, we have generated estimates directly, by calculating annual deductions and then discounting.

The reliance on a constant after-tax rate of return can be justified given the research of Fraumeni and Jorgenson [1980] and Holland and Myers [1980]. Estimates of the average aggregate real after-tax rates of return by Fraumeni and Jorgenson [1980] were: 4.32 percent for 1948–1952, 4.14 percent for 1953–1956, 3.13 percent for 1957–1959, 5.15 percent for 1960–1965, 6.05 percent for 1966–1968, 5.14 percent for 1969–1972, and 4.84 percent for 1973–1976. (These yield an average of 4.77 percent

Table 2-6. Asset Classes and Rates of Economic Depreciation

Asset Classes		*Rates*
Producers' Durable Equipment		
1.	Furniture and fixtures	.1100
2.	Fabricated metal products	.0917
3.	Engines and turbines	.0786
4.	Tractors	.1633
5.	Agricultural machinery (except tractors)	.0971
6.	Construction machinery (except tractors)	.1722
7.	Mining and oilfield machinery	.1650
8.	Metalworking machinery	.1225
9.	Special industry machinery (not elsewhere classified)	.1031
10.	General industrial equipment	.1225
11.	Office, computing and accounting machinery	.2729
12.	Service industry machinery	.1650
13.	Electrical transmission, distribution and industrial apparatus	.1179
14.	Communications equipment	.1179
15.	Electrical equipment (not elsewhere classified)	.1179
16.	Trucks, buses and truck trailers	.2537
17.	Autos	.3333
18.	Aircraft	.1833
19.	Ships and boats	.0750
20.	Railroad equipment	.0660
21.	Instruments	.1473
22.	Other	.1473
Private Nonresidential Structures		
1.	Industrial	.0361
2.	Commercial	.0247
3.	Religious	.0188
4.	Educational	.0188
5.	Hospital and institutional	.0233
6.	Other	.0454
7.	Public utilities	.0316
8.	Farms	.0237
9.	Mining exploration shafts and wells	.0563
10.	Other	.0290

Source: Hulten and Wykoff [1981a, and 1981c].

Table 2-7. Summary of Corporate Income Tax Rates: 1952-1986

Periods	*Tax Rates*	*Income Brackets*
1952–1963	30.0%	$0– $25,000
	52.0%	above $25,000
1964	22.0%	0$– $25,000
	50.0%	above $25,000
1965–1967	22.0%	$0– $25,000
	48.0%	above $25,000
1968–1969	24.2%	$0– $25,000
	52.8%	above $25,000
1970	22.55%	$0– $25,000
	49.2%	above $25,000
1971–1974	22.0%	$0– $25,000
	48.0%	above $25,000
1975–1978	20.0%	$0– $25,000
	22.0%	$25,000– $50,000
	48.0%	above $50,000
1979–1986	17.0%	$0– $25,000
	20.0%	$25,000– $50,000
	30.0%	$50,000– $75,000
	40.0%	$75,000–$100,000
	46.0%	above $100,000

Source: Pechman [1976], Commerce Clearing House [1980, 1981].

for 1952–1976.) Estimates of effective tax rates have also been made using real after-tax rates of return of 2 percent and 8 percent and they are presented in Tables 2–8 and 2–9, and in Figure 2–3. From these estimates it can be seen that while the assumed real after-tax rate of return does have an impact on the level of the effective tax rate, particularly for shorter-lived assets (i.e., equipment), the pattern of the movement of tax rates between 1952–1986 is preserved for these alternative assumptions. It should be emphasized that the view adopted in this paper is that effective tax rates are usefully interpreted as indices of the relative incentives inherent in the tax system. Therefore, undue attention should not be focused on their levels, but should be directed at the movement over time or the relationship between rates for plant and equipment.

As has been noted, we have relied on estimates for the expected rate of inflation for 1952–1980 developed by Schwab [1981]. These estimates, presented in Table 2–9, were estimated using a polynomial distributed lag

Table 2-8. Marginal Effective Corporate Tax Rates: 2% Real After-Tax Rate of Return* (Percentages)

Year	Statutory Tax Rate	Total Nonresidential Business			Manufacturing		
		Total	*Equipment*	*Plant*	*Total*	*Equipment*	*Plant*
1952	52.0	67.5	70.4	62.5	69.4	71.0	65.7
1953	52.0	64.5	67.0	60.1	66.4	67.6	63.5
1954	52.0	58.5	60.4	55.2	60.0	60.8	58.2
1955	52.0	54.6	56.2	52.0	56.1	56.6	55.1
1956	52.0	53.8	55.4	51.3	55.4	55.7	54.5
1957	52.0	57.0	58.8	54.0	58.6	59.2	57.1
1958	52.0	57.3	59.1	54.3	58.8	59.5	57.3
1959	52.0	58.7	60.6	55.4	60.2	61.1	58.4
1960	52.0	57.7	59.5	54.6	59.2	59.9	57.6
1961	52.0	54.6	56.2	52.0	56.1	56.6	55.1
1962	52.0	36.5	30.0	47.2	35.1	27.7	51.8
1963	52.0	35.9	29.5	46.6	34.5	27.1	51.2
1964	50.0	6.2	−15.8	42.9	−2.1	−24.3	48.2
1965	48.0	7.5	−12.9	41.8	0.1	−20.6	47.0
1966	48.0	30.2	21.2	45.3	28.3	18.8	49.9
1967	48.0	29.7	19.9	46.0	27.4	17.2	50.6
1968	52.8	39.5	30.9	53.8	37.6	28.5	58.1
1969	52.8	61.3	62.8	59.0	63.1	63.2	62.8
1970	49.2	59.6	61.3	56.6	61.4	61.8	60.4
1971	48.0	29.0	14.6	53.1	23.8	8.3	59.1
1972	48.0	29.0	14.6	53.1	23.8	8.3	59.1
1973	48.0	35.0	23.2	54.9	30.7	17.6	60.6
1974	48.0	44.9	37.1	57.9	42.1	32.9	63.1
1975	48.0	32.6	18.0	57.0	27.3	11.4	63.5
1976	48.0	31.1	15.8	56.7	25.6	9.0	63.3
1977	48.0	29.6	13.6	56.4	23.7	6.4	63.1
1978	48.0	31.2	15.9	56.7	25.6	9.1	63.3
1979	46.0	30.3	15.4	55.3	25.2	9.0	61.9
1980	46.0	36.4	24.4	56.5	32.4	19.0	62.8
1981–1982	46.0	−32.3	−76.1	41.1	−46.0	−86.3	45.5
1983–1986	46.0	5.1	−16.4	41.0	−2.5	−23.5	45.5

*Note, the estimates for 1981–1986 reflect an assumed rate of 6 percent inflation and the TEFRA provisions.

Table 2-9. Marginal Effective Corporate Tax Rates: 8% Real After-Tax Rate of Return* (Percentages)

		Total Nonresidential Business			*Manufacturing*		
Year	*Expected Rate of Inflation*	*Total*	*Equipment*	*Plant*	*Total*	*Equipment*	*Plant*
1952	2.95	57.3	58.9	54.7	58.6	59.6	56.4
1953	2.04	56.4	57.7	54.2	57.7	58.4	55.9
1954	1.69	51.8	52.1	51.2	52.8	52.9	52.5
1955	1.00	50.8	51.0	50.6	51.8	51.7	51.9
1956	0.88	50.7	50.7	50.5	51.6	51.5	51.8
1957	1.41	51.4	51.7	51.0	52.4	52.4	52.3
1958	1.46	51.5	51.8	51.0	52.4	52.5	52.3
1959	1.74	51.9	52.2	51.3	52.8	52.9	52.5
1960	1.53	51.6	51.9	51.1	52.5	52.6	52.4
1961	1.00	50.8	51.0	50.6	51.8	51.7	51.9
1962	0.81	42.1	38.4	48.3	42.2	38.5	50.6
1963	0.77	42.0	38.3	48.1	42.0	38.4	50.3
1964	0.63	35.7	29.7	45.7	35.3	29.6	48.1
1965	0.82	33.8	27.9	43.6	33.4	27.8	46.1
1966	1.42	37.5	33.5	44.3	37.6	33.7	46.5
1967	1.66	37.1	32.8	44.3	37.1	33.0	46.5
1968	2.50	42.4	38.1	49.6	42.4	38.3	51.8
1969	3.33	51.3	50.7	52.3	52.4	51.5	54.4
1970	3.91	48.3	47.9	49.0	49.4	48.8	50.9
1971	4.00	33.1	25.4	46.0	31.5	23.5	49.6
1972	4.00	33.1	25.4	46.0	31.5	23.5	49.6
1973	4.83	34.4	27.1	46.6	32.9	25.3	50.1
1974	6.85	37.0	30.6	47.7	35.8	29.1	51.0
1975	7.31	32.5	24.1	46.6	31.0	22.1	51.2
1976	7.08	32.2	23.6	46.5	30.6	21.6	51.1
1977	6.85	31.8	23.2	46.4	30.2	21.1	51.0
1978	7.09	32.2	23.7	46.5	30.6	21.6	51.1
1979	7.63	30.5	22.2	44.7	29.0	20.1	49.3
1980	8.83	32.0	24.1	45.2	30.7	22.3	49.7
1981–1982	6.00	16.7	5.5	35.6	13.3	2.5	37.8
1983–1986	6.00	21.5	13.2	35.5	18.6	10.2	37.8

*Note, the expected rates of inflation for 1952–1980 are from Schwab [1981] and the estimates for 1981–1986 reflect an assumed rate of inflation of 6 percent and the TEFRA provisions.

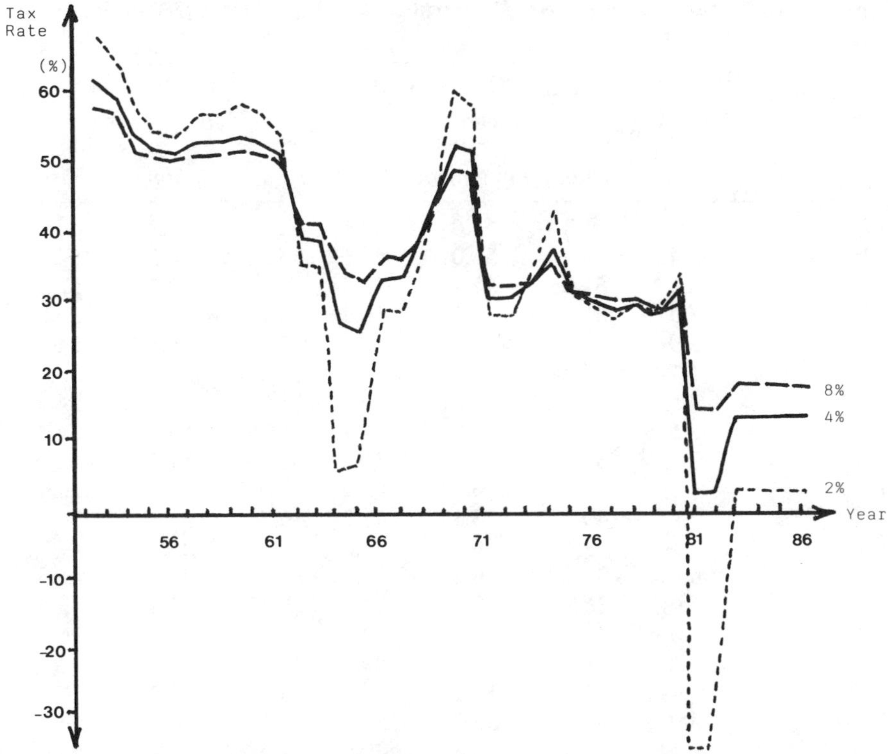

Figure 2-3. Marginal Effective Corporate Tax Rates for (Total Nonresidental Business) Plant and Equipment-Real Rates of Return of 2%, 4%, and 8%: 1952-1986

Sources: Tables 2-1, 2-8, 2-9.

formulation to generate estimates based on a moving average of actual inflation rates.

In addition to our estimates based on constant real after-tax rates of return, effective tax rates based upon historical real after-tax rates of return have been made. Estimates of the real tax rate of return by Feldstein, Poterba, and Dicks-Mireaux [1982] have been used. (Nominal rates of return are set equal to the real rates plus expected inflation as before.) The results, presented in Table 2–10 and Figure 2–4, generally follow the estimates based upon a constant 4 percent after-tax rate of return rather closely, except for 1974, when the real after tax rate of return fell to 1.3 percent. This decline can be attributed to a one-time revaluation of

Table 2-10. Marginal Effective Corporate Tax Rates: Using Real Rates of Return* (Percentages)

Year	Real Rate of Return	Total Nonresidential Business			Manufacturing		
		Total	Equipment	Plant	Total	Equipment	Plant
1953	2.9	61.3	63.6	57.6	63.1	64.2	60.6
1954	3.4	54.7	56.0	52.6	56.0	56.5	54.9
1955	4.6	51.5	52.1	50.5	52.6	52.6	52.5
1956	3.3	51.8	52.7	50.3	53.1	53.2	52.8
1957	3.0	54.4	55.7	52.2	55.7	56.1	54.7
1958	2.7	55.2	56.6	52.8	56.6	57.1	55.4
1959	3.8	54.3	55.4	52.4	55.5	55.9	54.5
1960	3.5	54.0	55.2	52.1	55.3	55.7	54.4
1961	3.7	52.0	52.8	50.6	53.2	53.3	52.9
1962	4.8	40.3	36.0	47.4	40.0	35.5	50.4
1963	5.2	40.4	36.3	47.2	40.2	35.8	50.0
1964	6.1	33.1	26.1	45.0	32.3	25.5	47.9
1965	6.9	32.6	26.2	43.3	32.0	25.8	46.0
1966	6.6	36.8	32.4	44.1	36.7	32.4	46.5
1967	6.0	35.9	31.1	44.0	35.7	30.9	46.6
1968	5.2	41.3	36.2	49.8	41.0	35.9	52.6
1969	4.0	54.8	55.1	54.2	56.2	55.7	57.2
1970	3.0	54.9	56.0	53.0	56.5	56.6	56.3
1971	3.6	31.0	20.6	48.5	28.0	16.7	53.6
1972	4.2	31.4	21.7	47.8	28.7	18.3	52.5
1973	3.6	34.1	24.8	49.8	31.4	21.3	54.6
1974	1.3	50.1	42.0	63.7	46.6	36.8	69.0
1975	2.7	32.2	19.5	53.6	28.3	14.4	59.9
1976	3.3	31.2	19.2	51.5	27.8	14.8	57.5
1977	3.6	30.5	18.5	50.6	27.2	14.4	56.5
1978	3.1	31.3	18.9	52.1	27.7	14.3	58.2
1979	2.7	30.1	17.1	51.8	26.3	12.3	58.2

*The real rates of return are from Feldstein, Poterba, and Dicks-Mireaux [1982]. See the text for details.

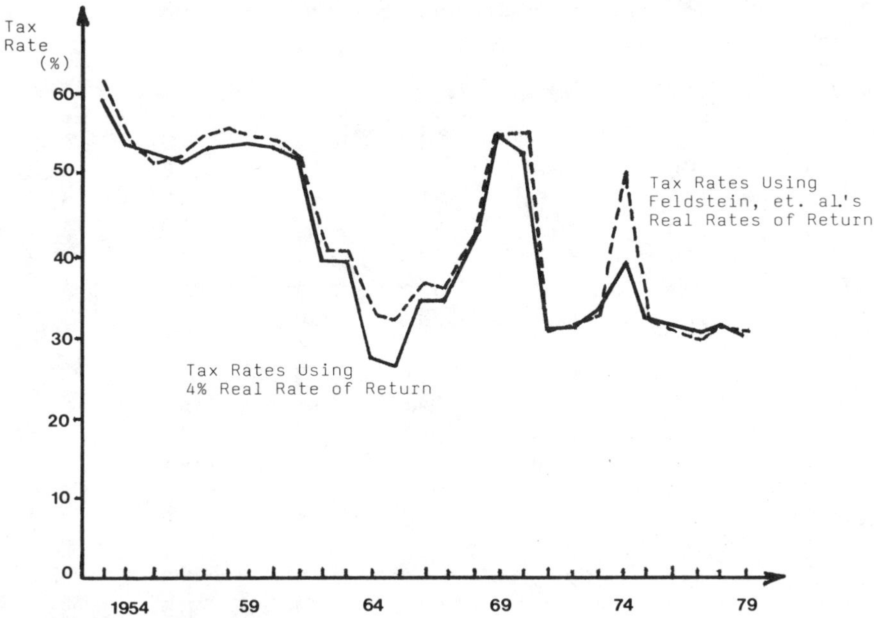

Figure 2-4. Marginal Effective Corporate Tax Rates for (Total Nonresidential Business) Plant and Equipment Using 4% and Feldstein et al.'s Real After-Tax Rates of Return

Sources: Tables 2-1 and 2-10.

inventories. These estimates would seem to suggest that the assumption of a constant real-after tax rate is not inappropriate.

Finally, we contrast our estimates with those developed in two previous studies; Hulten, Robertson, and Davies [1981] and Jorgenson and Sullivan [1981], (see Table 2–11). Beyond extending the coverage to include ERTA and TEFRA, our present estimates differ from those in our study with Sally Davies in several respects. In this paper we have adopted the half-year convention and have assumed that taxpayers use the double-declining balance method, with a switch to sum-of-years' digits for the period 1971–1980. (In this earlier study, a switch to straight-line was assumed.) The estimates in this paper are lower than those in Hulten, Robertson and Davies [1981], by one to two percentage points for 1952–1970 and by five to eight percentage points for 1971–1980, although the movement of effective tax rates during the period is similar in both studies.

Jorgenson and Sullivan [1981] estimate effective tax rates using the same

Table 2-11. Alternative Estimates of Marginal Effective Corporate Tax Rates

Year	*Total*[a]	*Equipment*[a]	*Plant*[a]	*Total*[b]	*Equipment*[b]	*Plant*[b]
1952	39.8	44.5	32.2	62.2	64.0	57.5
1953	41.8	46.0	34.8	60.2	61.8	56.2
1954	36.6	40.0	31.2	55.3	56.3	52.5
1955	37.0	40.5	31.1	53.1	53.9	51.0
1056	37.9	41.1	32.5	52.7	53.5	50.7
1957	39.4	42.9	33.5	54.4	55.4	51.9
1958	37.7	40.8	33.0	54.6	55.6	52.0
1959	41.2	44.4	35.5	55.4	56.5	52.6
1960	41.1	44.2	35.6	54.8	55.8	52.2
1961	39.7	42.8	34.6	53.1	53.9	51.0
1962	28.5	25.0	34.5	41.7	39.3	47.8
1963	26.3	21.9	33.9	41.4	39.1	47.4
1964	23.7	18.9	32.4	29.0	23.0	44.5
1965	21.4	16.0	31.0	27.7	21.9	42.8
1966	27.3	24.7	32.0	36.7	33.7	44.5
1967	36.7	24.0	31.8	36.3	33.0	44.7
1968	25.7	22.1	32.5	43.3	40.3	51.0
1969	37.1	37.8	35.7	56.5	57.2	54.7
1970	41.6	42.9	39.4	54.1	55.1	51.7
1971	28.9	24.4	36.7	37.5	33.1	48.7
1972	22.9	15.7	35.5	37.5	33.1	48.7
1973	25.6	18.8	37.9	40.0	36.2	49.8
1974	28.0	22.1	39.0	45.0	42.3	51.8
1975	21.1	13.1	35.7	40.4	36.6	50.9
1976	16.9	8.1	34.3	39.8	35.6	50.7
1977	13.5	4.1	33.1	39.3	34.9	50.5
1978	18.5	9.9	34.9	39.9	35.6	50.7
1979	19.8	12.1	34.3	38.4	34.3	49.0
1980	24.8	18.5	36.8	41.0	37.5	49.9

Sources: Hulten, Robertson, and Davies [1981] and Jorgenson and Sullivan [1981].
[a]Taken from Jorgenson and Sullivan [1981].
[b]Taken from Hulten, Robertson, and Davies [1981].

framework as is used in this paper, but with a somewhat different set of assumptions about tax lives and discount rates. Their tax rates are uniformly lower than the rates of this study, but the two series largely move together over time, and are thus consistent with the story told in this paper.

Table 2-12. Comparison of Alternative Estimates of Marginal Effective Tax Rates Under ERTA and TEFRA (Percentages)

Study	*PRE-ERTA*	*ERTA*	*(% Change)*	*TEFRA*	*1980 to TEFRA (% Change)*
Hulten-Robertson[a]	33.1	−11.6		15.8	(−52.3)
Fullerton-Henderson [1981][b]	23.3	N.A.		17.5	(−24.9)
U.S. Treasury [1982][c]	42.2	13.1	(−69.0)	28.4	(−32.7)
Gravelle-Esenwein [1983][d]					
Method 1	40.0	N.A.		29.0	(−27.5)
Method 2	25.0	N.A.		17.0	(−32.0)
Method 3	46.0	N.A.		36.0	(−27.8)
Method 4	34.0	N.A.		25.0	(−26.5)
Gravelle [1982][e]	33.1	16.0	(−51.7)	N.A.	N.A.

Note: N.A. means not available.

[a]Assumes a 6 percent rate of inflation after 1980. Note, the estimate for ERTA reflects the fully phased-in provisions of the Act.

[b]Fullerton and Henderson [1981] do not report aggregate marginal effective tax rates, although sectoral averages are presented. These aggregate estimates have been obtained by weighting their estimates of tax rates for 34 assets using 1978 investment shares presented in Jorgenson and Sullivan [1981].

[c]These estimates reflect a 4 percent after-tax rate of return and a 6 percent rate of inflation.

[d]Methods 1 and 2 use investment share weights; Method 1 averages the components of the rental price equation while Method 2 averages the pre-tax rates of returns. Methods 3 and 4 use capital stock weights and correspond to Methods 1 and 2, respectively. These estimates reflect a 4.0 percent after-tax rate of return.

[e]These estimates reflect a 4.6 percent after-tax rate of return.

Appendix Notes

1. The CTM contains data for 77 activities, but one, real estate, has been dropped as being inappropriate for this analysis.

2. It was pointed out in the text that the Treasury noted in 1962 that in practice, taxpayers had been claiming lives which were approximately 21% shorter than those stated in *Bulletin F*. We have used the effective (shorter) estimated of *Bulletin F* lives. Estimates of effective tax rates based on the stated *Bulletin F* lives are presented in Hulten, Robertson, and Davies [1981].

3 INFLATION AND PRODUCTIVITY GROWTH

Peter K. Clark

3.1. Introduction

During the past 15 years, the United States has experienced a dramatic decline in the growth of the productivity of its private enterprises. In the two decades before the mid-1960s, real output per hour of labor input grew at an average rate of about 2.5 percent per year, fueling a dramatic rise in both the amount of goods and services produced, and the average real wage of American workers. Since then, productivity performance has been much poorer, falling to about 2 percent per year in 1965–1973 and to about 1 percent per year in 1973–1978. Even this low level, about half of the twentieth century average of approximately 2 percent a year, is less worrisome than the downward movement in productivity that has occurred in the past three years. Since the fourth quarter of 1978, the Bureau of

---

This research was supported in part by a National Fellowship from the Hoover Institution on War, Revolution, and Peace at Stanford University. The views expressed in this paper are those of the author and do not necessarily represent the views of the Board of Governors or the staff of the Federal Reserve System

This paper was presented at Conference in Current Issues in Productivity at Rutgers The State University of New Jersey while the author was working at the Board of Governors of the Federal Reserve System.

Labor Statistics estimates that real output per hour in the private non-farm business sector has fallen almost continuously at a rate of nearly 1 percent a year. This decline is very similar to the one experienced in 1973 and 1974.

The deterioration of U.S. productivity performance has sparked a resurgence of interest in the sources of U.S. economic growth. However, the renewed research effort has not been able to find a convincing explanation for slow productivity growth. Edward F. Denison, the preeminent analyst of economic growth in the United States, has no trouble explaining the reduction in productivity growth after 1965 but before 1973,[1] but finds the collapse in productivity performance since 1973 completely mysterious. After estimating the effects of average labor quality, capital per worker, improved resource allocation, changes in the legal and human environment, and economies of scale, Denison finds that they neither individually nor collectively explain the drop in productivity growth that he isolates in the years since 1973. In conclusion, he states:

> The contribution of advances in knowledge and miscellaneous determinants to growth rates in nonresidential business, as measured by the residual series, fell from 1.4 percent per year in the 1948–73 period to −0.8 percent per year in the 1973–76 period. That I do not know why the record turned so bad after 1973 must be obvious, because the effects of all the output determinants I could measure continuously are excluded from the residual.[2]

In their 1979 Brookings study, Norsworthy, Harper, and Kunze come to exactly the opposite conclusion. They find that the difference in labor productivity growth between 1965–1973 and 1973–1978 can be attributed to slower growth in the capital intensity of production, but the difference between labor productivity performance between 1948–1965 and 1965–1973 remains a mystery.[3] I have taken an intermediate position between these two:

> ... 'the case of the missing productivity' is a two-part mystery extending through both the 1965–73 and 1973–78 periods.[4]

While a large number of hypotheses have been advanced about the productivity slowdown[5] very little attention has been paid to the fact that slower productivity growth in the United States has been closely correlated with the other major economic development since World War II: the shift from price stability before the mid-1960s to persistent inflation since that time.

In fact, the timing of reductions in productivity growth strongly suggests that the productivity slowdown is related to the inflationary process. Labor productivity started increasing more slowly in the mid-1960s, just as the current inflationary spiral gained momentum. In the 1970s, as inflation increased, productivity performance deteriorated even further. On a cyclically adjusted basis, the underlying trend in productivity growth seems to have been reduced in two stages, as shown in Figure 3–1A. The first stage starts in the mid-1960s and lasts until 1973; productivity growth in the private nonfarm sector dropped from about 2.5 percent to 2.0 percent per year. The second stage starts in 1973 and continues through the latest available observation in the fourth quarter of 1980. In the past seven years, the trend in labor productivity growth has fallen to a meager 0.5 percent per year. By the end of 1979, private output was fully one-sixth less than it would have if the 1948–1965 trend in labor productivity had been maintained.

Increases in the price level have followed a very similar pattern, as shown in Figure 3–1B. Between the wars in Korea and Vietnam, prices were very stable, with the annual increase in the GNP deflator averaging less than 2 percent per year between 1952 and 1965. In 1965–1973, these increases accelerated to 4½ percent per year, and since 1973 the GNP deflator has grown at almost an 8 percent annual rate.

Deviations of the price level and productivity from their pre-1965 trends are proportional, as shown in Figure 3–2. With vertical scales adjusted appropriately, the increases in the inflation rate closely track the reductions in productivity growth that the economy has experienced. *Over the past 15 years, each increase of 1 percent in the inflation rate has been associated with a reduction in productivity growth of about one-quarter of a percentage point per year.* In the rest of this paper I will argue that the correlation between inflation and productivity growth observed in the United States since 1948 is more than a statistical accident. A number of theoretical considerations support the hypothesis that inflation since the mid-1960s has been a major cause of slower growth in real output per unit of input.

3.2. Measurement Problems

Explanations of the high correlation between increases in the price level and decreases in productivity growth fall into two distinct categories: measurement errors and real efficiency losses. Any estimate of economy-wide productivity growth is subject to a wide spectrum of errors; measures of output, capital input and labor input could all be severely distorted. The

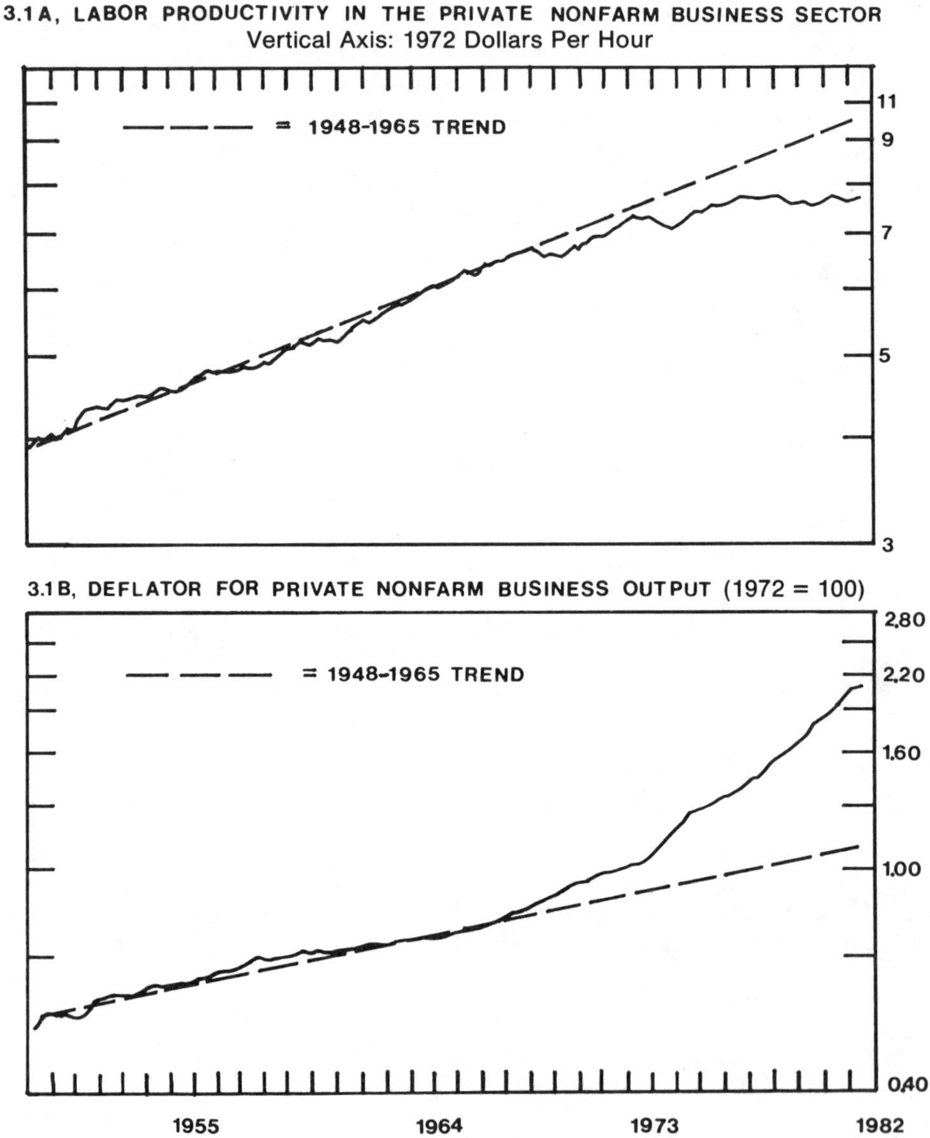

Figure 3-1. Labor Productivity and Prices, 1948-1982

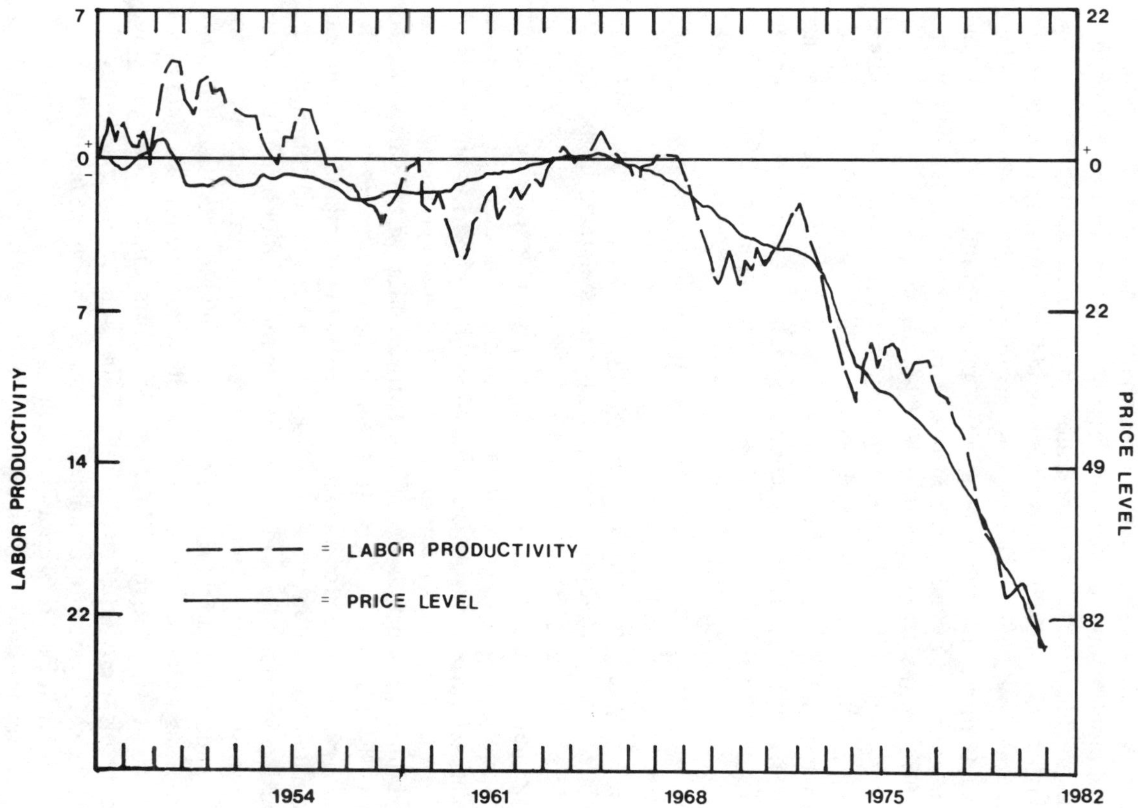

Figure 3-2. Deviations (in per cent) of Labor Productivity and the Price Level from 1948–1965 Trends

two basic problems are, first, the estimation of physical volumes of individual input or output items, and second, the construction of an index of these individual items that represents a meaningful aggregate.

By far the most likely place for inflation-induced measurement errors to enter labor productivity statistics is in the estimation of individual components of real output. Almost all of private nonfarm nonresidential output is estimated by the Department of Commerce by deflating nominal expenditure figures. That is, current-dollar estimates of expenditures are divided by a price index based on the Consumer Price Index, the Producer Price Index, or prices from some other source. Any upward bias in the price series used to deflate nominal expenditures would be translated on a one-for-one basis into a spurious reduction in productivity. Between 1965 and 1980, the deflator for nonfarm nonresidential output increased nearly 150 percent. If 20 percentage points (or less than one-sixth) of this increase was fictitious, it would totally explain the apparent slowdown in labor productivity.

There are good reasons for suspecting that the nominal GNP is overdeflated and real output growth has been understated in the past 15 years. First, the ratio of list prices to transaction prices has probably increased, imparting an upward bias to those price indexes which are based on list prices. High rates of inflation bring with them an increased probability of price controls, and one obvious method for businesses to avoid these controls is a system of high list prices and variable discounts. If the government decides to freeze prices, transaction prices can be raised while the list price is held constant. Since the list price is typically the maximum price charged for an item, an increase in the inflation rate should be associated with an increase in the difference between list price and the average of prices actually paid. While the Bureau of Labor Statistics tries to obtain transaction prices in all cases, many prices are estimated from voluntary submissions by firms who have a number of incentives to report list prices only. One specific example of this phenomenon is discussed in Appendix 3–1: In 1974, the PPI for electric motors jumped 27 percent after price controls were lifted, while unit value indexes increased only 17 percent. This 10 percentage point difference is probably related to large increases in both list prices and discounts.

The deflator for consumption expenditures on durables could also have been biased by a widening gap between list and transaction prices, although the quality adjustment for pollution abatement equipment creates a bias in the other direction that could more than offset it.[6] Prices of consumer nondurables and services are less likely to have been affected by rising list price/transaction price differentials, since BLS samples the actual prices paid in these areas. The segment of real output represented by expenditures for both residential and nonresidential structures may be contaminated by substantial deflation errors; for example, the Census Bureau's hedonic price index for single family homes is a major component of the deflator for shopping center construction.

Unbiased errors in the measurement of the output price deflator could also lead to the observed negative correlation between inflation and productivity growth. Suppose that real output $\tilde{Y}$ is unobservable and that it is related to a set of explanatory variables in the standard way:

$$\log \tilde{Y}_t = \beta_0 + \beta_1 X_{1t} + \beta_2 X_{2t} + \xi_t$$

Also assume that the "true" price level $\tilde{P}$ is unobservable, and is estimated by an output deflator P that varies around $\tilde{P}$:

$$\log P_t = \log \tilde{P}_t + \eta_t.$$

Then if the observed value of real output Y is obtained by dividing nominal output (YN) by the deflator P, we have:

$$\log \mathrm{YN_t} - \log \tilde{P}_t = \beta_0 + \beta_1 X_{1t} + \beta_2 X_{2t} + \xi_t, \text{ or}$$

$$\log YN_t = \beta_0 + \beta_1 X_{1t} + \beta_2 X_{2t} + \log \tilde{P}_t + \xi_t \qquad (3-1)$$

Thus, in a logarithmic regression of nominal output on the price level and variables that explain real output, the coefficient on the price level is 1.0. However, if the "true" price level $\tilde{P}$ in equation (3–1) is replaced by the error-contaminated deflator P:

$$\log YN_t = \beta_0 + \beta_1 X_{1t} + \beta_2 X_{2t} + \gamma \log P_t + \xi_t, \qquad (3-2)$$

its regression coefficient, γ, will be biased toward zero. The ordinary least squares estimate of γ has an expectation less than 1.0; the greater the dispersion of errors in the deflator P, the closer γ will be to zero.

At low price levels, there are some high estimates of real output that are generated by estimates of the price level that are too low; at high price levels, there are low estimates of real output generated price level estimates that are too high. This "stretching" of observed values in (Y, P) space causes the least squares regression fit to underestimate the true derivative of nominal output with respect to price. It is very unlikely that the observed *longer-run* negative correlation between productivity and the price level shown in Figure 3–2 could be explained by unbiased deflation errors, unless these errors persisted over long periods of time. If, for example, quarterly deflation errors are uncorrelated, short-run changes in productivity growth would be negatively related to short-run changes in the price level, but longer-run trends would not be related.

However, there are a number of reasons for believing that errors in deflation might persist over long periods of time. First, the "linkage" procedure used for updating items actually priced in the CPI should generate a high error autocorrelation. If, for example, a new model is introduced and an old one discontinued, a continuous price series is constructed by assuming that the difference in price between the new and old product in a time period where both are sold is exclusively a quality difference. An error in the price of a discontinued item in the time period when the linkage is made would persist forever. Second, errors generated by faulty procedures (rather than mistakes in data transcription or manipulation) are likely to be carried over from one time period to the next. Thus, a substantial downward bias in the estimate of real output generated by unbiased (but positively correlated) errors in price measurement cannot be ruled out.

Finally, there is also a possibility that the increase in the relative price of energy has increased the amount of quality improvement that is not reflected in the price indexes used for the deflation of nominal expenditures.[7] Improvements that increase a durable product's energy efficiency are likely to be counted as inflation, rather than as an increase in real output, because the price reflects only initial capital cost, rather than the value of services it can render. Gordon [1979] provides an extensive discussion of one such case: the price deflator for the output of commercial aircraft.

In 1958, the first generation of commercial jet aircraft were introduced, replacing older piston-engine planes. Since only piston-engine planes were produced before 1958, and only jet planes were produced after 1960, the C.A.B. had to "link" the prices of the two types of aircraft in the price index it compiles for aircraft. This linkage was performed in the standard way, by measuring the change in unit price for each type of aircraft delivered in adjacent years, and counting only the observed price differential in the "changeover" year as a quality improvement. However, in terms of cost per seat-mile, the quality change was substantially greater than the price differential for the two types of aircraft in 1958. On a net revenue basis, Gordon calculates a deflator that is four times as large in 1957 as the official BEA deflator.[8]

This implies that output of the aircraft industry in efficiency units is substantially underestimated by the B.E.A., or equivalently, that measured productivity growth in that industry has a serious downward bias. Of course, the linkage method used by the B.E.A. in the construction of deflators does not by itself explain the observed productivity slowdown; the same method has been used both before 1965 and after 1973. However, as a result of the shift in the relative price of energy after 1973, more of this sort of bias has probably entered the standard measure of real output. The energy efficient versions of almost every type of durable equipment that have been introduced since 1973 should generate the same sort of problem that aircraft posed in 1958.

All of these considerations lead to one conclusion: There is a reasonable chance that much of the apparent slowdown observed in the United States since the mid-1960s is a product of the method used for measuring aggregate productivity, rather than a significant slowing of the engine of progress. As an index of the physical volume of output, "GNP at constant prices" must be viewed with some skepticism; only a few components of the total index are based on observed volumes of physical output. In inflationary times, percentage changes in real output are the difference of two much larger numbers: the percentage changes in nominal expenditures and prices. It should not be surprising that the small difference between two larger estimates has a relatively large variance.

3.3. Real Efficiency Losses

While errors in the measurement of real output may explain part of the negative correlation between inflation and productivity growth, there are a number of sound reasons for believing that the poor performance of the economy is more than a statistical artifact, and that the observed resistance to further productivity gain is related to high rates of inflation.

It has been widely observed that the inflationary process does not leave relative prices unchanged.[9] Both adjustment costs and institutional arrangements dictate that many individual prices increase in discrete increments rather than continuously. Since the "jumps" in prices are not synchronized, increases in the aggregate price level are accompanied by substantial movements in relative prices. In fact, there is a strong positive correlation between the rate of price increase and the dispersion of relative price change. In Figure 3–3, the quarterly rate of change in the fixed-weight price index for private final expenditures less net exports is plotted alongside a measure of the dispersion of increases in the components that make up this index.[10] Over the past 15 years, the dispersion of relative price change has increased substantially as the aggregate inflation rate has risen.

Since the price system is an intricate signaling mechanism used by firms in deciding how much to produce and in selecting production techniques, it

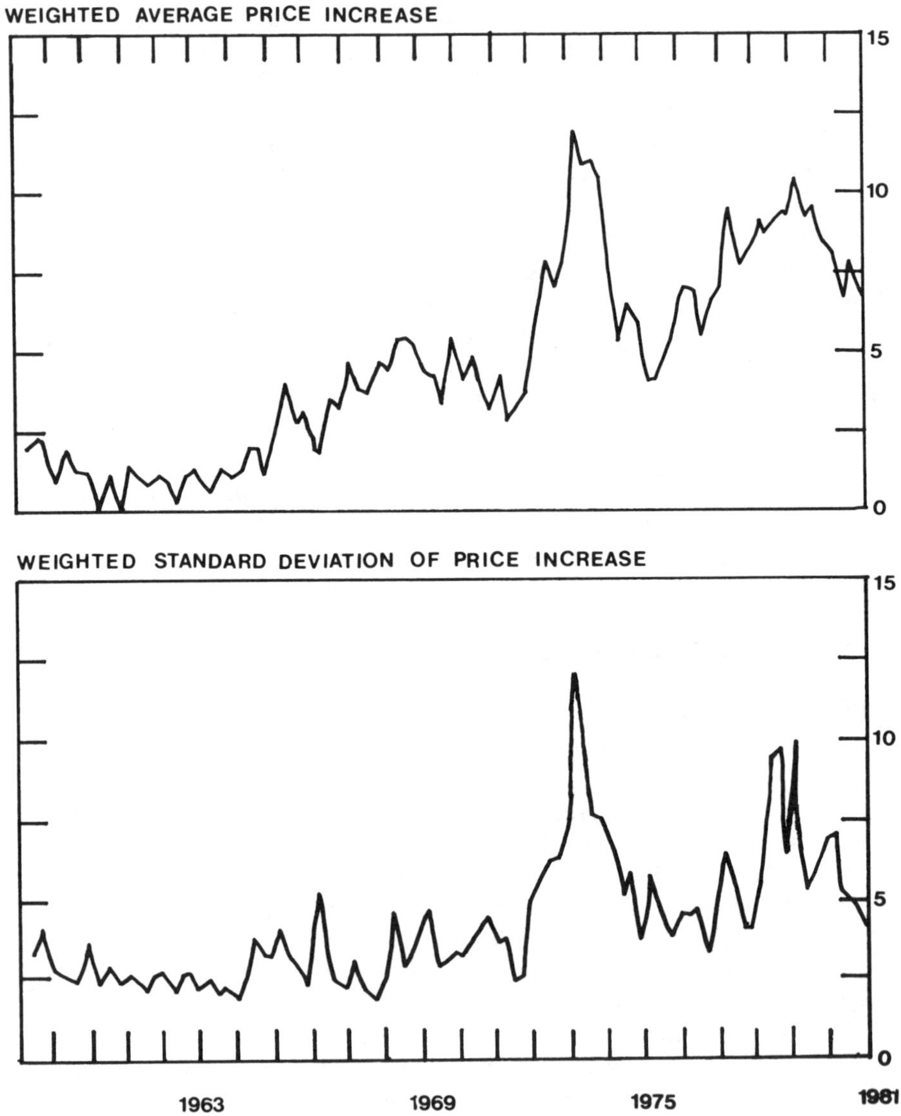

Figure 3-3. Mean and Standard Deviation of Changes in Prices. (Vertical axes indicate percent per year)

is clear that the introduction of more "noise" in the set of signals should lower production efficiency. For example, consider production decisions in an environment of relative price stability. If the price of an input rises by 10 percent, firms can be fairly certain that the price increase reflects a change in relative prices and will alter their production techniques accordingly. On the other hand, if the overall rate of inflation is about 10 percent a year, a 20 percent price increase for a particular input is a much weaker signal. Firms using the input must make an estimate of the proportion of the increase that can be attributed to the general rise in prices. This involves the extraction of a signal from information that contains noise. When the dispersion of relative prices is higher, price signals are noisier, making the extraction of the signal costlier and subject to more error.[11]

Thus, an increase in the dispersion of relative prices generates three types of efficiency loss which would result in slower growth in measured labor productivity. First, when the information content of the price system is degraded by the introduction of additional noise, firms make more mistakes. Aggregate output of any given good is more likely to be larger or smaller than necessary, generating shortages or inventory costs. Even if aggregate production is still about right, the distribution of output across firms is likely to be less efficient than it would have been if relative prices were less variable. On the input side, suboptimal techniques of production are likely to be more prevalent.

Second, increased variation in relative prices creates an incentive for firms to choose flexibility over absolute efficiency in the production processes they select. For example, if the prices of different fuels are expected to vary substantially, a firm may install equipment that allows the use of both oil and natural gas, even though it is not as efficient as single-fuel equipment. And since labor is the most flexible input to many production processes, more flexibility is likely to involve more labor and lower labor productivity.

Finally, an analogous argument can be made with respect to information about prices. In an environment of irregularly changing prices, some suppliers may increase their margins knowing that it is costly for their customers to search out a lower price on the same or similar items. Other suppliers may hold prices constant for longer periods of time, hoping to maintain customer relations. The dispersion of prices for inputs would therefore increase. Firms would have to allocate more real resources to the search for lower prices, thus lowering the level of productivity. In Okun's terminology, the "customer market" nature of many transactions makes the inflation process both irregular (with discrete adjustment of prices) and costly (since it requires more search and estimation of price distributions on the part of customers).[12]

It should also be noted that higher aggregate rates of inflation are usually accompanied by higher variance in this aggregate rate.[13] Thus, a higher rate of inflation should generate more uncertainty about the future, complicate planning and investment decisions, and impair the attainment of higher levels of productive efficiency even if uncertainty about relative prices has not increased.

While all these considerations make it clear that higher rates of inflation have cut into productivity performance in the past 15 years, neither the functional relationship between inflation and efficiency nor the magnitude of the induced productivity loss is clear. At one extreme, the increased variability associated with higher rates of inflation might be handled by incurring a once-and-for-all expenditure. For example, new procedures might be instituted for sampling prices in different regions of the country; computer programs might be written to automatically average out variations in prices over time. In this case, the costs of a shift from a noninflationary to an inflationary environment are like a reduction in output.[14] The reaction of labor productivity should be a temporary drop, followed by a return to its previous trend level.

At the other extreme, the increased variation in both relative prices and the absolute price level could be continuously siphoning off managerial talent and labor resources that would otherwise have gone into reducing production costs. In this case, each increase in the rate of inflation could be associated with a decline in the rate of productivity growth, as more and more effort is permanently diverted toward handling financial uncertainty and instability.

It seems likely that the reaction of productivity growth to increased inflation lies between these two extremes, with each increase in the rate of inflation requiring further adjustment and a temporary lowering of productivity growth. In other words, the second derivative of prices should be related to the first derivative of output. Once constant inflation rate is reached, productivity growth would return to its underlying trend rate. Superficially at least, this seems to argue that the relationship between inflation and productivity growth shown in figure 3–2 and estimated empirically in Appendix 3–2 was not generated by real efficiency losses.

Productivity growth is negatively related to the inflation rate, not changes in the inflation rate. However, efficiency losses caused by higher price variance would probably be spread out over a long period of time, rather than being concentrated during the quarter or year in which the inflation rate increased. In this case, reductions in productivity growth should be a long distributed lag of past changes in the inflation rate. In a standard linear regression model, it would be hard to distinguish this sort of relationship and one between productivity growth and inflation itself.[15]

If the measurement of real output has been biased downward by overdeflation, a negative relationship between the price level and real output (or inflation and productivity growth) should be observed. Thus, the empirical evidence leans toward measurement error as the primary cause of the relationship between inflation and productivity growth, although real efficiency losses cannot be ruled out.[16]

3.4. Energy Price Effects

One intuitively appealing explanation for the slowdown in productivity growth since 1973 is that dramatic increases in the relative price of energy, first in 1973–1974 and again in 1979–1980, have made substantial amounts of energy-intensive capital obsolete, and have generated massive substitution of labor for energy and capital. Exponents of this view include Edward Hudson and Dale Jorgenson, who have estimated that between 1972 and 1976, real GNP was reduced 3.2 percent, energy consumption was reduced 8.8 percent, and labor input was reduced 0.5 percent as a result of energy price increases.[17] Using an entirely different methodology, Robert Rasche and John Tatom came to the conclusion that a 4 percent reduction in the level of output in 1974 is a conservative estimate of the effect of higher energy prices.[18] While these large reductions in the level of output would explain almost all of the observed slowdown in productivity growth since 1973, it is hard to see how the doubling of energy prices in 1973–1974 generated such an immediate reduction in labor productivity.[19]

If, like Rasche and Tatom, one assumes that the elasticity of substitution between energy and other factors of production is unity, then a doubling of energy prices could reduce output per unit of labor input by 4 percent if owners of energy resources received 8 percent of GNP as royalties. But such a dramatic substitution of capital and labor for energy also implies that energy consumption must fall immediately by 50 percent; all the available evidence indicates that the reduction in the industrial use of energy since 1973, while substantial, is certainly not that large. In addition, as Denison points out, if energy is counted as a factor of production (separate from land, labor, and capital), it probably accounted for much less than 8 percent of GNP in 1972.[20]

At the other extreme, if it is assumed that the elasticity of substitution between energy and other factors is zero, then an increase in energy prices would not affect labor productivity, even if all energy were imported. This is because real output is typically measured using 1972 (pre-increase) prices;[21] adverse movements in the terms of trade, while reducing domestic command over goods and services, do not directly lower measured real output.

Other hypotheses linking the recent productivity slowdown to the rise in energy prices are a little harder to dismiss. The Hudson-Jorgenson model allows only small changes in the ratio of energy to capital, but substantial substitution between labor and combinations of these two factors. If capital and energy must be consumed in a fixed ratio, then an increase in the relative price of energy acts just like an increase in the rental price of capital services. If, for example, capital's share is 20 percent, energy's share is 8 percent, and the elasticity of substitution between labor and energy/capital is 1.0, doubling of energy prices should cut capital (and energy) input over 20 percent in the long run, and reduce labor productivity by about 6 percent. However, investment data for the past seven years do not indicate that capital formation has fallen below the level that could have been expected, given the path of output and the other determinants of investment.[22] If the capital-energy complementarity argument is correct, then the adjustment to a lower capital/labor ratio is taking a very long time and the reduction in productivity growth should have been taken much longer.

The problem with both these explanations of the post-1973 productivity slowdown is that they exclusively on factor substitution and ignore the fact that more than half of all labor productivity growth before 1973 was not attributable to any specific factor of production. The primary contributor to productivity growth is a "residual" or "advances in knowledge not elsewhere classified." Most observed growth in labor productivity is not a consequence of more capital per worker, but rather the gradual accretion of improved organizational structure, quality improvements in capital equipment, and other forms of learning that are not well adapted to precise measurement.

It seems likely, then, that if the shift to higher energy prices is lowering productivity growth, it is doing so by interfering with these learning processes and quality improvements. For example, suppose that a substantial fraction of the growth in total factor productivity between 1948 and 1973 was the result of firms learning how to take advantage of the low and falling relative price of energy. When the price of crude quadrupled, and the prices for other energy sources began to rise as a result, the rules of the cost-saving game were completely changed. Instead of continuing to exploit the energy-intensive "experience curve" that existed before 1973, firms had to discover new techniques for reducing costs by reducing energy inputs instead of increasing them. In such a scenario, labor productivity growth could easily be eliminated during a period of adjustment to the altered economic environment. If this "learning pause" theory is correct, productivity growth should reemerge some time after the price of energy has stabilized. Any empirical evidence of such a "learning pause" would have to be gleaned from microeconomic data; it is impossible to construct a good explanation for a slowdown in an "unexplained residual" at the aggregate level.

3.5. Conclusions

Over the past 30 years, real output per hour of labor in the U.S. private sector has shown a remarkable correlation with the price level. *On the average, a 1 percent increase in the price level has been associated with a .20 to .30 percent decrease in output, holding capital and labor input fixed.* The slowdown in productivity growth, which began in the mid-1960s and accelerated after 1973, has closely paralleled the evolution of the double-digit inflation the United States is now experiencing. Although the mechanism connecting inflation and productivity growth is not well understood, it is a reasonable guess that the virtual disappearance of productivity growth in the United States for the past eight years is intimately connected to high rates of inflation and shifts in the structure of relative prices.

Explanations of the relationship between inflation and productivity growth fall into two categories: measurement errors and real efficiency losses. Measurement errors could have generated part of the apparent productivity slowdown if nominal output has been systematically over-deflated when prices rise, or if unbiased errors in the estimated price level have created a downward bias in the observed relationship between nominal output and prices. It is also possible that part of the price increases for some types of durable equipment have been related to improved energy efficiency, rather than just price inflation.

Real efficiency losses could have been caused by inflation in a number of ways. First, increased variance in relative prices may have resulted in output decisions that were inefficient in an *ex post* sense. Second, as the inflationary process added noise to the signals in the price system, more resources may have been used to obtain price information and predict prices. Third, rising variation in the aggregate price level could have complicated investment decisions, making them less efficient. And finally, the extraordinary rise in energy prices may have created a whole new environment for production; adjustment of learning and efficiency improvement to this environment may still be far from complete.

At this time, the relative weight of each of these factors is unknown. The fact that the slowdown in productivity growth is closely linked with increases in the inflation points toward measurement error as the primary explanation. However, disentangling all the various interactions between inflation and productivity growth is likely to be a monumental task requiring the examination of data relating outputs, inputs, and prices at a very disaggregated level. If it is discovered that even a small part of the negative correlation between inflation and productivity growth is real efficiency loss that can be eliminated by returning to price stability, then the real costs of inflation are very high.

Notes

1. Denison, pages 92–93. A careful examination of Denison's results indicates that he attributes almost all of the 1965–1973 slowdown to reduced intensity of production. This reflects his choice of 4 percent unemployment as a benchmark for input utilization.
2. Denison, page 122.
3. Norsworthy, Harper, and Kunze, page 421.
4. Clark, page 431.
5. For a good discussion of range of possible causes, see Denison, chapter 9, or the Boston Fed conference volume.
6. Increases in the cost of new automobiles for mandatory anti-pollution and, safety equipment are treated as a quality improvement by BLS even though they may represent an inconvenience (quality reduction) to new car buyers. See Denison, p. 70.
7. "Quality" in this context means value to the user or purchaser of a particular item. For example, the replacement of a metal part with a more durable plastic alternative should be counted as a quality improvement even though the plastic part costs much less to produce.
8. Gordon, Table 4. Both deflators are computed on a 1972 basis ($P_{1972} = 1.000$).
9. See Barro, Cukierman (1979), Clements and Nguyen, Fischer, Hercowitz, Parks, and Vining and Elwertowski for discussions of this issue.
10. Figure 4 is similar to Figure 1 in Vining and Elwertowski.
11. These considerations have led Friedman to argue that the long-run Phillips curve should have a positive slope.
12. See Okun. Okun makes an eloquent argument for the case that inflation is costly because it destroys the customary relationship between buyer and seller. It is only a short step from Okun's thesis to the realization that some of the cost should be reflected in poorer productivity performance.
13. See Balk, Blejer, Foster and Logue and Willet.
14. The output associated with this "capital" expenditure would not have been counted in GNP, because it can be expensed instead of depreciated (items which can be expensed by business are, by convention, counted as raw materials, regardless of their useful life).
15. This is because the inflation rate is one particular (very long) distributed lag on its own first differences.

16. In principle, the effect of measurement error and real efficiency loss on productivity could be disentangled by frequency domain methods. Under reasonable assumptions, measurement error would be indicated by high coherence between output and the price level at high frequencies, while real efficiency loss should show up a higher power at lower frequencies.

17. Hudson and Jorgenson. Also see Berndt and Wood.

18. Rasche and Tatom.

19. A number of observers have pointed this out, including Fellner and Denison.

20. Denison, p. 139.

21. This statement applies when a Laspeyres quantity index is used for measuring real output; if a Tornquist or other index employing variable price weights is used to estimate productivity growth, price shifts obviously matter.

22. Clark found that the relatively low ratio of business fixed investment to output after the 1973–1974 energy shock could be explained by the reduced output during the period. Since that paper was written, National Income and Product Account estimates of business fixed investment have been revised upward by a substantial amount strengthening the argument that capital spending was not surprisingly low in the years after 1973.

References

Ashley, Richard, "Inflation and the Distribution of Price Changes Across Markets: A Causal Analysis," *Economic Inquiry*, October 1981, pp. 650–660.

Balk, B.M., "Inflation and Its Variability," *Economics Letters*, 1978:1, pp. 357–360.

Barro, Robert J., "Rational Expectations and the Role of Monetary Policy," *Journal of Monetary Economics*, January 1976, pp. 1–32.

Berndt, Ernst R. and D. O. Wood, "Technology, Prices and the Derived Demand for Energy," *Review of Economics and Statistics*, August 1975, pp. 259–268.

Blejer, Mario I., "Inflation Variability in Latin America," *Economics Letters*, 1979:2, pp. 199–210.

Blejer, Mario I. and L. Leiderman, "On the Real Effects of Inflation and Relative-Price Variability: Some Empirical Evidence," *Review of Economics and Statistics*, November 1980, pp. 539–544.

Clark, Peter K., "Capital Formation and the Recent Productivity Slowdown," *Journal of Finance*, June 1978, pp. 965–975.

———, "Investment in the 1970's: Theory, Performance, and Prediction," *Brookings Papers on Economic Activity* 1:1979, pp. 73–113.

———, "Issues in the Analysis of Capital Formation and Productivity Growth," *Brookings Papers on Economic Activity* 1979:2, pp. 423–431.

———, "Inflation and the Productivity Decline," *American Economic Review*, May 1982, pp. 149–154.

Clements, Kenneth W. and P. Nguyen, "Inflation and Relative Prices: A System-Wide Approach," *Economics Letters*, 1981:7, pp. 131–137.

Cukierman, Alex, "The Relationship Between Relative Prices and the General Price

Level: A Suggested Interpretation," *American Economic Review*, June 1979, pp. 444–447.

———, "Relative Price Variability, Inflation, and the Allocation Efficiency of the Price System," *Journal of Monetary Economics*, March 1982, pp. 131–162.

Cukierman, Alex and P. Wachtel, "Differential Inflationary Expectations and the Variability of the Rate of Inflation," *American Economic Review*, September 1979, pp. 595–609.

Denison, Edward F., *Accounting for Slower Economic Growth: The United States in the 1970's*, the Brookings Institution, Washington, D.C., 1979.

Federal Reserve Bank of Boston, *The Decline in Productivity Growth*, Conference Series No. 22, June 1980.

Fellner, William, "The Declining Growth of American Productivity: An Introduction Note," *Contemporary Economic Problems 1979*, American Enterprise Institute, Washington, D.C., 1979.

Fischer, Stanley, "Relative Shocks, Relative Price Variability, and Inflation," *Brookings Papers on Economic Activity*, 2:1981, pp. 381–431.

Fischer, Stanley, and F. Modigliani, "Towards an Understanding of the Real Effects and Costs of Inflation," *Weltwirtschaftliches Archiv*, Band 114 (1978), pp. 810–833.

Foster, Edward M., "The Variability of Inflation," *Review of Economics and Statistics*, August 1978, pp. 346–350.

Friedman, Milton, "Nobel Lecture: Inflation and Unemployment," *Journal of Political Economy*, June 1977, pp. 451–472.

Glesjer, Herbert, "Inflation, Productivity, and Relative Prices—A Statistical Study," *Review of Economics and Statistics*, February 1965, pp. 76–80.

Gordon, Robert J., "Energy Efficiency, User Cost Change, and the Measurement of Durable Goods Prices," National Bureau of Economic Research, Working Paper 408, November 1979.

Hercowitz, Zvi, "Money and the Dispersion of Relative Prices," *Journal of Political Economy*, April 1981, pp. 328–356.

Hudson, Edward A. and D.W. Jorgenson, "Energy Prices and the U.S. Economy 1972–1976," *Natural Resources Journal*, October 1978, pp. 877–897.

Jaffee, Dwight and E. Kleiman, "The Welfare Implications of Uneven Inflation," in E. Lundberg (ed.), *Inflation Theory and Anti-Inflation Policy*, (London: Macmillan, 1977), pp. 285–307.

Logue, Dennis E. and T.D. Willett, "A Note on the Relation Between the Rate and Variability of Inflation," *Economica*, May 1976, pp. 151–158.

Lucas, Robert E., "Some International Evidence on Output-Inflation Tradeoffs," *American Economic Review*, June 1973, pp. 326–334.

Marquez, Jaime and D. Vining, "Inflation and Relative Price Behavior: A Survey of the Literature," Discussion Paper #500, Department of Economics, University of Pennsylvania, March 1982.

McKee, Michael J., "Computer Prices in the National Accounts: Are Our Economic Problems a Computer Error?" Council of Economic Advisors mimeo, September 1981.

Norsworthy, J.R., M.J. Harper and K. Kunze, "The Slowdown in Productivity Growth: Analysis of Contributing Factors," *Brookings Papers on Economic Activity* 1979:2, pp. 387–421.

Okun, Arthur M., "Inflation: Its Mechanics and Welfare Costs," *Brookings Papers on Economic Activity* 2:1975, pp. 351–390.

Panel to Review Productivity Statistics, *The Measurement and Interpretation of Productivity*, National Academy of Sciences, 1979.

Parks, Richard W., "Inflation and Relative Price Variability," *Journal of Political Economy*, February 1978, pp. 79–95.

Rasche, Robert H. and John A. Tatom, "Energy Resources and Potential GNP," *Federal Reserve Bank of St. Louis Review*, June 1977, pp. 10–24.

U.S. Bureau of the Census, *Current Industrial Reports MA-36H, Motors and Generators*, annual issues from 1960 to 1978.

U.S. Council of Economic Advisers, *Economic Report of the President*, 1979 and 1980.

Vining, Daniel R. and Thomas C. Elwertowski, "The Relationship Between Relative Prices and the General Price Level," *American Economic Review*, September 1976, p. 699–708.

APPENDIX 1 TO CHAPTER 3 INDUSTRIAL ELECTRICAL MOTORS—AN EXAMPLE OF THE LIST PRICE/TRANSACTION PRICE BIAS IN THE PRODUCER PRICE INDEX

The Bureau of Labor Statistics (BLS) currently prices three A.C. electric motors that can be classified as "industrial": 3 H.P., 10 H.P., and 50 H.P. Although BLS claims that it receives transaction prices from domestic motor manufacturers, the constancy of their series for months at a time argues otherwise; it is likely that a sizeable fraction of the firms in their sample report list price minus a published discount, a price which is substantially higher than that charged large customers that have a wide knowledge of the motor market. In periods where published prices are rising rapidly, but are offset by widening discounts, the PPI for industrial electric motors is likely to be biased upward.

The data shown in Figure 3–4 seem to confirm this hypothesis. Each of the three panels compares the Producer Price Index for a specific motor with a unit-value index for motors of the same size constructed from Census Bureau data.[1] In each case, the Producer Price Index has increased much more since 1965 than the associated unit value index. The divergence is sharpest in 1974; in the last nine months of that year, the PPI for the three motors shown in Figure 3–4 rose an astounding 35 percent. This price explosion coincided with the removal of price controls that had been in place since August 1971. As measured by the PPI, prices of industrial electric motors were 27 percent higher in 1974 than in 1973. In contrast,

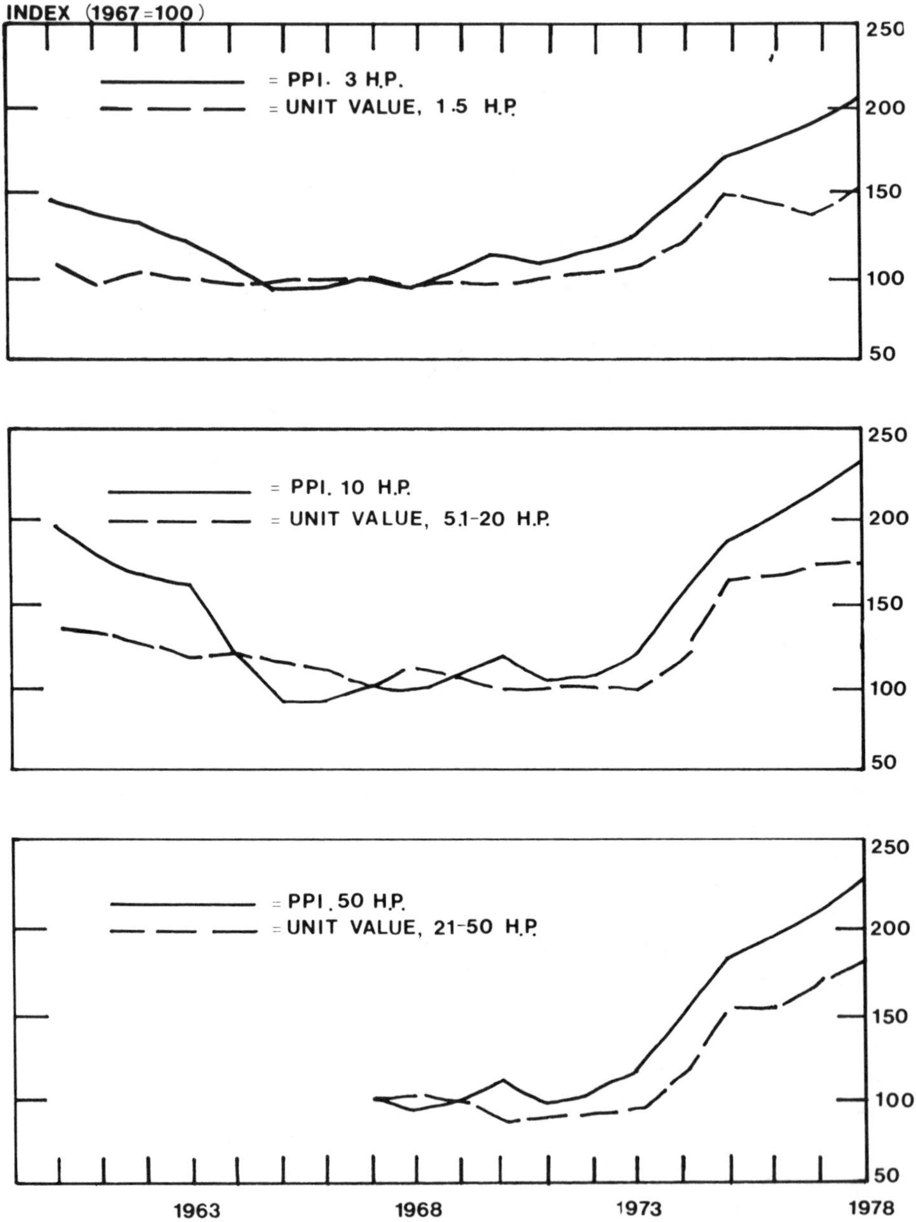

Figure 3-4. Producer Price Indexes and Unit Value Indexes for A.C. Electric Motors

the unit value indexes for similar motors increased only 17 percent. While it is possible that the mix of motors in each horsepower class used to construct the unit value indexes could have changed enough to generate the disparity in Figure 3–4, an alternative explanation is probably better: the PPI overstates the increase in the price of electric motors. The disparity was greatest in 1973–1974, when list prices were probably being raised faster than transaction prices in anticipation of the reimposition of price controls.

Note to Appendix 3.1

1. Each unit-value index is dollar volume of sales divided by number of units sold. These data are published annually in Current Industrial Reports, [25].

APPENDIX 2 TO CHAPTER 3 EMPIRICAL ESTIMATES OF THE RELATIONSHIP BETWEEN PRODUCTIVITY GROWTH AND INFLATION

While a rough measure of the historical relationship between increases in the price level and reductions in productivity growth can be obtained by inspection of Figure 3–2, additional insight is gained from the following 3-equation model:

Potential Hours

$$\log H_t = \log H_t^* + A(s)Z_t + \varepsilon_t \qquad (3A\text{–}1)$$

Cyclical Movement of Labor Demand Around Trend

$$\log\left(\frac{H_t}{H_t^*}\right) = B(s)\log\left(\frac{Y_t}{Y_t^*}\right) + \eta_t \qquad (3A\text{–}2)$$

Long-Run Production Function

$$\log Y_t^* = \text{Constant} + \alpha \log K_t + (1-\alpha)\log H_t^* + \gamma t - \delta \log P_t + \nu_t \qquad (3A\text{–}3)$$

H_t = observed hours of labor input
H_t^*= potential, or trend level hours
$Z_t = U_t - U_t^*$= excess of actual unemployment rate over its potential level U_t^*, the benchmark unemployment rate
Y_t = observed level of real output for the private nonfarm nonresidential business sector
Y_t^*= potential level of Y_t.
K_t = gross capital services, a weighted average of equipment, structures, and inventories.[1]
t = time trend
P_t = price level, defined as the deflator associated with Y_t

$A(s)$, $B(s)$ are lag operators; in general,

$$B(s)x_t = \sum_{s=-m}^{n} \beta_s x_{t-s}$$

ε_t, η_t, ν_t are error terms.

The first equation states that the difference between actual and potential hours of labor input is a function of the unemployment rate. Although some time lags may be involved, the sum of the lead and lag coefficients in $A(s)$ should be negative, so that if unemployment is above its benchmark, hours are below their trend level. This equation incorporates the cyclical movement of hours as well as labor force participation.

The second relationship is a dynamic factor demand equation, which is used to explain the cyclical relationship between hours and output which generates the "short-run increasing returns to labor" phenomenon that has been widely studied. The only difference here is that leads as well as lags are allowed in the regression of hours on output. The contemporaneous and lagging coefficients are expected to be positive, reflecting the fact that more output requires more labor in the short run, but the sum of the coefficients is not necessarily 1.0, reflecting that fact that in a dynamic situation, it may be optimal to make incomplete adjustments of inputs if adjustment costs are involved.

The third equation specifies a Cobb-Douglas production function with neutral technical progress for the relationship between the long-run or trend value of real output and capital and labor inputs. The extra term included in (3A–3) is $\delta \log P_t$, which allows the trend level of output to vary with changes in the price level. Thus, the regression coefficient δ is the statistical measure of the relationship between productivity and the price level depicted in Figure 3–2.

The model outlined above includes the potential levels of unemployment, hours, and output: U_t^*, H_t^*, and Y_t^*. By combining the three equations, two of these "unobservable" series can be eliminated. First, equation (3A–1) can be substituted into equation (3A–), yielding

$$A(s)Z_t + \varepsilon_t = B(s)\log\left(\frac{Y_t}{Y_t^*}\right) + \eta_t$$

Solving this expression for log Y_t^*;[2]

$$\log Y_t^* = \log Y_t - B^{-1}(s)A(s)Z_t - B^{-1}(s)(\varepsilon_t - \eta_t)$$

Substituting this relationship and equation (3A–1) into equation (3A–3),

$$\log Y_t - B^{-1}(s)A(s)Z_t - B^{-1}(s)(\varepsilon_t - \eta_t) =$$

$$C + \alpha \log K_t + (1 - \alpha)\left[\log H_t - A(s)Z_t - \varepsilon_t\right] + \gamma t - \delta \log P_t + \nu_t,$$

or

$$\log Y_t = C + \alpha \log K_t + (1 - \alpha)\log H_t + D(s)Z_t + \gamma t - \delta \log P_t + w_t, \tag{3A–4}$$

where

$$D(s) = [B^{-1}(s)A(s) - (1 - \alpha)A(s)], \text{ and}$$

$$w_t = B^{-1}(s)(\varepsilon_t - \eta_t) - (1 - \alpha)\varepsilon_t + \nu_t.$$

Equation (3A–4) is a standard Cobb-Douglas production function in logarithmic form with two important differences. First, the inclusion of leading, contemporaneous, and lagged excess unemployment ($D(s)Z_t$) adjusts for the cyclical variation of output per unit of input over the business cycle. Without this term, regression estimates of α are usually negative. Second, the "technological progress" term contains not only a time trend, but a price level term, reflecting the observed relationship between inflation and productivity growth. The one "unobservable" variable, U_t^*, which remains in equation (3A–4) as part of $Z_t = U_t - U_t^*$, is the benchmark unemployment rate published by the Council of Economic Advisers.[3]

Least-squares estimation of equation (3A–4) (with constant returns to scale imposed as a constraint), yields the following result:

$$\log(Y_t/H_t) = \underset{(.35)}{-2.61} + \underset{(.09)}{.22}\log(K_t/H_t) \underset{(.0013)}{-.0068} Z_{t+1} \tag{3A–5}$$

$$\underset{(.0023)}{-.0077} \quad Z_t + \underset{(.0014)}{.0053} \quad Z_{t-1} \underset{(.021)}{-.225} \log P_t^* \underset{(.0028)}{.0252t}$$

S.E. = .0060

$d - w = 2.02$ (standard errors in parentheses)

[sample interval = 1950–1978]

The t-statistic of the price level is higher than that of any other variable in equation (3A–5), confirming the close correlation between reductions in productivity growth and increases in the price level. The regression estimate of the elasticity of real output with respect to the price level is .225, almost exactly the same as the "eyeball" estimate obtained from Figure 3–2.

The price level variable in equation (3A–5) has taken the place of time-trend dummies that are usually included to allow the regression to track productivity growth since the mid-1960s. Typically, two dummies are included, one to allow productivity growth to decline in about 1965, and another to permit a further reduction after 1973, as in equation (3A–6).

$$\log\left(\frac{Y_t}{H_t}\right) = \underset{(.59)}{-1.98} \quad \underset{(.15)}{+.09}\log\left(\frac{K_t}{H_t}\right) \underset{(.0014)}{-.0084} Z_{t-1} \underset{(.0034)}{-.0053} Z_t \tag{3A–6}$$

$$\underset{(.0015)}{+.0052} Z_{t-1} \underset{(.004)}{+.0239t} \underset{(.0038)}{-.0049T1} \underset{(.0036)}{-.0105T2}$$

S.E. = .0071 d.w. = 2.04

$T1$ = 0, . . . , 0 until 1965, then 1,2,3 . . . .

$T2$ = 0, . . . , 0 until 1973, then 1,2,3 . . .

Since a standard time trend variable is included in equation (3A–6), the regression coefficients on $T1$ and $T2$ measure the *difference* in residual productivity growth emerging in 1965 and 1973. In terms of equation (3A–6), growth output per unit of labor and capital input fell a small amount, (one-half percent per year) in the mid-1960s, and plummeted an additional 1 percent per year after 1973.

To compare the "price correlation" view of equation (3A–5) and the "broken time trend" view of equation (3A–6), both the price term and the broken time trend terms can be included in one regression equation:

$$\log\left(\frac{Y_t}{H_t}\right) = \underset{(.52)}{-2.16} \quad \underset{(.13)}{+.09} \log\left(\frac{K_t}{H_t}\right) \underset{(.0015)}{-.0060} Z_{t+1} \tag{3A–7}$$

$$-.0050\ Z_t + .0050\ Z_{t-1} - .311\ \log P_t$$
$$(.0029) \quad (.0014) \quad (.118)$$

$$+.0034\ T1 - .0020\ T2 + .030t$$
$$(.0033) \quad (.0045) \quad (.004)$$

S.E. = .0063 d.w. = 2.08

In spite of the multicollinearity between the price level term and the broken time trend, the data indicate that price increases explain the productivity slowdown better than an *ad hoc* broken time trend. While this demonstration of the strong negative correlation between inflation and productivity growth is not proof of a causal connection between the two phenomena, it is striking enough to warrant an investigation of possible linkages between them.

Notes to Appendix 3.2

1. See Clark [1979:2] for a comparison of this series with other measures of capital input.
2. $B^{-1}(s)$ is the inverse of the lag operator $B(s)$, so that $B^{-1}(s)\ B(s)\ x_t = x_t$. When lag operators are allowed to be two-sided, such an inverse always exists.
3. See the Economic Report of the President, 1979 and 1980.

PART TWO

4 NIPA
A MODEL FOR NET INCOME AND PRODUCTIVITY ANALYSIS

M. Ali Chaudry, Malcolm Burnside, and Dan Eldor

4.1. Introduction

A firm's performance can be measured in many ways. The traditional financial analyses commonly measure performance in terms of ratios of certain accounting data contained in the income statement and the balance sheet. The key result management is most interested in is growth in earnings. Thus, it would be very helpful to know more about the factors which underlie that growth and to be able to quantify the impact of those factors on earnings. Conventional accounting measures provide a good deal of such information. However, the income statement data on sales, costs, and profits include the effect of price changes as well as changes in physical volumes over time. Moreover, many of the balance sheet accounting measures are composites of real volumes and price changes over time and do not necessarily reflect current economic relationships. The conventional financial measures, therefore, could mask a decline in efficiency of the enterprise or fail to provide correct indications of improvements that might be taking place.

On the other hand, productivity analysis, which seems to be gaining popularity at the firm level, focuses on a physical measure of efficiency. It is usually measured by the percentage change in output per employee hour, often called labor productivity (*LP*), and in some cases, by total productivity (*TP*).[1] The pattern of productivity growth provides a general indicator of how the firm's productivity performance compares with its past trend, that in the industry in which it operates, or that in the economy as a whole. Often, the use of productivity indexes is limited to such comparisons which are made for public relations or regulatory purposes. However, productivity measures have not been widely used in management decision-making or in planning in general. One reason may be that there remains a large gap between productivity measures and the financial measures that management is used to looking at.

We have attempted to build a bridge to close that gap and provide a link between the two types of measures. Figure 4-1 shows the financial as well as physical flows that management has to deal with. In order for management to fully understand the reasons for changes in overall performance of the firm, it is essential that an integrated analysis of both types of flows be developed. The Net Income and Productivity Analysis (NIPA) model (described below) permits a decomposition of the total change in net income into quantity effects and price effects. The real quantity effects are reflected in the total productivity measure and in the physical growth of capital, while changes in output and input prices are reflected in the "price effects" variable. Changes in taxes and purely financial variables such as depreciation and interest on debt are handled in a separate module. By explicitly identifying the various factors and quantifying their contribution to the growth in net income, this model provides the management a better appraisal of the firm's performance and a perspective on the sources and quality of its earnings. In particular, it translates the productivity gain, which is traditionally measured in terms of percentage growth, into dollar terms which, in turn, can be directly related to the bottom line.

The factor affecting net income can be accounted for among the following categories:

1. Income augmenting factors are those directly contributing to growth in net income. These include productivity or improvement in efficiency of the firm; growth in the physical capital stock; changes in product prices; and "other income" (not directly associated with the physical operations of the firm).
2. Income absorbing factors are those inversely related to growth in net income. These include changes in prices of materials and services purchased from other firms; changes in labor input prices due to changes in wages and benefits; changes in non-income (indirect) taxes

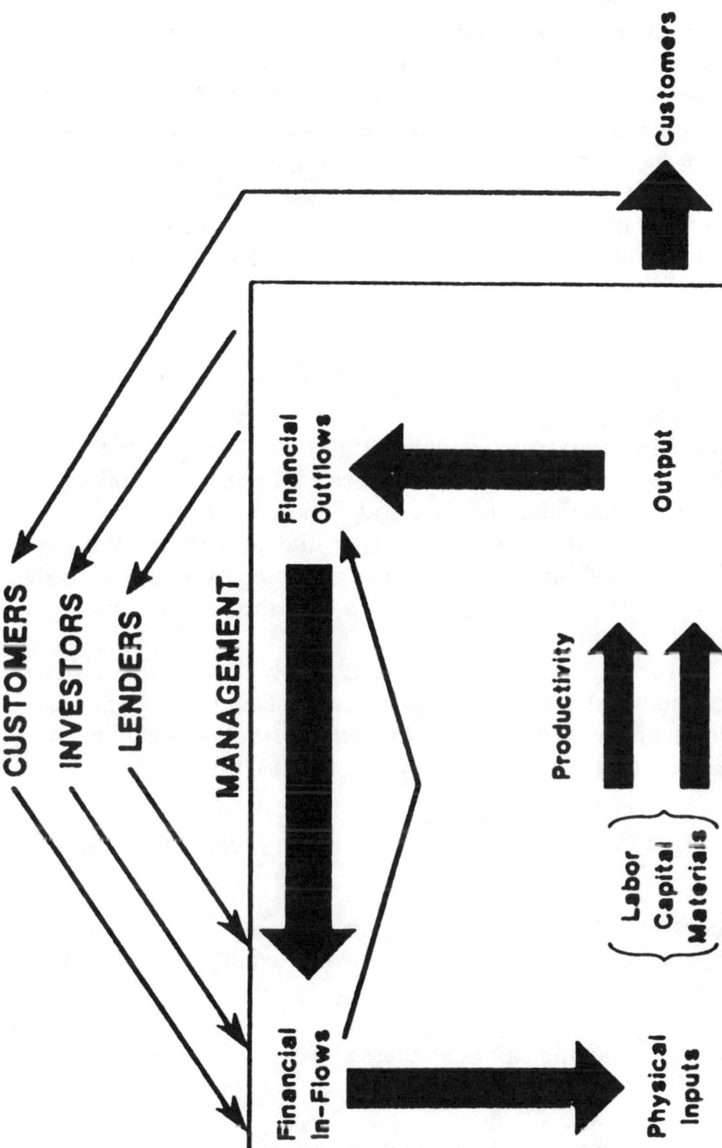

Figure 4–1. Physical & Financial Resource Flows of a Firm

due to change in the tax rates; changes in depreciation expenses; and changes in income taxes and other financial factors.

The rest of the paper is organized as follows: In section 4.2, we develop the conceptual framework of the NIPA model and discuss the rationale for classifying the factors affecting net income growth. In section 4.3, we describe the key data items for a company called XYZ. Although we have changed the name of the corporation in order to protect proprietary information, we have provided a detailed description of the data sources which exist in most large corporations. In section 4.4 we describe an effective method of presenting the NIPA results in the form of an "arrow chart," and in Section 4.5, we discuss some of the possible uses of this model and its results.

4.2. The Model

The NIPA Model consists of five submodules as shown in Figure 4–2. They are: Productivity Module; Output Price Module; Capital Growth Module; Input Price Module; and Tax and Financial Module.

The following theoretical development of the underlying framework starts from the basic definition of net income and, step by step, specifies the structure of the above modules which will be described in their operational form later in this section.

By the usual broad definition, net income is simply the difference between total sales revenue and total expenses or costs. Defining revenue as all financial inflows and expenses as all financial outflows, including taxes, etc., we have

$$NI = R - C' \tag{4-1}$$

where
NI = Net income
R = Total sales revenue
C' = Total operating costs (excluding return to equity capital including preferred stock).

Thus, change in net income can be expressed as:

$$\Delta NI = \Delta R - \Delta C' \tag{4-2}$$

where Δ indicates a change in the respective variable from one year to the next, measured in dollars as shown on the income statement. Time

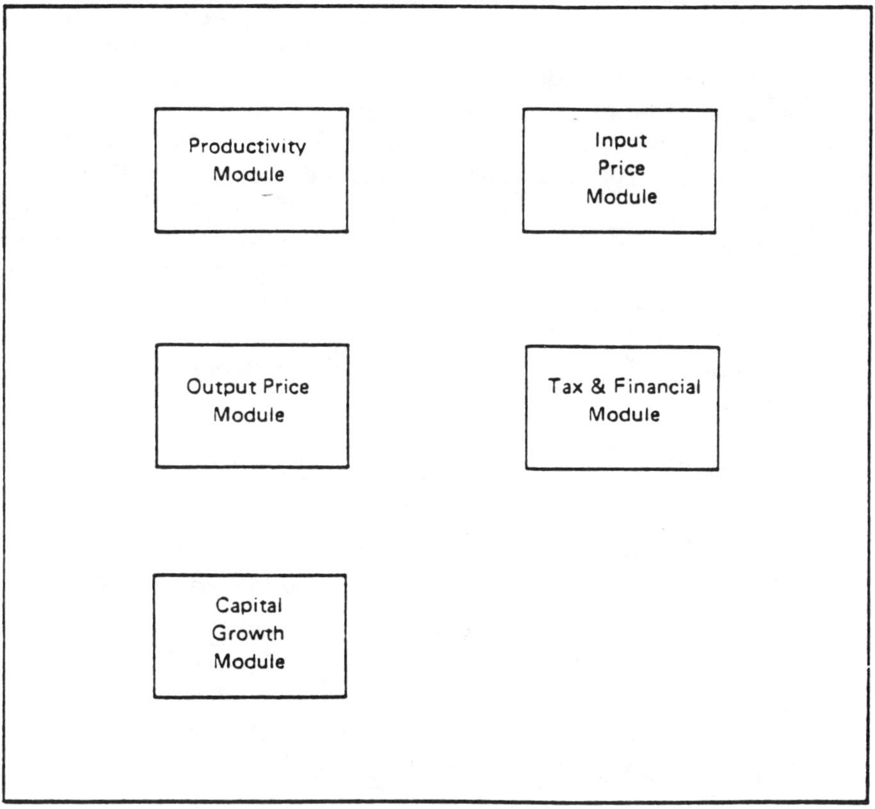

Figure 4-2. NIPA Model Components

subscripts have been omitted here for simplicity of notation and will be used subsequently as needed.

Since the changes in revenue and costs, and therefore in net income, reflect the combined effect of price and quantity changes, we need to further decompose the total change in each variable into its price and quantity components. Only then can we measure productive efficiency in terms of the real output and real inputs and account for the price effects separately.

It should be noted that the productivity calculation in NIPA is different from the fixed base-year methodology which is used in standard TP measurement. Since we are attempting to account for the growth in net income from one year to the next, we are dealing with the quantities (or volumes of output and inputs, respectively), and their corresponding prices for two consecutive years. Thus, the measures of output and inputs for the current year (t) must be constructed in terms of prices of the previous year ($t - 1$). Similarly, any effects attributable to changes in output prices or input prices must be measured with reference to the previous year. This means that all computations of this type to be made within the NIPA framework employ a changing base year as contrasted with the fixed-base-year indexes of the traditional productivity studies, e.g., Kendrick [1977].

In order to develop the framework for decomposition of revenue and costs, we begin by restating the conventional accounting definition of net income in terms of a model of the firm which assumes that all revenue is distributed among the various factors of production, stock holders and government taxes. Thus, using a more general definition of costs as:

$$C = C' + NI \tag{4–3}$$

we may now write that model requirement as an equality between total revenue and total cost, or

$$R = C \tag{4–4}$$

It then follows that

$$\Delta R = \Delta C \tag{4–5}$$

where

$$\Delta R = P(Q) \cdot \Delta Q + \Delta P(Q) \cdot Q \tag{4–6}$$

(with $P(Q)$ representing the base year price of base year output Q)

and

$$\Delta C = P(X) \cdot \Delta X + \Delta P(X) \cdot X \tag{4–7}$$

where $P(X)$ is the base year cost (price) of base year input. Thus, we have

$$P(Q) \cdot \Delta Q + \Delta P(Q) \cdot Q = P(X) \cdot \Delta X + \Delta P(X) \cdot X \tag{4–8}$$

where

$$P(Q) \cdot \Delta Q \text{ and } P(X)\, \Delta X \tag{4–9}$$

represent the effects of changes in quantities of outputs and inputs (aggregated by base year prices)

and

$$\Delta P(Q) \cdot Q \text{ and } \Delta P(X) \cdot X \tag{4–10}$$

represent the effect of changes in prices of outputs and inputs aggregated by base year quantities. By definition, total productivity is

$$TP = \text{Change in real output} - \text{Change in real inputs} \quad (4\text{–}11)$$

or

$$TP = P(Q) \cdot \Delta Q - P(X) \cdot \Delta X, \quad (4\text{–}12)$$

defined in terms of quantity changes.

The accounting identity (4–8) above can be written as

$$P(Q) \cdot \Delta Q + \Delta P(Q) \cdot Q - P(X)\, \Delta X - \Delta P(X) \cdot X = 0 \quad (4\text{–}13)$$

$$P(Q) \cdot \Delta Q - P(X) \cdot \Delta X + \Delta P(Q) + Q - \Delta P(X) \cdot X = 0 \quad (4\text{–}14)$$

Substituting (4–12) in (4–13), we get

$$TP + \Delta P(Q) \cdot Q - \Delta P(X) \cdot X = 0 \quad (4\text{–}15)$$

Alternatively, substituting (4–12) in (4–14),

$$TP = \Delta P(X) \cdot X - \Delta P(Q) \cdot Q \quad (4\text{–}16)$$

which is a definition of *TP* in terms of prices. Substituting individual input prices explicitly, we can write the total income change due to changes in these prices as

$$\Delta P(X) \cdot X = \Delta P(K) \cdot K + \Delta P(L) \cdot L + \Delta P(M) \cdot M. \quad (4\text{–}17)$$

The identity (4–15) can now be written as

$$TP + \Delta P(Q) \cdot Q = \Delta P(K) \cdot K + \Delta P(L) \cdot L + \Delta P(M) \cdot M. \quad (4\text{–}18)$$

In addition to the quantities and prices of the three major input factors, we also need to take into account indirect taxes and a number of financial factors. In defining output for calculating *TP*, deflated indirect non-income taxes (*NIT*) are generally subtracted from deflated revenues.[2] These include (a) property taxes, (b) capital stock taxes, (c) gross receipts taxes, and (d) other non-income taxes.

The first two categories are related to the real investment in plant and equipment, while the last two are related to sales revenue. Total change in these taxes (ΔNIT) consists of real change ($\Delta NITR$) and the "price change" effect which, in this case, means the change resulting from a change in the tax rate ($\Delta NITP$), i.e.,

$$\Delta NIT = \Delta NITR + \Delta NITP. \quad (4\text{–}19)$$

The real effect, $\Delta NITR$, has been implictly accounted for in the definition of output and, therefore, of *TP*,[3] but we also need to account for the "price effect." This is done by expanding the $(\Delta P(X) \cdot X)$ vector to add $\Delta NITP$ to the right hand side (RHS) of equation (4–18).

Since the capital input change is a deduction in the *TP* calculation, but is included (in part) in the net income, we need to reflect this in our model.

Adding $P(K) \cdot \Delta K$ to both sides of the equation, we get

$$
\begin{aligned}
TP + \Delta P(Q) \cdot Q + P(K) \cdot \Delta K = {} & (\Delta P(K) \cdot K + P(K) \cdot \Delta K) \\
& + \Delta P(L) \cdot L + \Delta P(M) \cdot M \\
& + \Delta NITP \qquad (4\text{–}20)
\end{aligned}
$$

where $P(K) \cdot \Delta K$ is the growth of physical input and $\Delta P(K) \cdot K + P(K) \cdot \Delta K = \Delta(P(K) \cdot K)$ is the current undeflated value of change in capital input. For the present expository purpose this may be interpreted as including depreciation (*DEP*), interest charges on debt (*INT*), income taxes (*FIT* + *SLIT*), return to equity investors, i.e., the net income (*NI*) and other miscellaneous financial factors such as uncollectibles (*UNC*), miscellaneous deductions from income (*MDI*) and extraordinary and delayed charges and credits-net (*E&D*).

Substituting these factors for $\Delta(P(K) \cdot K)$, and adding other income (*OI*) to the left hand side (LHS) (as it has not been included in the system of equations relating to the productive system and since it is a part of net income (*NI*) on the RHS), we obtain the fundamental equation underlying NIPA as

$$
\begin{aligned}
TP + \Delta P(Q) \cdot Q + P(K)\Delta K + \Delta OI = {} & \Delta P(L) \cdot L + \Delta P(M) \cdot M + \Delta NITP \\
& + \Delta DEP + \Delta FIT + \Delta SLIT \\
& + \Delta INT + \Delta UNC + \Delta MDI \\
& + \Delta E\&D + \Delta NI \qquad (4\text{–}21)
\end{aligned}
$$

Now, the change in net income can be expressed as the difference between two sets of factors affecting the growth in net income as follows:

	$\Delta NI =$	change in net income
	TP	total productivity
Income	$+ \Delta P(Q) \cdot Q$	value of product price changes
Augmenting	$+ P(K) \cdot \Delta K$	earnings on capital expansion (growth)
Factors	$+ \Delta OI$	change in other income

	$-\Delta P(L)\cdot L$	change in labor input prices
	$-\Delta P(M)\cdot M$	change in prices of purchased materials
	$-\Delta NITP$	change in non-income taxes due to changes in tax rates
	$-\Delta DEP$	change in actual book depreciation
Income	$-\Delta FIT$	change in federal income taxes
Absorbing	$-\Delta SLIT$	change in state and local income taxes
Factors	$-\Delta INT$	change in interest on debt
	$-\Delta UNC$	change in uncollectible revenues
	$-\Delta MDI$	change in miscellaneous deductions from income
	$-\Delta E\&D$	change in extraordinary and delayed items-net

(4–22)

A Note on Capital Growth

As the foregoing model development shows, the change in capital input (= Earnings on Capital Growth) is counted among the income augmenting factors, a procedure which might appear to be counter-intuitive. In accounting terminology, capital is a cost item. However, while interest (related to debt capital) and depreciation charges, are included in the conventional accounting model, no specific allowance is made for the return to equity as a cost item in the income statement because it is a part of the net income. As shown in Figures 4–3 and 4–4, the NIPA model has to account for all the factors that determine net income growth, including the real return on capital expansion.[4] The contribution of earnings on capital expansion is computed by applying the base (previous) year rate of return to the growth of total deflated capital. The other effect of capital growth, namely that which is due to the change in the rate of return itself, is captured by other factors, such as output price changes or productivity. If capital expansion were not accounted for in this way, the change in net income attributed to the other factors would be overstated.

Symbol Definitions

NI = net income in a year
R = total revenue
R_i = revenue from the ith product

	NIPA	INCOME STATEMENT
	Change In Net Income =	Change in Net Income =
TP	Revenue (Deflated)	Change in Revenues[1]
TP	− Non-Income Taxes	− Change in Non-Income Taxes[1]
TP	− Labor Input	− Change in Labor Costs[1]
TP	− Capital Input	− 0.0[2]
TP	− Materials Input	− Change in Materials Costs[1]
	+ Output Price Changes	(See Footnote 1)
	+ Capital Expansion	+ 0.0[2]
	− Inflation in Materials	(See Footnote 1)
	− Inflation in Labor	(See Footnote 1)
	− Inflation in Non-Income Taxes	(See Footnote 1)
	+ Change in Other Income	+ Change in Other Income
	− Change in Depreciation	− Change in Depreciation
	− Change in Federal Income Tax	− Change in Federal Income Tax
	− Change in State & Local Income Tax	− Change in State & Local Income Tax
	− Change in Interest	− Change in Interest
	− Change in Uncollectibles	− Change in Uncollectibles
	− Change in Misc. Deductions	− Change in Misc. Deductions
	− Change in Extra. & Del. Items—Net	− Change in Extra. & Del. Items—Net

Notes
1. These items are in nominal terms and thus include price changes.
2. In the income statement, there is no deduction for capitalized investment expenditures. Thus the return to capital is a part of net income.
3. TP = Total Productivity. See text for definition.

Figure 4-3. Relationship Between NIPA and the Income Statement

P_i = price index (deflator) for the ith product
Q = total output
C = total cost
PC = the value of output price changes from the previous year
X_j = quantity of jth input
P_j = price of the jth input
M = purchased materials and services (deflated)

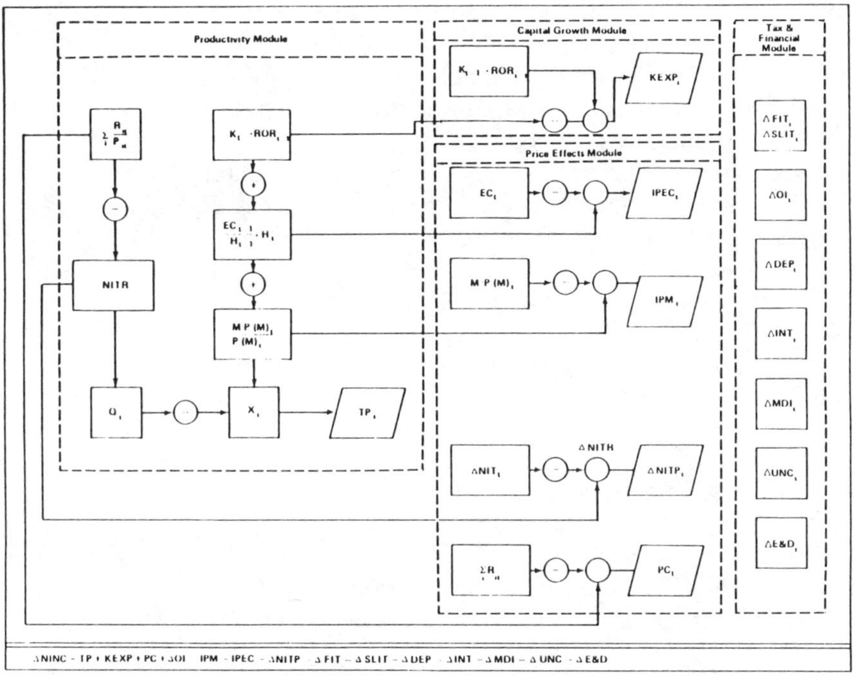

Figure 4-4. Net Income and Productivity Analysis (NIPA)

$P(M)$ = implicit deflator for purchased materials and services
IPM = effect of inflation in materials prices
EC = total employee compensation, including social security taxes
$IPEC$ = effect of the change in labor input prices
H = total employee hours
w = effective hourly rate of remuneration
= EC/H
TP = total productivity gain
$GPI(K)$ = gross capital price index
$PROPT$ = property taxes
GRT = gross receipts taxes
CST = capital stock taxes
$ONIT$ = other non-income taxes
NIT = total non-income taxes
$= TPROP + TGR + TCS + TONI$

$NITR$ = real component of non-income taxes at the previous year's tax rate
$NITP$ = "price" (tax rate change) component of non-income taxes
$KGPE$ = gross invested capital in plant and equipment
KAC = average cash component of capital
KNR = average net receivables component of capital
KMS = average materials and supplies component of capital
GK = average total capital for the year ($= KGPE + KAC + KNR + KMS$)
K = deflated total capital ($= GK/GPI(K)$)
ROR = rate of return on total capital for the firm (actual) $= P(K)$
$KEXP$ = earnings on capital expansion
FIT = federal income tax
$SLIT$ = state and local income taxes
INT = total fixed (interest) charges
DEP = depreciation expense (book)
OI = other income
MDI = miscellaneous deductions from income
$E\&D$ = extraordinary and delayed charges & credits—net
UNC = uncollectible revenues

4.3. The Data

In this section we briefly describe the data for XYZ Corporation for the four years, 1975 through 1978. XYZ is a large nationwide domestic corporation primarily involved in the provision of five different types of services, both in the household and the business markets.

The degree of computational complexity will obviously vary among firms, depending on the nature of the operations. For a single-product firm operating in a single market, the task of collecting the data for *NIPA* is relatively simple. However, for multi-product firms operating in multinational markets, it would require some system aggregation or consolidation of the many data series on outputs and inputs into corporate totals. In such situations, while an overall corporate NIPA study may be of interest to the upper management of the firm, it may also be useful to apply NIPA to some of the individual divisions or profit centers. NIPA can be applied to any part of the firm, which is required to produce an income statement.

Output

XYZ sales revenues are reported separately for five sales categories. For purposes of calculating physical output of the firm, each revenue stream is deflated by the service-specific deflator. Using the definition of revenue

$$R = P \cdot Q \tag{4–23}$$

we define deflated revenue as

$$Q'(t) = \sum_{i=1}^{5} (R(it)/P(it)) \tag{4–24}$$

where

$R(it)$ = Revenue from the ith service category in year t;
$P(it)$ = Price deflator for the ith service category; and
$Q'(t)$ = Total deflated revenue for year t, stated in terms of the previous year's prices.

Note that $P(it - 1) = 1$ since NIPA requires that deflated revenues be stated in terms of prices of the previous year.

Total output for the firm is then defined as

$$Q(t) = Q'(t) - NITR(t) \tag{4–25}$$

where $NITR(t)$ is the value of real non-income taxes for year t as defined in connection with equation (4–19) above.

Capital Input

Capital input is derived using the flow of services concept. It represents the return foregone on alternative investment opportunities for the entire capital stock of the firm. This capital stock is the embodiment of investor's capital in physical and financial assets. Alternatively, capital input can be thought of as the rental value of these capital resources.

Measurement of capital for a firm is a very difficult task and perhaps the most complex part of developing the necessary data for a total productivity study. It is even more difficult to accurately measure the opportunity cost of capital. Since the many conceptual as well as measurement issues in this area are beyond the scope of this paper, the reader is referred to Usher [1980].

To obtain our measure of capital, the current value of all surviving physical plant and equipment is estimated by type and vintage of plant, taking historical book costs and multiplying them by an appropriate investment price index. Aggregate plant under construction along with plant held for future use is also included. (The rate of return computed for the total capital stock is also applied to this plant for purposes of calculating earnings on expansion.) The resulting value is subsequently restated in terms of investment prices of the previous year.

Working capital consists of (a) average net receivables, (b) average cash, and (c) average inventories of materials and supplies. Net receivables can be thought of as future revenues and thus are deflated by a composite output deflator for XYZ Corporation. The other two components are deflated by the implicit deflator for Gross National Product (GNP). The sum of physical plant and the real working capital is the total value of capital resources (K) of the firm.

Capital input is then derived by applying the firm's actual[5] rate of return (r) in the previous year to the real value of capital stock (K) as

$$\text{Capital input } (t) = r(t-1) \cdot (K(t)). \tag{4–26}$$

Thus, the change in capital input is $r(t-1) \cdot \Delta(K(t))$.

Labor Input

Labor input represents the value of all human resources employed within the firm. These resources are measured by first estimating total hours committed to the productive process and then multiplying them by the previous year's average hourly compensation, including the employer's contribution to Social Security taxes. To capture the total hours along with any improvements in labor quality, XYZ employees are classified into several occupational categories (n) and cross-classified into a number of seniority groupings (m). Actual hours are calculated for each of the job-seniority cells and weighted by their respective relative weights in the base year. It should be noted that the job-seniority weighting is very valuable in capturing the change in the true labor input, especially for firms that experience a significant change in the work force mix.

These hours are finally converted to dollar cost in terms of the previous year's rate of pay, $w(t-1)$. That is

$$\text{Labor input} = w(t-1) \cdot \sum_{i}^{n} \sum_{j}^{m} \lambda\, ij(t-1) \cdot Hij(t) \qquad (4\text{–}27)$$

where

$w(t-1)$ = Average hourly compensation for all employees in the previous year.
$\lambda(ijt-1)$ = Relative weight for the ijth cell.
$H(ijt)$ = Total hours in the ijth cell in the current year.

The relative weights, (λij) represent the ratio of average hourly compensation for the ijth cell in the base year $(w(ij))$ to the average hourly compensation of the entire workforce in the base year (w).

Thus, for the base year,

$$\lambda(ij) = w(ij)/w. \qquad (4\text{–}28)$$

Note that these weights are normalized, so that

$$\sum_{i}^{n} \sum_{j}^{m} \lambda(ij)/(n \cdot m) = 1. \qquad (4\text{–}29)$$

Materials Input

All materials and services purchased from other enterprises are included in this category. These include energy, paper, computer rentals, and so on. Wherever possible, each component is deflated by an appropriate deflator. Where no specific deflators are available, the general implicit deflator for GNP is used to remove the effects of inflation in costs of these materials and services. Of course, in each case the deflator represents an index with a value of unity in the previous year so that the deflated items are volumes in terms of prices of the previous year.

4.4. The Results

Organization

A summary of the key results for 1975 through 1978 is presented in Table 4–1. For each year, the table shows the quantitative magnitude of the impact of each factor affecting net income growth. We have organized these factors into two groups: the income augmenting and income absorbing factors described in section 4.1. Factors which generally contribute positively to the growth of earnings when they increase—namely, productivity, output price changes, capital growth, and other income—have been designated as "income augmenting" factors. On the other hand, factors which generally reduce net income when they increase have been designated as "income absorbing" factors. These include three

Table 4–1. XYZ Corporation Net Income and Productivity Analysis Summary (Thousands of Dollars)

	1975	*1976*	*1977*	*1978*
Total productivity gain	576	747	561	871
Earnings on capital expansion	180	251	382	448
Value of price changes	803	979	568	620
Other income	−126	46	159	84
Total income augmenting factors	1,433	2,023	1,670	2,023
Price effects in:				
Materials costs	204	138	184	240
Labor costs	742	775	407	607
Non-income taxes	73	83	41	31
Change in:				
Depreciation	229	227	322	285
Federal income taxes	29	295	180	308
S&L income taxes	15	17	35	20
Interest charges	139	61	24	110
Uncollectibles	13	7	21	46
Misc. deduc. from income	—	—	1	—
Extra. & del. items—net	−2	16	31	−41
Total income absorbing factors	1,442	1,619	1,246	1,544
Estimated change in net income	−9	404	424	479
Actual change in net income	−9	404	424	479

under inflation—materials, labor, and non-income taxes—showing the portion of increase in the respective cost categories resulting purely from inflation (i.e., other than the increase in volume of activity). They also include changes in depreciation, interest charges, income taxes, and a number of other financial factors. Within each group we have constructed subtotals for income augmenting and income absorbing factors, with the change in net income defined as the difference between these subtotals.[6]

At the bottom of the table, we show that the NIPA model estimate of the change in net income is identical with the change actually reported. This means that the model has fully accounted for the growth in net income for each of the years analyzed.

While these results refer to historical years, the model is equally well-suited to projected budgets for future years. In fact, the model is very useful for analyzing corporate budget plans, as it can sound advance warnings about potential problems in the projections. It enables management to determine the expected contribution of each of the factors and makes it possible to evaluate trade-offs among the key relevant variables. One can also ask the usual "what if" questions and perform sensitivity analyses of the planning assumptions. We shall return to possible uses of the model in the next section.

Graphical Presentation

The NIPA results can also be presented in the form of an "arrow chart" (see figure 4–5). The length of each arrow shows the magnitude of the impact of each factor upon the change in net income for the year under study and the point of the arrow indicates the direction of the impact. The income augmenting factors are shown first in a cumulative fashion, followed by a cumulative netting out of the income absorbing factors, with the difference exactly matching the change in net income for the year. Note, however, that one of the income absorbing factors in this figure—non-income taxes—acted to increase net income, since in this year these taxes were actually lower relative to the real capital stock and revenue (on which they are based) than they were in the previous year.

For brevity, a number of financial factors have been combined with income taxes and shown on the arrow chart as "Tax and Financial" factors. Of course, if desired, each of the underlying variables could be shown separately in this figure, including components of the productivity calculation. However, the detail might clutter the chart; if a picture is supposed to be worth a thousand words, it had better be crisp and clear.

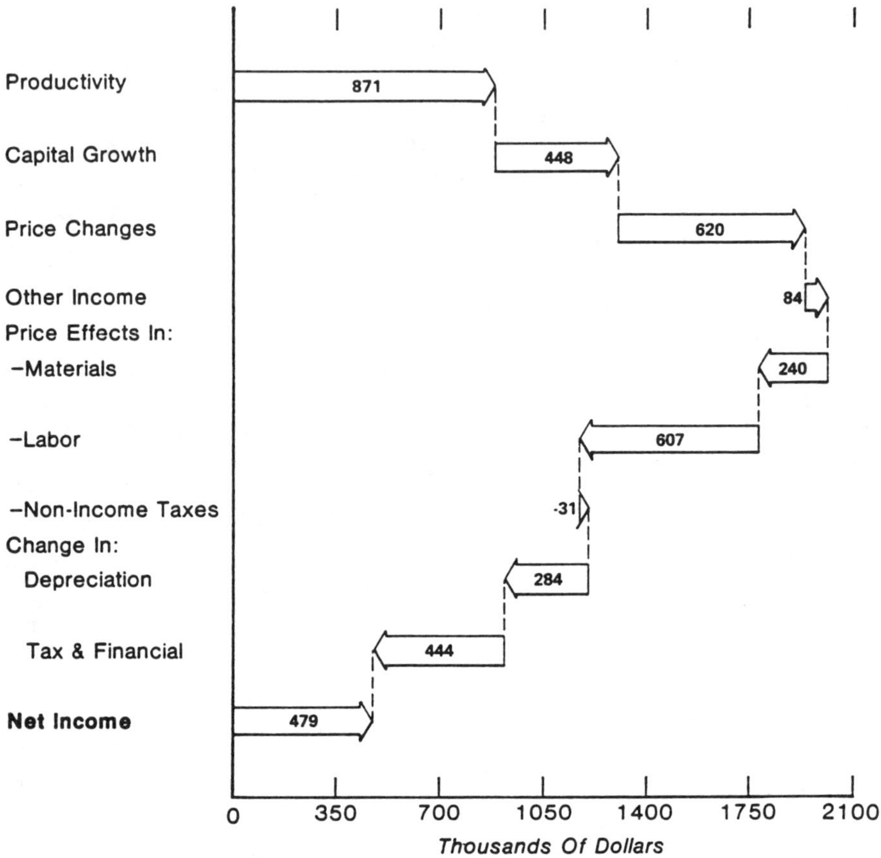

Figure 4–5. NIPA "Arrow Chart" Net Income and Productivity Analysis for XYZ Corporation—1978

Analysis

As shown in Table 4–1, over the four-year period (1975–1978) the dollar contribution of productivity to the growth of net income was very substantial—ranging from $576,000 dollars in 1975 to over $871,000 in 1978—accounting for more than one-third of the total income augmenting factors. (For a comparison of the dollar contribution of productivity to the conventional percentage growth measure of productivity see Table 4–3.) Price changes also played an important role, contributing between just under a million dollars in 1976 and $620,000 in 1978. In 1975 and 1976, that factor amounted to 56 percent and 48 percent respectively of the total for all income augmenting factors. (Table 4–2 gives the percentage distribution of the respective factors in the positive and the negative groupings. Figures 4–6 and 4–7 give the dollar contribution and percentage shares of each major factor over time.) The third important income augmenting factor—capital growth—increased its share of the income augmenting factors from 13 percent in 1975 to 32 percent in 1978, equal to those of productivity and price changes considered separately. While the dollar values of these factors may depend on the level of activity in a given year, these percentage distributions seem to offer a good way to look at trends over time.[7]

Among the income absorbing factors, the largest was the increase in the rate of employee compensation throughout the period analyzed. This is followed by income taxes, depreciation, and materials inflation. In terms of percentage impact, labor price increases ranged from 32 percent of the total

Table 4–2. XYZ Corporation Net Income and Productivity Analysis Summary

	1975	*1976*	*1977*	*1978*
	% Of Income Augmenting Factors			
Total productivity gain	40	38	39	32
Earnings on capital expansion	13	11	17	32
Value of price changes	56	48	34	32
Other income	−9	3	10	4
Total income augmenting factors	100	100	100	100
	% Of Income Absorbing Factors			
Price effects in:				
Materials costs	14	9	15	16
Labor costs	51	48	32	38
Non-income taxes	5	5	4	−3
Change in:				
Depreciation	16	14	26	19
Federal income taxes	2	18	14	21
S&L income taxes	1	1	3	1
Interest charges	10	4	2	8
Uncollectibles	1	0	2	3
Misc. deduc. from income	0	0	0	0
Extra. & del. items—net	−0	1	2	−3
Total income absorbing factors	100	100	100	100

Table 4-3. Comparison of Traditional Total Productivity and NIPA Measures

	Traditional Productivity (%)	*NIPA Productivity ($000)*	*Dollar Value of 1% Gain in Productivity ($000)*
1975	2.1	576	274
1976	3.2	747	233
1977	2.8	561	200
1978	3.7	871	235

Notes: 1. The traditional measure is derived from a fixed base-year index of total productivity (Output/(Capital + Labor + Materials)) constructed for XYZ corporation.

2. Since the base year for NIPA changes every year, its productivity gain in terms of dollars will not necessarily follow the growth pattern of the traditional productivity study.

income absorbing factors in 1977, to 51 percent in 1975. Combined federal and state and local income taxes ranged from 3 percent in 1975 to 22 percent in 1978. Increases in depreciation expense ranged from 14 percent in 1976 to 26 percent in 1977. Inflation in Materials costs accounted for between 9 percent and 16 percent of the total income absorbing factors.

Although NIPA requires a decomposition of the total nominal change in some of the variables into quantity and "price" components, not all of these components appear in the summary, Table 4–1. The remaining components can be displayed as a natural byproduct of the basic NIPA model application. Figure 4–8 contains the dollar distributions of total nominal changes between the price effects and real volume changes for revenue, labor costs, and materials costs.

The price component of the revenue change over the period dropped from as much as $979,000 of the revenue increase in 1976 down to $568,000 in 1977 and $620,000 in 1978. Thus, volume growth has accounted for more and more of the overall growth in revenues, increasing from $814,000 in 1975 to over $2 million in 1978.

Labor costs present an interesting picture. Since total employee hours actually fell by 1 percent and 7 percent in 1975 and 1976, respectively, the estimated inflationary increases in labor costs were $742,000 and $775,000. These increases were both above the nominal change in total labor costs. In other words, nominal increases would have been even higher, had it not been for the decline in the number of hours (possibly reflecting an actual decline in the work force or a decline in the average hours per week, or both).

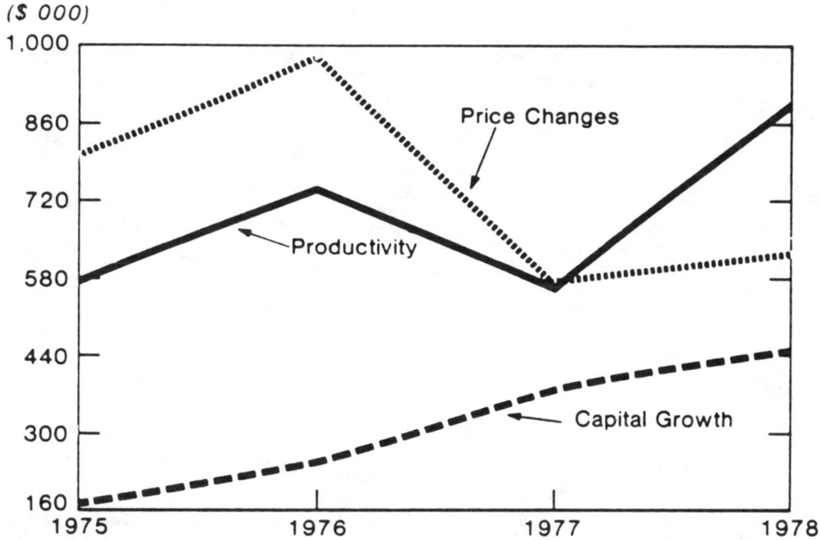

Percentage Distribution of Productivity, Capital Growth and Price Changes (% Of Income Absorbing Factors)

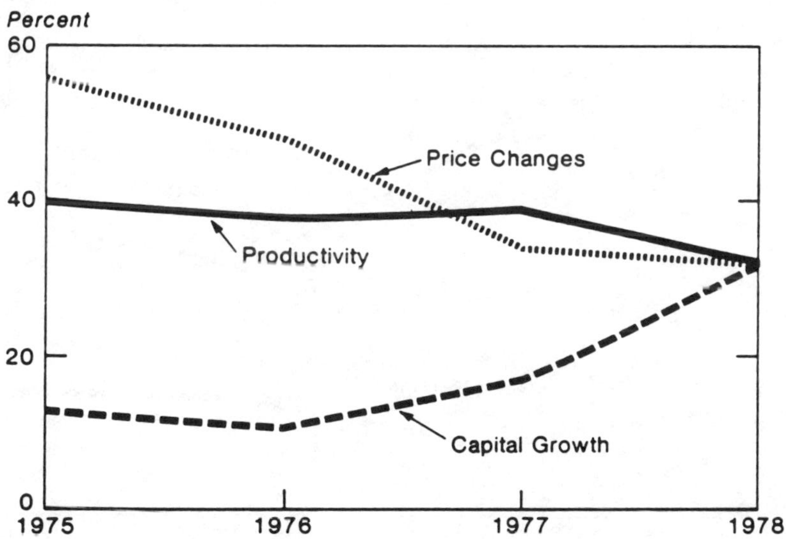

Figure 4-6. Productivity Gain, Capital Growth and Price Changes

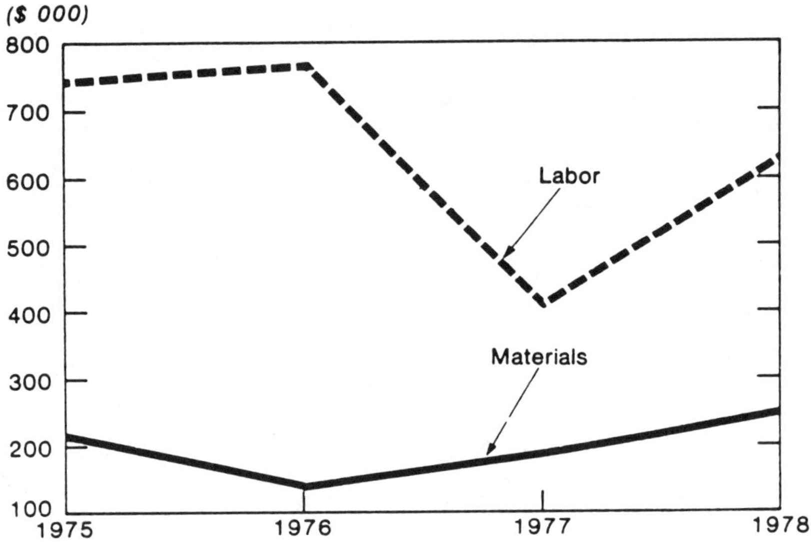

Percentage Distribution of Price Effects in Labor and Materials (% Of Income Absorbing Factors)

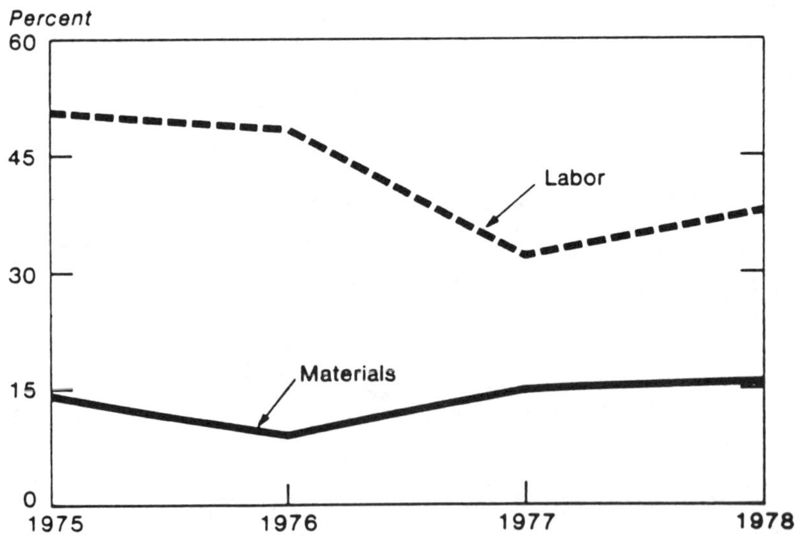

Figure 4-7. Price Effects in Labor and Materials

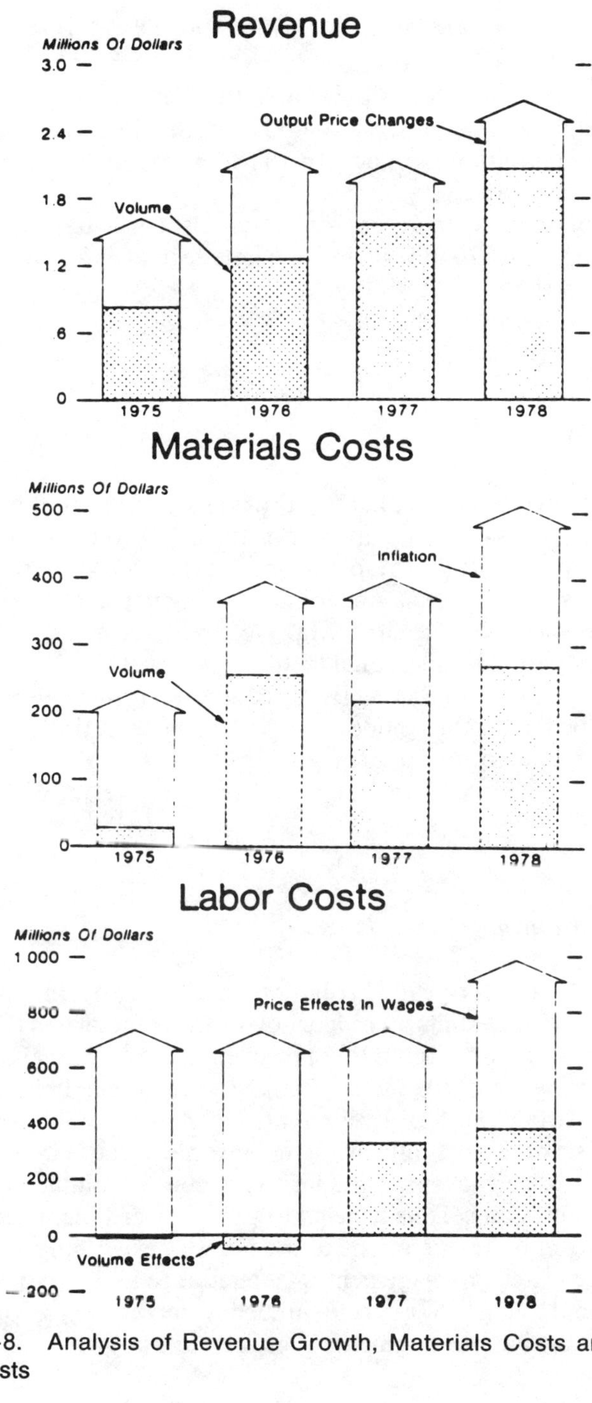

Figure 4-8. Analysis of Revenue Growth, Materials Costs and Increases in Labor Costs

In 1977 the increases in hours accounted for $328,000 of the increase in total compensation. The other $407,000 of the increase was due to increases in compensation per hour. In 1978, the increases were $279,000 and $607,000, respectively.

The effect of volume increases on materials costs has ranged from $27,000 in 1975 to $270,000 in 1978. The effect of inflation was much stronger in 1975 than in 1978.

4.5. Uses of NIPA

While the traditional financial analyses provide a good deal of information for management decision-making, most of them ignore the real (physical) side of the story. NIPA, on the other hand, takes both the real and the financial aspects into account and offers the manager a more comprehensive "report card" on the firm. Many of the data items in NIPA are familiar to managers. The additional factors will, hopefully, fill the gap that has existed for some time. Since NIPA reduces everything to dollars and cents, it is hoped that this model will find some practical uses by the decision makers and corporate planners.

The following are some of the important possible uses of NIPA.

Comparison of Earnings Trends

By providing a year-over-year distribution of factors affecting the growth of net income, NIPA permits a comparison of these factors as they impact on the earnings trend over time. It supplements the traditional accounting analysis of earnings, which generally looks at the nominal changes in net income and other factors. NIPA represents an improvement over the usual variance analysis of factors influencing net income because it separates the changes due to price movements from those due to volume changes for both outputs and inputs. Thus it helps to point toward inefficiency which may be creeping into the operations of the firm. By examining productivity or efficiency separately, management is better able to focus on those factors which may be having an adverse influence on earnings, or on any component factor, income-augmenting or -absorbing.

Analysis of Sources of Net Income Growth

The standard NIPA summary table provides a fairly complete picture of a number of key factors such as productivity, capital growth, output price changes on the positive side, and materials costs, labor costs, depreciation and income taxes (among others) on the negative side, affecting net income growth. A knowledge of their individual trends and their relative (percentage) contributions can be very helpful in assessing the reasonableness of future budgets or corporate plans.

Corporate Planning Uses

Currently, most large-scale corporate planning models rely almost entirely on the conventional accounting framework. While being very useful for the general purpose for which they are designed—financial analysis of the income statement and the balance sheet—these models frequently ignore the productivity story underlying the financial statements. NIPA can easily be incorporated into a corporate planning model and can be a very useful enhancement. To establish a track record, NIPA results should be examined for a number of historical years so that managers become familiar with the underlying strength of the model. In any case, care should be taken in using NIPA in the context of a planning model so as to avoid misuse of the results. This means that the analyst has the responsibility for creating a proper understanding of the tool and its limitations.

As mentioned earlier in this paper, NIPA provides a more comprehensive picture of the factors affecting the health of a corporation in that it explicitly shows the dollar contribution of productivity, price changes, capital growth along with the dollar impact of inflation on the bottom line. Thus, NIPA could be a valuable tool for examining the possible alternative scenarios in terms of the well-defined determinants of net income growth.

More importantly, NIPA can be used for deriving quantitative policy recommendations for achieving prespecified management goals and numerical targets.

Sensitivity Analysis of Assumptions

Future budgets are essentially pegged to some key assumptions about technological developments, economic growth, prices of investment goods, wage contracts, taxes, prices of output, and prices of inputs. However, the budgets are generally devoid of any explicit assumptions about the underlying productivity trends. NIPA provides a tight, logical, and quantitative framework where all assumptions must be made explicit. Thus it would permit a sensitivity analysis of, for example, the inflation assumption. By varying the assumed rate of inflation, we can examine the incremental impact on net income growth. Similarly, we can examine the effect of a different output growth pattern in the future, or a new labor contract, or a different cost of capital in the future.

Useful By-Products

In order to develop the NIPA results, it is obvious that a great deal of new information has been collected and a fairly comprehensive data base established. These data may also be valuable for a variety of analyses within or outside the NIPA framework. This data base is particularly useful in economic and financial analyses, as it contains data generated by a complete economic model of the firm. Thus the data are developed on a consistent basis which can be used for a number of applications. Selected examples of such byproducts were shown in Figure 4–8.

Trend Comparison with Macroeconomic Indicators

This would permit us to make comparisons between, say, the implicit output price increases of the firm with the general price level or with the projected price behavior of some other relevant entity.

An important and apt comparison, often made with the traditional productivity measures, is between the implicit productivity trend projected for the firm and that of the industry or the economy as a whole. This type of comparison, however, should only be made if the total productivity measure for the firm is comparable in concept to the one used for the economy or the industry. Productivity measures for the economy are usually based on gross value added while measures for certain industries may be developed on gross value added or on a gross output basis. (See Kendrick and Grossman [1979].) Given the degree of interdependence between the firm and the environment in which it operates, the projected trends in the economy may serve as a guide or the boundaries within which the firm can achieve an acceptable rate of return and an overall performance.

Notes

1. The total productivity (TP) concept used in this paper refers to the ratio of total output to the combined capital, labor, and materials inputs for a firm. This is distinguished from measures of Total Factor Productivity based on Value Added (TFPVA), which is a ratio of Value-Added Output to the weighted sum of just primary inputs, namely capital and labor.

2. Indirect or non-income taxes are subtracted from revenue since their variation is not directly identified with any particular input in the production process; i.e., they are not considered a part of the cost of the inputs. This exclusion may be justified if one accepts the U.S. Treasury Department's definition of a tax as "a compulsory payment for which no specific benefit is received in return." On the other hand, if these taxes are viewed as payments for state and local government services, such as roads, fire protection and police, a case could be made for not subtracting NIT from revenues. If so, real NIT would become part of total input costs.

3. In terms of tax-adjusted output and real inputs, in this paper we shall define total productivity as:

$$TP = \underbrace{P(Q)\cdot\Delta Q}_{\substack{\text{Total}\\ \text{Deflated}\\ \text{Revenue}}} - \underbrace{\Delta NITR}_{\substack{\text{Deflated}\\ \text{Non-Income}\\ \text{Taxes}}} - \underbrace{P(K)\cdot\Delta K}_{\substack{\text{Real}\\ \text{Capital}\\ \text{Input}}} - \underbrace{P(L)\cdot\Delta L}_{\substack{\text{Labor}\\ \text{Input}}} - \underbrace{P(M)\cdot\Delta M}_{\substack{\text{Materials}\\ \text{Input}}}.$$

4. "Capital expansion" in this paper refers to addition to aggregate physical capital and change in real working capital during the accounting period under study. Therefore, the return on capital expansion as calculated here does not reflect return on any individual projects started in the period under study. Typically, expansion projects take longer than a year to complete and to generate any return. In NIPA, capital additions accrue earnings when they are put on the books, whenever that might be permitted by the prevailing accounting practices of the industry in which the firm operates.

5. Note that NIPA requires the use of actual rate of return in the previous year rather than some alternative opportunity cost of capital. This is necessary to properly and fully account for the change in net income actually realized (rather than some hypothetical income which would result, had the alternative investment opportunity been used).

6. A negative sign for any item within each group indicates a decline in the level of that variable during the current year. Thus, while Other Income contributed positively to net income in 1976, 1977, and 1978, it had declined in 1975, thus reducing the sum of the income augmenting factors and hence net income. A −31 for Non-Income Taxes (NIT) in 1978, on the other hand, indicates that these taxes would have declined by 31,000 had the 1977 tax rates remained in effect. This −31 reduced the sum of the income absorbing factors in 1978 and thus acted to increase net income. The change in net income is defined as: total income augmenting factors less total income absorbing factors.

7. The idea of decomposition of variables per se is not new. A separation of the real and price changes is often developed to discern trends. However, many of these accounting type decomposition procedures rely on different ad hoc measures of the "real" or physical volume changes for different variables. Thus, it is not uncommon in these situations that parts may add up to more or less than the whole. The principal advantage of the NIPA model is that, by employing the structure of an economic model, it ensures a complete accounting of the total change in an internally consistent manner.

References

Craig, C. E. and Harris, R. C. [1973], "Total Productivity Measurement at the Firm Level," *Sloan Management Review*, Spring, pp. 13–28.

Kendrick, J. W. [1977], *Understanding Productivity: An Introduction to the Dynamics of Productivity Change*, The Johns Hopkins University Press.

Kendrick, J. W. and Grossman, E. S. [1979], *Productivity in the United States, Trends and Cycles*, The Johns Hopkins University Press.

Kraus, J. [1978], "Productivity and Profit Models of the Firm," *Business Economics*, September pp. 10–14.

Tilanus, C. B. (ed.) [1976], *Quantitative Methods in Budgeting*, Martinus Nijhoff, Leiden.

Usher, D. [1980], *The Measurement of Capital*, NBER Studies in Income and Wealth, Volume 45, The University of Chicago Press.

Werner, E. [1979], "Productivity Based Planning Model for Teleglobe Canada," A Working Paper.

5 PRODUCTIVITY MEASURES: DESCRIPTIVE AVERAGES VERSUS ANALYTICAL NEEDS

Bela Gold

5.1. Introduction

The past decade's sharp increase in studies of changes in industrial productivity has clearly enriched the perspectives provided by the earlier surge in such efforts during the 1930s, which was similarly stimulated by widespread concern about the declining competitiveness of domestic industries. But the more recent analyses by economists have been broadened to consider capital as well as labor inputs, have used better measures of output, and have applied more sophisticated methodologies, including econometric and input-output models. Nevertheless, the results have remained more serviceable as descriptions of past magnitudes and of gross relationships than as sources of analytical insights into the causes of observed changes, or of persuasive guides to the development of programs to improve productivity performance.

These fundamental limitations derive from two characteristics of most such studies.[1] One involves continued dominant reliance on highly

Bela Gold is the Fletcher Jones Professor of Technology and Management, Claremont Graduate School, Claremont, California.

aggregative statistics. The second involves continued concentration on simply determining the average relationship over some past period between the total magnitudes of given inputs and of total outputs, without serious efforts to probe more deeply into the reasons for changes in resulting findings—resting such explanatory efforts instead on *ex post* logical speculations and rationalizations which have seldom been tested by careful analyses of the actual processes involved.

Because these limitations have an important bearing on the validity of the performance evaluations and policy recommendations based on such studies, the following discussion will review the nature of resulting vulnerabilities before suggesting some more effective means of meeting managerial and governmental needs.

5.2. On the Vulnerability of Aggregate Measures of Productivity

Growing concern about the apparent decline in the competitiveness of American manufacturing has led to an increasing array of studies of the changing "productivity" of such industries during recent years as well as of comparisons of their "productivity" with major foreign competitors. Reliance on national aggregates in such industry studies, however, has encouraged unfounded and even misleading interpretations.

On the Significance of Industry Averages

For example, a variety of studies have been made of the relative "productivity" of the Japanese, American, and Western European steel industries. But in fact the steel industry of most countries is nothing more than a statistical artifact. It usually encompasses a broad array of plants with widely varying operating characteristics and capabilities. Moreover, such national industries do not compete with other national industries, for competition tends to be sharply focussed by products in particular markets. Nor can productivity performance be meaningfully aggregated beyond the plant and firm, for these alone represent the outcome of unified managerial programs to maximize the utilization of available resources towards achieving specified economic objectives—often at the expense of their domestic as well as foreign competitors.

A number of purposes can, of course, be served by using the aggregative industry data published by government agencies, trade associations, and trade journals. Their availability provides a breadth of informational coverage which few, if any, individual researchers would have the resources to duplicate, even in the unlikely event that they could get access to individual plant and firm operating data. The resulting statistics relating to total inputs of labor, capital, and other supplies and to total outputs of major products, as well as to associated changes in revenues, costs, profits, and prices, provide essential foundations for studies of adjustments in the magnitude of operations of defined industry categories *as a whole*. But the ready availability of such data has also tempted many analysts to use them in ways which are open to serious question.

Plants and firms are obviously grouped into particular statistical categories on the basis of some defined similarities. But the resulting "industry" classifications are usually broad enough to encompass a wide range of differences among the operations covered in respect to such important characteristics as: capacity, product-mix, product quality, technological processes, modernity of facilities, capacity utlization rates, relative costs, primary markets and other determinants of the operating effectiveness, competitiveness, and profitability of the plants and firms included within that category. This raises a serious question concerning what purposes can be effectively served by analyzing changes in the *average relationships* among statistical aggregates of inputs and outputs for such changing arrays of heterogeneous components.

Results are obviously of little use to investors, or customers, or suppliers, or even competitors. Nor have government and academic analysts been notably successful in utilizing such superficial aggregates to identify the specific loci, magnitudes, and causes of various industry problems as the basis for developing remedial policies effectively adapted to the distinctive urgencies of different sectors within major industries. To meet the practical needs of these various groups would require analysis of the internal differences within industry aggregates associated with such firm and plant characteristics as were noted immediately above.

The wide range of differences within national totals for an industry may be illustrated by the following comparisons of man-hours per ton of finished products in the steel industry of Japan. This was estimated for the American Iron and Steel Industry to approximate 9 for Japan at about 90 per cent of capacity in the mid-1970s [25]. My own detailed estimates for five Japanese mills, which represented the leading edge of their international competitiveness and which accounted for 40 per cent of their national capacity, ranged between 2.09 for Oita and 4.93 for Kashima to average 3.48 in 1975–1976, or more than 60 percent below the estimated average for the whole industry.[14] And it is equally important to recognize that, even within this newest and most efficient sector of the Japanese steel industry, Oita's output per man-hour was more than double that of Kashima—attributable less to differences in performing identical operations than to the significance of disparities in the composition of their respective outputs. Moreover, this intra-industry range apparently became even broader in 1980, when the *Wall Street Journal* (April 7, 1981) estimated that the newest mill, Ohgishima, had reduced man-hours per unit of output to 1.1.

On the Limitations of Industry Measures

The heterogeneity of operations encompassed within most industry categories also undermines the significance of resulting aggregate measures. The most meaningful measure is probably total man-hours, although even this tends to be inadequate in two respects. For example, it ignores differences in the skill composition of the labor force, which has been changing. It is also often based on employment levels in selected periods, thus understating seasonal fluctuations. Even more important, it encourages misinterpretations of productivity gains by ignoring recent trends towards shifting functions from wage earners to salaried employees. For example, the ratio of salaried employees to wage earners in the domestic iron and steel industry rose from 17.6 percent in 1950 to 36.8 percent in 1980.[1]

Changes in total material inputs present even more difficult problems of interpretation. One reason is that the quality of inputs, especially those involving natural resources, is subject to changes. A second is that the composition of material inputs may be altered substantially as a result of changes in technologies, in product specifications, and in the relative prices of substitutable materials and energy. And a third is that the levels of processing and fabrication of purchased supplies and components may also be adjusted over time, especially within particular sectors of an industry, as a result of forward or backward integration.

Capital investment data are the source of still more perplexing problems. Because capital goods prices tend to be subject to substantial fluctuations, because the facilities and equipment of given plants tends to reflect an array of acquisitions in different periods and, hence, at different price levels, and because net investments are the result of diverse patterns of depreciation allowances over differing periods, net changes in resulting aggregates are difficult to interpret. But it is even more difficult to assess attendant changes in the "productivity" of net fixed investment because of the general absence of persuasive data concerning the changes in plant capacity, flexibility, and quality capabilities contributed by intermittent acquisitions of various types of capital goods.

The latter consideration also calls attention to significant uncertainties concerning the estimates of capacity which are often used to assess the impacts of additional investments as well as the rate of capacity utilization. It is apparent, for example, that capacity tends to vary with different product mixes, because not all equipment is capable of producing all products, and because progressive shifts in product-mix tend to erode the relevance of facilities whose economic contributions are limited to products in declining demand. Economic capacity also tends to be affected by changes in manufacturing technologies, as well as by alterations in the level of processing at which materials and components are acquired. In the absence of specific information concerning these sources of potential changes in capacity, published estimates may be at substantial variance with competitive capabilities. For example, it is quite conceivable that current estimates of capacity in the steel industry may be 20–25 percent greater than is likely to prove competitively viable even after reasonable recovery from currently depressed demand.

Output measures, too, have certain limitations which are often glossed over. When calculated by means of relative price weights for various products, the result does indeed reflect changes in total product value not due to changes in prices relative to some base period. But it ignores the nature and magnitude of changes in the quality and service capabilities of products which have not been paralleled by accompanying price adjustments. In many cases, such product improvements are the result of significant advances in technological processes and production methods as well as of substantial investments in new equipment—and yet may fail to effect any comparable gains in price because of competitive pressures, thereby leading to underestimates of associated advances in productive efficiency. Calculations of changes in the physical output of an industry also tend to be weakened by reliance on relatively broad categories of product prices which cannot take account of the very differences in qualitative specifications within each product group which may elicit significant price differentials as well as competitive advantages.

How important are these limitations of industry-level measures of inputs and outputs? The answer depends primarily on the homogeneity of the plants within the category and on the similarity of their experiences and responses during the period studied. It should be emphasized, however, that truly extensive similarities are so unlikely in most industries that a substantial burden of proof rests on any analyst making such claims. In the absence of persuasive evidences of homogeneity, these aggregative data could still be utilitized for certain general historical purposes, such as would be involved in reviewing long-term changes in the broad dimensions of an industry. But it would be very difficult indeed to justify their use in seeking to evaluate changes in the productive efficiency or competitiveness of the industry or in seeking to explain the causes of observed changes in average relationships. For such purposes, it is necessary to undertake more detailed explorations of the characteristics of component plants, of the differential impacts on them of product and input market pressures, and of their responsive adjustments.

One of the most troublesome aspects of such a review of the limitations of the data commonly used to appraise productivity changes at the level of industries is that the serious weaknesses which have been noted are readily apparent to qualified analysts—and yet are widely ignored in the rush to provide ostensibly relevant analyses of problems of major public concern.[2]

5.3. On the Vulnerability of Analyses and Interpretations of Industry-Level Changes in Productivity

Most analyses and interpretations of changes in "productivity" relationships at the level of industry aggregates are subject to five sources of vulnerability.

1. They cannot define the managerial objectives that led to the observed changes in productivity relationships.
2. They cannot specify the initiating causes of such observed changes.
3. They cannot trace the successive linkages between changes in inputs and outputs.
4. They cannot identify interactions between internal operating adjustments and external pressures and changes.
5. They cannot determine the effects of productivity changes on such more critical aspects of operating performance as: total unit costs; profitability; and market share.

On Managerial Objectives in Seeking to Change Productivity Relationships

Most productivity studies by economists rest on a set of assumptions which, though vulnerable, are so widely accepted as to remain unstated. One of these is that managements are continuously seeking to increase output per man-hour as well as per unit of other inputs. A second assumption is that such reductions in unit input requirements will yield lower unit costs. And a third is that lower unit costs increase profitability.

Such motivations and expectations certainly do exist, but only as part of a larger system of objectives and pressures. Among the more important of these would be included: marketing pressures for higher quality, lower prices, and new or improved products; procurement pressures involving shortages or higher prices for material inputs; labor pressures to raise wage rates and maintain employment; and financial pressures to conserve capital, minimize risks, and safeguard dividends. Hence, management's primary commitment to at least maintain satisfactory profitability means that it would prefer increases in unit costs by means which promise larger sales at higher prices because of product improvements as over against decreases in unit costs by means of product improvements as over against decreases in unit costs by means threatening comparable reductions in sales volume and product prices because of less competitive products.

Moreover, managements are well aware that the benefits of reductions in unit input requirements are often offset by increases in factor prices. For example, increases in output per man-hour have quite commonly been paralleled by gains in wage rates; and reductions in materials requirements per unit of output have frequently been offset either by higher prices for the more demanding materials specifications permitting such improvements, or by lower prices for the products resulting from skimping either on the quality or quantity of materials. It is also important to bear in mind that productivity increases are often a defensive response to external pressures which threaten disadvantages. Thus, rising wage rates, energy prices, and other input prices may require substantial productivity improvements merely to moderate resulting increases in unit costs, thus yielding no decreases at all. Alternatively, price reductions by competitors may necessitate gains in productivity merely to help minimize any reductions in unit profits due to the enforced matching decrease in product prices.

In short, managements have higher priority objectives than increasing productivity. This means that observed changes in productivity may often be the by-products of other more urgent objectives; that these may entail decreases as well as increases in specified productivity relationships under given circumstances; and, hence, that assuming common motivational objectives for all firms at all times in seeking to interpret industry-level productivity results is likely to be wholly unwarranted.[3]

On the Causes of Changes in Productivity Relationships

Because of their location at the heart of manufacturing operations, changes in productivity relationships may represent reactions to pressures from input factor markets, or to pressures from product markets, as well as the outcome of internally-generated efforts to improve such performance. Specifically, changes in productivity relationships may be attributable to a wide array of developments, including:

1. changes in product designs, in product quality, and in product-mix;
2. changes in output levels and in the length of production runs for individual products;
3. changes in technological processes, in the modernity of facilities, and in the scale of operations;
4. changes in labor motivations, skills, and work rules;
5. changes in production planning and control, in maintenance, and in work-in-process inventory levels; and
6. changes in the availability and quality of purchased materials as well as in the level of prior processing of incoming supplies.

Although all plants in an industry could be affected by any of these sources, the relative urgency of such pressures and opportunities are bound to differ, especially within the perspectives of each management. Hence, comparative studies of individual plants within an industry, and even within a multi-plant firm, commonly reveal wide differences in productivity improvement efforts and results. Accordingly, efforts to attribute industry-level productivity adjustments to one or a few particular developments can seldom be persuasively justified in view of the wide variety of such developments in various stages of diffusion within any given period, in view of the disparate emphases among such alternatives in different plants, and in view of the usual dispersion in the effectiveness of such efforts in different managerial environments.[4]

On the Linkages Between the Causes and Effects of Productivity Changes

Recognition of the complexities of production processes and of variations in product-mix emphasizes the impracticality of directly linking changes in any given input category, such as labor or materials or fixed investment, to changes in total output even at the level of the single plant, much less at the level of an entire industry.

The problems involved may be illustrated by systematic consideration of the basic means whereby managements seek to improve production performance in respect to *each* product. With respect to the initial stages of inputs, attention may be given to possible changes in the quality of each specific category of purchased materials as well as in the combination of different materials and supplies used. And similar appraisals are necessary in respect to each of the other major inputs. But performance improvement efforts must also consider possible substitutions among input categories, including the reduction of labor and capital requirements through purchasing more highly processed materials and components, for example, or substituting capital for labor through increases in mechanization, automation or computerization. Incidentally, such substititions are commonly misinterpreted by statistical analyses as indicating an increase in the productivity of the factors being replaced (as in the case of resulting increases in output per man-hour) rather than as a reduction in the productive contributions of such factors.

Consideration of possible sources of improvements in production operations must be extended further, however. For example, attention must be given to possible interactions between changes in the quantity or quality of each input and their respective factor prices in order to determine resulting changes in such unit costs. Moreover, in order to maximize consequent decreases in total unit costs, prospective choices among alternative sources of improvements must also take account of the relative proportions of total cost likely to be affected by each. Finally, and often most important of all, efforts must be made to assess the effects of contemplated changes on the attractiveness of resulting products to customers, as reflected by likely changes in the quantities which could be sold and in the prices which could be charged for them. This analytical framework is summarized in Figure 5-1.

In order to trace the sources of plant-level changes in productivity, cost and profit relationships, all of the preceding analyses for each product must then be supplemented by allowances for changes in product-mix within each period covered. The critical importance of such adjustments in the composition of output derives from the wide differences which often exist within the range of products made in respect to factor proportions, productivity relationships, relative cost levels and resulting profit margins as well as output volumes and variability. As a result, changes in such performance measures are frequently attributable in much greater measure to adjustments in product-mix than to changes in these measures which are common to all products. For example, output per man-hour can fluctuate significantly at plant and industry levels because of changes in the proportions of output accounted for standardized products using highly mechanized production processes as over against products which are more labor-intensive—even if each product's operations are unchanged during the period.[5]

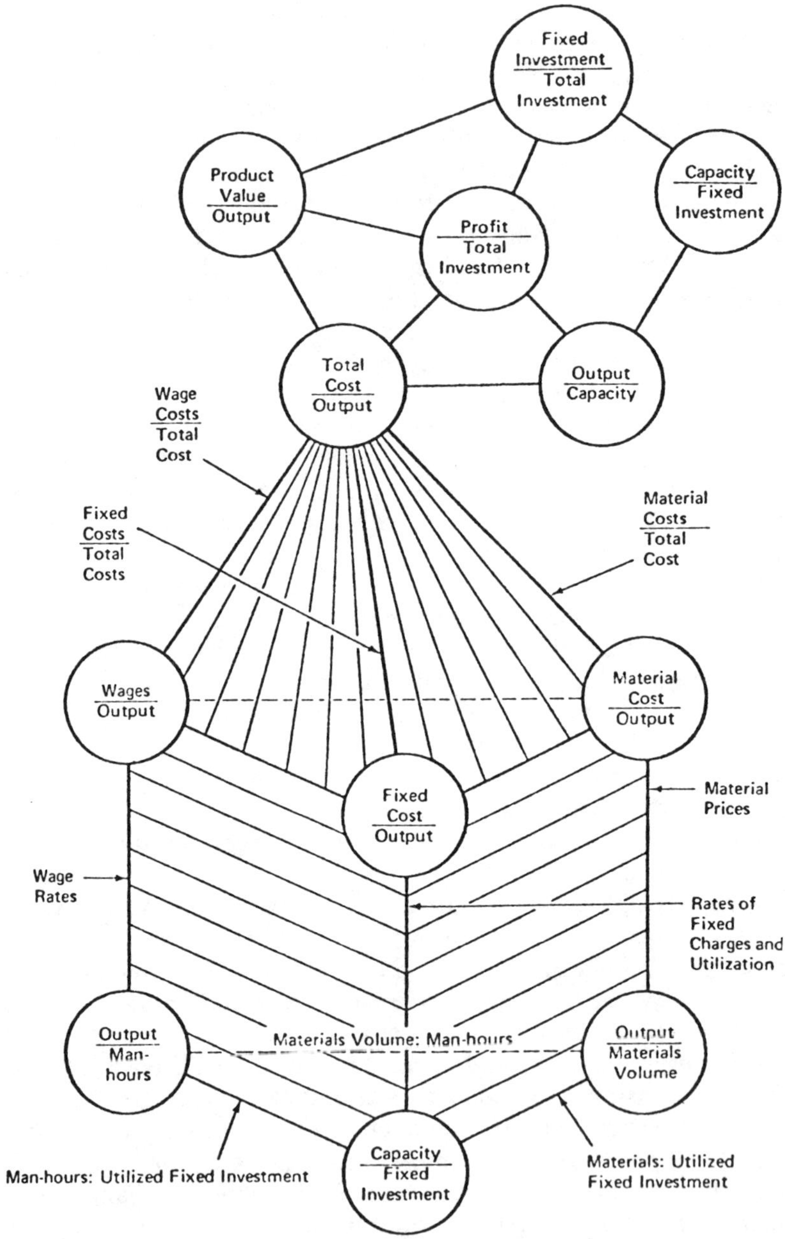

Source: Reprinted with permission from *Omega, International Journal of Management Science* 1 (February 1973). © Pergamon Press, 1973.

Figure 5.1. Productivity Network, Cost Structure, and Managerial Control Ratios

Nevertheless, even after all such analytical requirements have been met, the results would still fall far short of explaining industry-level changes in productivity relationships, costs and profitability, because these are the outcome of distinctive adjustment patterns among all plants in the industry in respect to most of the multiple levels of interactions which have been identified. Hence, there is little professionally authoritative basis for diagnosing the specific causes of observed changes in such industry-level measures of performance in the absence of detailed investigations of the nature and relative importance of interplant and inter-product differences in the large array of interacting factors shaping them. Nor do such industry-level studies provide persuasive bases for appraising the prospective effects of specified changes in productivity relationships and hence for recommending such remedial measures to operating managements or to government officials.

5.4. Elements of a More Effective Approach to the Diagnosis and Improvement of Productivity Performance

Basic Approach—Differentiating Criteria According to Aggregation Levels

Efforts to maximize performance efficiency are limited to systems which are centrally directed to advance specified management objectives by integrating the contributions of all component operations. Hence, although data can be collected covering all of the inputs and outputs of groups of the differently oriented and unintegrated plants or firms comprising most "industry" categories, resulting input-output or revenue-cost relationships must be regarded as merely the happenstance averages of the disparate relationships which are actually generated only within each plant or firm. Indeed, the more favorable performance of some is often achieved at the expense of competitors also encompassed by such averages. Because changes in these averages are the resultants of a wide variety of interacting factors operating at different levels of aggregation, effective diagnoses, evaluations, and planning for improvements requires a systematic disaggregation and decomposition of such outcomes.

One approach which has proven useful begins by regarding all industry aggregates as the passive summation of data representing the resource allocations and performance levels resulting from management decisions limited to individual plants and firms. All production input, output, and cost data can then be analyzed on a plant-by-plant basis, but other revenue, cost, and investment data often cannot be completely disaggregated below the firm level in the case of multi-plant operations. Plant level input, output, and cost data may then be disaggregated on a product-by-product basis, on an operation-by-operation (or departmental) basis, or both, although investment and staff personnel data often cannot be fully allocated in the same way. Finally, cost data may then be decomposed as among the major categories of outlay and then into their respective factor price and quantity determinants.

Such an analytical process facilitates identifying the actual initiating sources of change and then tracing the subsequent interactions which have directly shaped past findings at the level of plants and firms and, through them, have indirectly accounted for industry-level adjustments. Only by means of such more detailed probing can highly vulnerable speculative deductions be replaced by more practically rooted insights into the determinants of changes in performance at higher levels of aggregation. But this approach can also strengthen the bases for estimating the prospective effects of contemplated changes in inputs, production processes, product-mix, and other potential sources of external market pressures, or of internal improvement efforts, on various aspects of performance.

Some Illustrative Empirical Findings

The Productivity-Cost Profitability (P-C-P) analytical framework has been applied to a wide range of industries in the United States and abroad at the level of departments, product lines, plants, firms, and even entire industries.[6] For present illustrative purposes, it may suffice to present sample findings for a machinery manufacturing plant in the Midwest and for an integrated steel mill in Great Britain.

Results in a Machinery Manufacturing Plant. In this illustration, the primary focus will be on disaggregating plant-level results by product lines to show the wide range of differences in their performance. But before reviewing such results, Panels A and B of figure 5–2 demonstrate the importance of uncovering the shorter-term variability which often underlies the reasonably stable adjustment patterns presented by annual data. By indicating the factors fluctuating most and the specific timing of their increases and decreases, such findings help to identify the areas of greatest sensitivity to be considered in future planning, as well as to focus efforts on uncovering the causes of such variations.

Panels A, B, and C of Figure 5–3 illustrate the wide range of differences

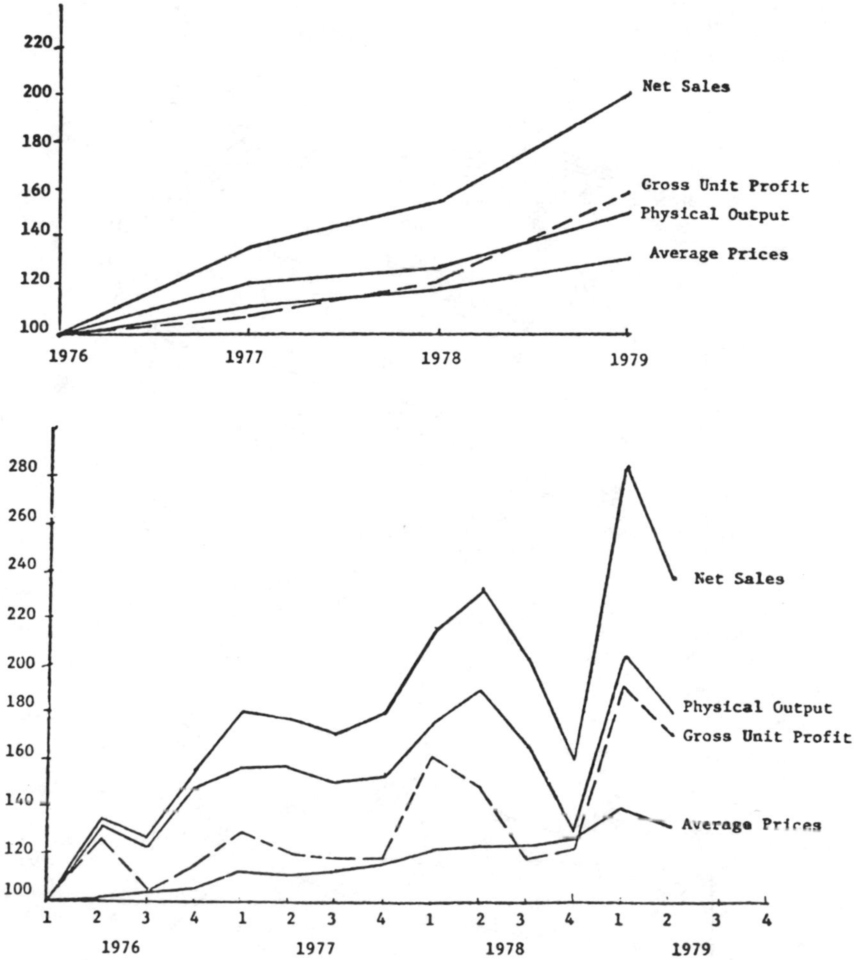

Figure 5–2. Net Sales, Physical Output, Gross Unit Profit and Average Prices Annual and Quarterly

among products in respect to output, unit cost of sales, and gross profits per unit of output which may underlie the plant-level adjustments in these variables. And Panels A, B, and C of Figure 5–4 illustrate the wide range of differences among products which underlie aggregate changes in unit wage costs and output per man-hour.

Thus, by monitoring changes in profitability, costs, and productivity

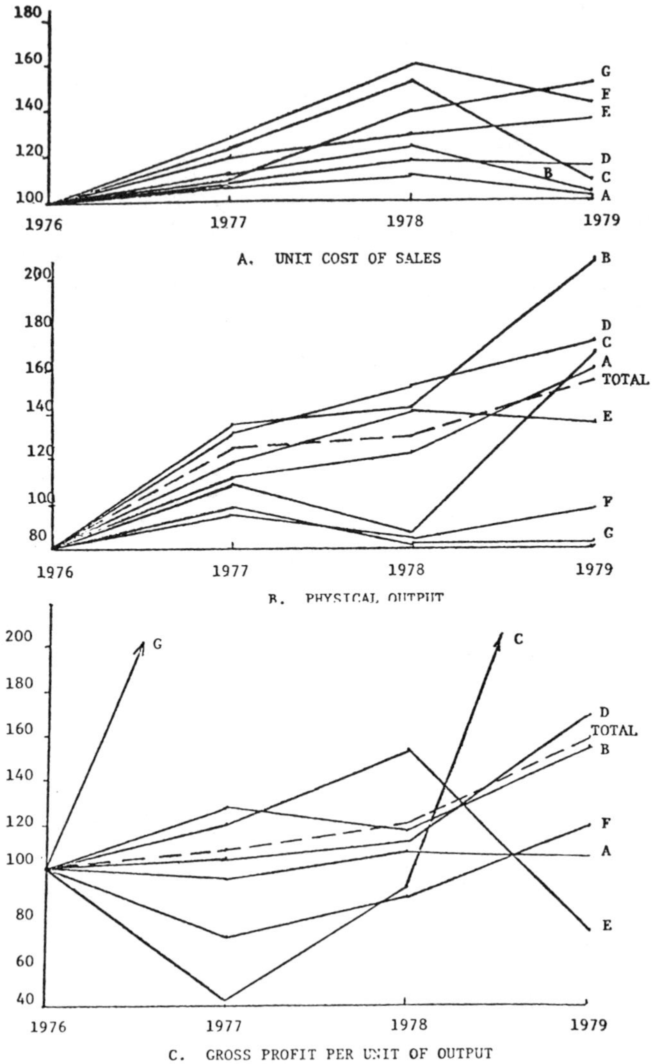

Figure 5-3. Unit Cost of Sales, Output, and Gross Unit Profits by Products—Annual

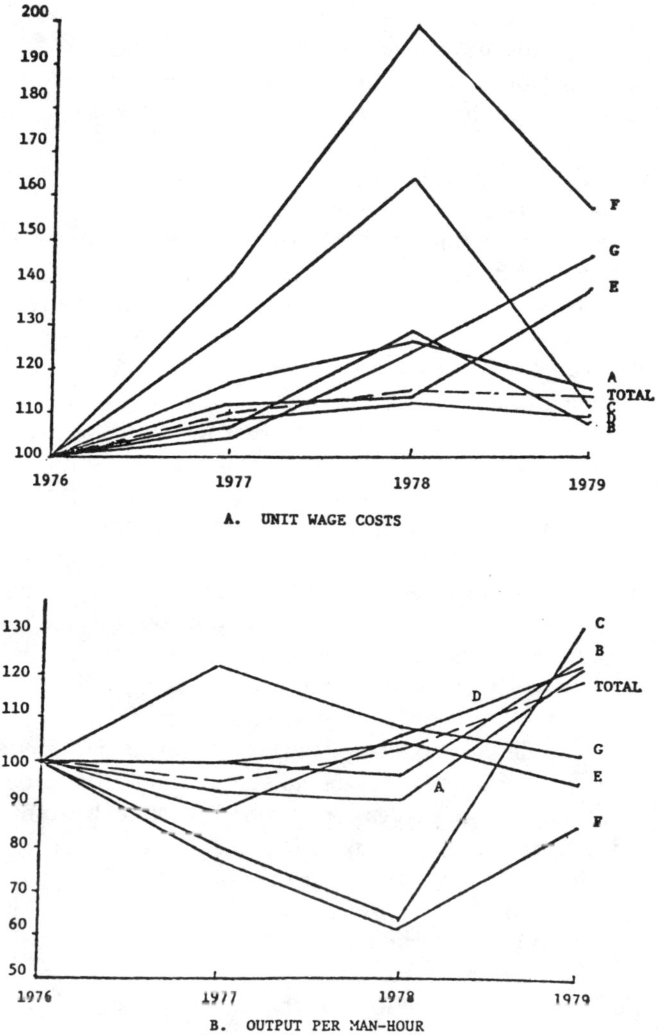

Figure 5-4. Unit Wage Costs and Output per Man-Hour by Products—Annual

quarterly, and perhaps even monthly, the application of the P-C-P System facilitates uncovering the sources as well as the effects of advances and regressions in performance. And by subdividing aggregate adjustments among products, such efforts are strengthened markedly.

Results in a British Steel Mill. In order to illustrate the application of the P-C-P framework to disaggregating plant level results through successive levels to reveal the structure of changes in different departments and even within cost centers, findings in one of the largest integrated steel mills of the British Steel Corporation—its Port Talbot Works—will be reviewed.

Figure 5–5 shows that a steady decline in the rate of profits on total investment during the first four years was accentuated during the fifth, only to be sharply reversed during the last two years covered by our study. The major reason for the outcome during the first five years was that total unit costs rose more rapidly than prices, and this burden was intensified during the fourth and fifth years by lower capacity utilization rates. During the last two years, the rate of profits on total investment rose sharply because a downturn in unit costs was accompanied by rising prices and some recovery in utilization rates. Accordingly, efforts to explain these developments may concentrate primarily on the factors responsible for observed changes in total unit costs, which were dominated by materials and wages, averaging 49–55 percent and 15–18 percent, respectively.

Figure 5–6 demonstrates the need to dig beneath plant aggregates by showing the wide differences in unit cost adjustment patterns among the three operating departments. Specifically, total unit costs rose over the seven-year period by 70 percent in ironmaking and by only about 25 percent in steelmaking and finishing. More particularly, unit material costs rose by 40, 30, and 20 percent, respectively, in these sequential departments, while unit wage cost covered a much wider range, rising by 56 percent in ironmaking, declining by 29 percent in steelmaking, and increasing by 26 percent in finishing.

The major technological change in this plant during the period studied was the replacement of the open-hearth furnaces and the smaller capacity "very low nitrogen" (VLN) furnaces with the basic oxygen furnaces (BOF) during the fifth and sixth years. This changeover involved two major changes in materials inputs: halving the ratio of scrap to pig iron, and replacing the former 70 to 75 percent reliance on fuel oil for energy by almost complete reliance on oxygen, as shown in Figure 5–7. As a result, conversion costs were expected to decline by 20 percent, assuming certain capacity-utilization rates, scrap ratios, and material prices.

Figure 5–7 shows that such expectations were not realized. As often

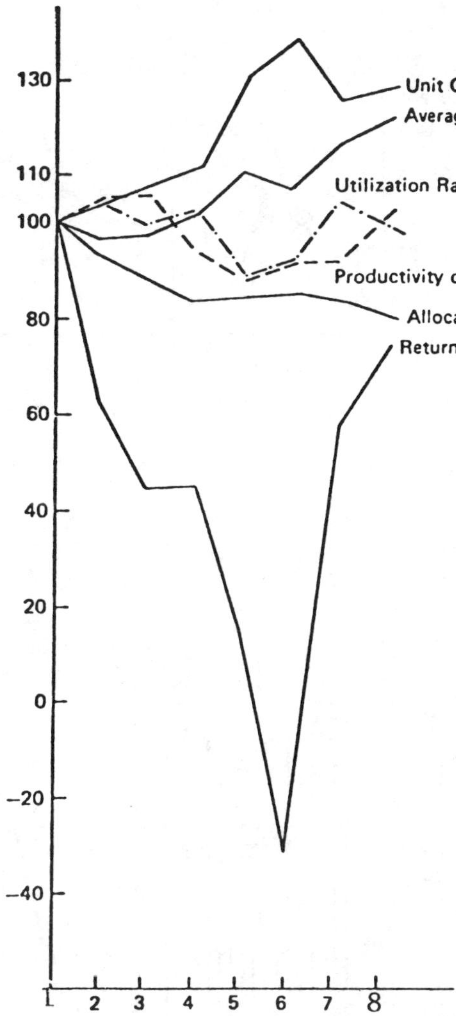

Figure 5-5. Managerial Control Ratios: Steel Mill

Source: S. Eilon, B. Gold, and J. Soesan, *Applied Productivity Analysis for Industry* (Oxford: Pergamon, 1976). Reprinted with permission.

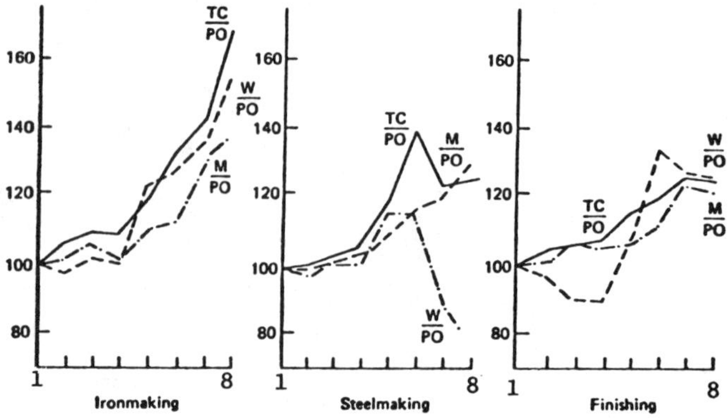

Source: S. Eilon, B. Gold, and J. Soesan, *Applied Productivity Analysis for Industry* (Oxford: Pergamon, 1976). Reprinted with permission.

Figure 5-6. Total Unit Costs, Unit Material Costs, and Unit Wage Costs by Departments

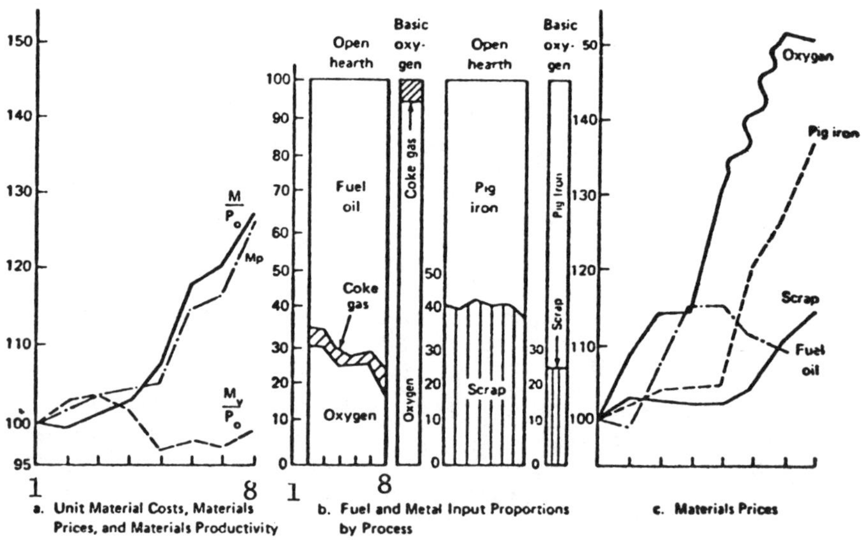

Source: S. Eilon, B. Gold, and J. Soesan, *Applied Productivity Analysis for Industry* (Oxford: Pergamon, 1976). Reprinted with permission.

Figure 5-7. Unit Materials Costs and Their Determinants in Steelmaking

happens, this was due not to erroneous technological estimates, but rather to accompanying economic adjustments. Although the relationship between pig-iron and scrap prices had been reasonably stable for some years preceding the changeover, pig-iron prices rose twice as much as scrap prices during the last three years, as shown in Figure 5–7. Similarly, although increases in fuel oil and oxygen prices were about the same during the first three years, fuel oil prices declined gradually thereafter while oxygen prices rose by one-third. As a result, unit materials costs rose sharply instead of declining, reflecting not only the price increases just mentioned, but also the decrease in materials productivity (or increase in materials volume per unit of output, as shown in Figure 5–7a), owing to the fact that materials inputs, like product outputs, are aggregated into a combined index of changes in total volume by weighting the quantities of each in each year by their average prices in the base and comparison years, thus responding to their disparate price adjustments.

Figure 5–8b shows that the technological innovation also had a major

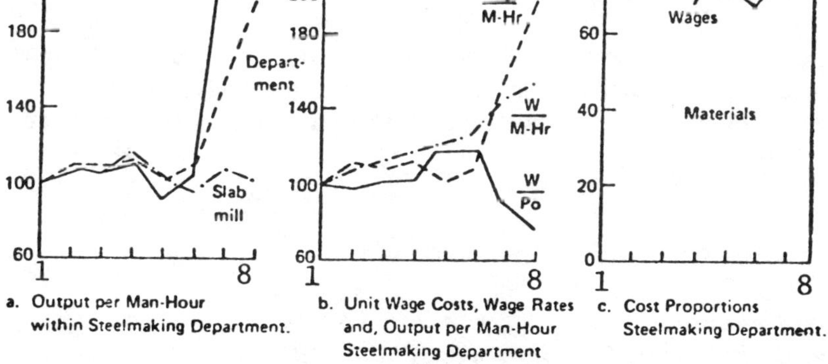

Source: S. Eilon, B. Gold, and J. Soesan, *Applied Productivity Analysis for Industry* (Oxford: Pergamon, 1976). Reprinted with permission.

Figure 5-8. Steelmaking Department: Unit Wage Costs, Output per Man-Hour, Wage Rates, and Cost Proportions

effect on wage costs, reducing them by one-third, despite an increase in wage rates of 15 percent during the last two years. This was attributable to a spectacular tripling of output per man-hour in steel furnace operations combined with no change in labor productivity in the slab mill, which constitutes the remaining half of the department's operations. Unfortunately the effect of the reduction in unit wage costs was minimized by the fact that they account for only about 4 percent of total costs, as shown in Figure 5-8c, while the impact of the increase in unit material costs on total unit costs was multiplied by its dominant proportion of total costs.

In short, it has been possible to identify the direct impacts of the technological innovations and to trace their interactions with other input factors and with factor price adjustments as the basis for determining their effects on the network of productivity relationships and the structure of costs. Moreover, one could easily trace these effects on steelmaking costs further on to the unit costs of finished products and profit margins.

It also should be emphasized, however, that such results represent only the short-term effects of the innovation. Accordingly, this same analytical framework can be used to estimate the probable effects of future increases in the utilization of the new furnaces, which were capable of producing one-third more than the final year's output. In addition, the framework also can be used to estimate the effects of prospective changes in pig-iron, scrap, and oxygen prices.

Finally, presentation of the parallel analyses for each department's operating units—which is not feasible here—would permit an even more detailed mapping of the entire anatomy of plant operations; the tracing of all major innovations, as well as of external impacts, through the entire system over the seven-year period studied; and the development of increasingly persuasive estimates of the prospective effects of any additional contemplated innovations and possible adjustments in product and factor markets.[7]

5.5. Some Concluding Observations

Changes in the Ratio of Any Input to Any Output Can Be Interpreted as Reflecting Changes in the "Productivity" of That Input Only Under Certain Limiting Conditions Which Are Often Violated.

Specifically, such interpretations are justifiable only under the following conditions: if the input and the output are part of an integrated production process; if all of the input is used to produce the given output; if no use is made of any other source of the contributions provided by that input; and if there is no change in the quality or composition of the input or of the output. These conditions are never met at levels of aggregation beyond individual plants and are seldom fulfilled for extended periods even within individual plants.

Even within individual plants, changes in total output relative to the volume of some input tend to represent the net resultant of a wide array of interactions among changes in such factors as: the capacity and rate of capacity utilization; the product composition of output (including the size, design, and quality of individual products as well as the proportions of different products); the quality and level of fabrication of purchased materials and components; the level of mechanization of manual operations and the scale, modernity, and degree of specialization of such facilities and equipment; the skill levels, working conditions, and motivations of direct and of indirect labor; and the proportion and capabilities of technical and managerial personnel.

At the level of industries, and even of multi-plant firms, comparisons of total output with total inputs of labor or other factors of production are also affected by what are often very wide ranges of inter-plant differences among all of the variables cited above, in addition to differences in immediate performance objectives and in relevant material, labor, capital, and product market conditions. Such considerations also make comparisons among the seemingly similar industries in different countries vulnerable to serious weaknesses. Finally, efforts to interpret differences among nations in their respective ratios of gross inputs to gross outputs require still further expansions of the already complex analytical framework which has emerged as a result of efforts to keep broadening the coverage of these measures.

Hence, Determination Of the Causes of Observed Changes in Apparent Productivity Relationships, As Well As Of Resulting Adjustments In Costs and Profitability, Requires Comprehensive Sophisticated Analyses.

There is seldom any shortage of instant "explanations" offering conflicting claims for credit in cases of favorable results, and divergent allocations of blame to others for unfavorable results. Although each of these may be correct in some degree, significant changes in apparent productivity relationships are usually the outcome of interactions among a variety of external as well as internal readjustments. Failure to explore all potentially relevant factors at successively lower levels of aggregation is likely to encourage interpretations which support vulnerable and even futile means of seeking future improvements. Hence, even analyses of associated variations in other statistical series as means of identifying the factors influencing changes in input-output relationships must be supplemented with detailed explorations of modifications in the procurement, production, marketing, and financial aspects of the operations involved.

No System of Productivity Analysis Is Likely To Prove Of Continuing Value For Performance Evaluation and Improvement Unless Its Users Learn To Interpret the Complex Relationships Underlying the Oversimplified Results Which Have Commonly Been Reported In the Past.

Thus, industrial managers must learn to examine the network of productivity relationships at successively lower (or higher) levels of aggregation and to press for persuasive analyses of the relevant internal and external influences involved, as well as for analysis of the effects of past efforts to effect improvements. And government officials must also learn to press for more penetrating determinations of the extent to which past results have been affected by government-influenced developments as well as of the ways in which future government policies and measures might facilitate further improvements in industrial performance.

Notes

1. For example, see Kendrick [22]; Baird [2]; Boylan [3]; Erdilek [9]; Denison [4]; Jorenson[21]; Gollop and Jorgenson [19]; Dogramaci [6] and Norsworthy [29].
2. For further discussion, see [15, pp. 103–113].
3. For related discussion, see [16, pp. 25–26].
4. For more detailed discussion, see [11, pp. 109–165].
5. For a fuller discussion, see [17].
6. For illustrative applications, see [15, chapters 9, 10, and 11].
7. For fuller analysis and discussion of this case, see [8, chapters 5 and 6].

References

1. American Iron and Steel Institute, *Annual Statistical Reports* (Washington, D.C.: 1955, 1981).

2. R. N. Baird, "Production Functions, Productivity and Technical Change" in [13].
3. M. G. Boylan, "Reported Economic Effects of Technological Changes" in [13].
4. E. F. Denison, *Accounting for Slower Economic Growth: The U.S. in the 1970's* (Washington, D.C.: The Brookings Institution, 1979].
5. A. Dogramaci, "Perspectives on Productivity" in [6].
6. ———, (ed.), *Productivity Analysis: A Range of Perspectives* (Boston, MA: Martinus Nijhoff, 1981).
7. A. Dogramaci and A. Nabil (eds.) *Macroeconomic Productivity Analyses* (Boston, MA: Martinus Nijhoff, 1982).
8. S. Eilon, B. Gold, and J. Soesan, *Applied Productivity Analysis for Industry* (Oxford: Pergamon Press, 1976). Russian translation Moscow—*Economika*, 1980. Chinese translation: Beijing—*The Technical Economy and Modernization of Management Institute*, 1982.
9. A. Erdilek, "Productivity, Technical Change and Input-Output Analysis in [13].
10. B. M. Fraumeni and D. W. Jorgenson, "Capital Formation and U.S. Productivity Growth, 1948–1976" in [6].
11. B. Gold, *Foundations of Productivity Analysis: Guides to Economic Theory and Managerial Control* (Pittsburgh, PA: University of Pittsburgh Press, 1955, 1956).
12. ———, "Research, Technological Change and Economic Analyses: A Critique of Prevailing Approaches," *Quarterly Review of Economics and Business*, Spring 1977. Reprinted in [18].
13. ———, (ed.) *Research, Technological Change and Economic Analysis* (Lexington, MA: D.C. Heath—Lexington Books, 1977).
14. ———, "Steel Technologies and Costs in the U.S. and Japan," *Iron and Steel Engineer*, April 1978. Reprinted in [15]. Japanese translation: Jōhō Shūhō (Tokyo), July 1978.
15. ———, *Productivity, Technology and Capital: Economic Analysis, Managerial Strategies and Governmental Policies* (Lexington, MA: D.C. Heath—Lexington Books, 1979, 1982).
16. ———, "Changing Perspectives on Size, Scale and Returns: An Interpretation," *Journal of Economic Literature*, March 1981.
17. ———, "Improving Industrial Productivity and Technological Capabilities: Needs, Problems and Suggested Policies" in [6].
18. B. Gold, G. Rosegger, and M. G. Boylan, *Evaluating Technological Innovations: Methods, Expectations and Findings* (Lexington, MA.: D.C. Heath—Lexington Books, 1980).
19. F. M. Gollop and D. W. Jorgenson, "U.S. Productivity Growth in Industry: 1947–1973" in [23].
20. J. D. Hogan (ed.), *Dimensions of Productivity Research* (Houston, TX: American Productivity Center, 1980), Volume I.

21. D. W. Jorgenson, "U.S. Productivity Growth: Retrospect and Prospect" in [20].
22. J. W. Kendrick, *Postwar Productivity Trends in the U.S., 1948–1969* (Princeton, N.J.: Princeton University Press, 1973).
23. J. W. Kendrick and B. Vaccara (eds.), *New Developments in Productivity Measurement* (Chicago, IL: University of Chicago Press, 1980).
24. J. R. Norsworthy, "The Role of Capital Formation in the Recent Productivity Slowdown," in [7].
25. Putnam, Hayes and Bartlett Inc., *Economics of International Steel Trade—Policy Implications for the United States: An Analysis and Forecast for the American Iron and Steel Institute* (Newton, MA: May 1977) p. 33.

6 ANALYZING THE EFFECTS OF COMPUTER-AIDED MANUFACTURING SYSTEMS ON PRODUCTIVITY AND COMPETITVENESS

Bela Gold

6.1. Introduction

I am reasonably familiar with the extensive literature reporting the results of statistical studies of the factors associated with changes in so-called productivity levels, and have made a number of such studies myself at the level of firms as well as of industries.[1] But I have become increasingly dissatisfied with the unpersuasiveness of the causal interpretations of such findings. And my doubts about the analytical insights offered by such reliance on average relationships over extended periods among three or four or five bits of data torn out of their multi-dimensional operating context have been reinforced by two considerations. One has been their demonstrated vulnerability in estimating future productivity changes. Another has been their patent inapplicability to guiding managerial choices among the array of specific decision alternatives available in seeking to improve the effectiveness of operations.

Accordingly, I have focussed more sharply in recent years on more direct efforts to trace the successive linkages by means of which changes in capital investments, adoptions of major technological innovations, and other developments have affected what I have called "the network of productivity relationships," as well as associated interactions with the other determinants of changes in costs and profitability. The following discussion will summarize the results of a year-long field study designed to develop a more effective approach to analyzing the effects on productivity and production capabilities of one of the most important technological advances in recent decades: computer-aided manufacturing systems.[2]

6.2. Study Objectives

Computer-aided manufacturing (CAM) offers major potentials for providing urgently needed advances in the productivity and competitiveness of a wide array of industries. Despite the pioneering development of this powerful new technology in this country, domestic adoption rates have fallen far short of exploiting resulting opportunities and even threaten to lag behind the utilization of these new capabilities by foreign competitors.

The speed with which technological innovations diffuse among prospective users obviously depends on a variety of factors. Three of the most important of these seem to be: the criteria used by management to choose among alternative proposals for the allocation of available resources; the processes relied on to develop such proposals; and the effectiveness with which the potentials of adopted innovations are harnessed.

In industries that have had experience with successive technological innovations, proposal-development, selection, and evaluation processes have come to be highly systematized. Because most such arrangements have emerged from efforts to deal with the continuing flow of incremental improvements, however, they are not likely to be effectively applicable to the relatively uncommon challenges of major advances in technology. Our field research suggests that this limited applicability of standardized approaches has led to a serious underestimation of the prospective benefits of CAM and, hence, to unduly slow rates of adoption.

This exploratory project was designed, therefore, to develop an approach to managerial evaluations of CAM systems which would be more effective in capturing their distinctive capabilities and requirements than the capital budgeting procedures commonly used for appraising proposed acquisitions of new equipment. It involved development of an evaluation model through studies of seven applications of CAM systems (including computer-aid design or CAD) in the automobile, machinery, and electrical equipment industries. Supplementary insights were provided by discussions with vendors as well as other users of such systems. It is hoped that the availability of such a more directly relevant evaluation model, together with the more thorough understanding of CAM potentials likely to be engendered in the course of utilizing this analytical framework, will help to accelerate recognition of additional rewarding applications of this powerful new technology.

6.3. Some Common Elements in Evaluations of Major Equipment Acquisitions

Decisions about the adoption of CAM systems are still widely based on applications of relatively standard capital budgeting methods. These have evolved through long experience in appraising proposals for acquiring capital equipment. For this very reason, however, such methods are rooted in unrecognized assumptions and restrictive perspectives that are unsuited to the evaluation of CAM systems and tend to encourage erroneous evaluations of their potential benefits.

Most efforts to appraise proposals for equipment acquisitions in industry tend to share certain common assumptions about the general characteristics of such additions. One of these is that the equipment under consideration would be directly applicable to, and would exert all or most of its effects within, particular narrow subsectors of production. A second is that the capabilities of the equipment and of its embodied technology are known and will not change after installation except for eventual decline. A third is that its contributions to the effectiveness of operations and to cost improvements can be estimated within reasonably close margins. And a fourth is that the prospective advantages and limitations of such an acquisition can best be understood and evaluated by the managerial and technical specialists familiar with that subsector.

Such assumptions have accordingly encouraged broad reliance on processes for generating and choosing among equipment acquisition proposals involving common elements. Thus, most or all proposals to be considered by top management tend to be originated or approved by officials of the operating subsectors which would be affected. In addition, proposals are generally appraised independently of one another as top management seeks to allocate available capital resources among competing equipment as well as non-equipment proposals. Finally, their choices tend to be based on the relative attractiveness of the estimated economic returns among all proposals that exceed some minimum "hurdle rate."

Under the foregoing conditions, it is apparent that the nature and volume of the equipment acquisition proposals submitted to top management tend to be heavily influenced by the technical background and motivations as well as the innovativeness of the subsectoral managerial and technical staffs. Their incentives obviously center around potential financial and status rewards. But the directions in which improvements are likely to be sought often tend to avoid innovations that may threaten to undermine rather than to reinforce the technological authority and organizational security of the specialists guiding the search and evaluating resulting possibilities.

The preceding assumptions, expectations, and procedures undoubtedly remain relevant for evaluating many kinds of equipment acquisition proposals. Nevertheless, each element of the above approach tends to prevent the effective development and appraisal of CAM potentials.

6.4. On the Distinctive Capabilities of Computer-Aided Manufacturing

The basic reason why the traditional approach to evaluating capital allocation proposals results in underestimating the potential benefits of CAM is that this represents a form of "contagious" technology, which presses to surmount the boundaries of given applications and thereby to "infect" adjacent sectors of operations and controls. Thus, it should be recognized as an essentially general process of progressive advances in technological capabilities and productive efficiency rather than as additional cases in the familiar succession of independent, locally restricted equipment acquisitions. Computerization may, of course, be applied beneficially to particular operations. But its major potentials derive from providing means of achieving increasingly effective integration: among successive production operations; between production operations and related material flows and maintenance services; and between manufacturing activities as a whole and the encompassing systems of managerial planning, control, and performance evaluation—even including procurement, inventory management, and distribution.

To illustrate these broad potentials, one may begin with CAD. In such applications, engineers develop new designs on the screen of a terminal by specifying certain points on the screen and tapping in instructions concerning the shapes and dimensions of the configurations to be drawn

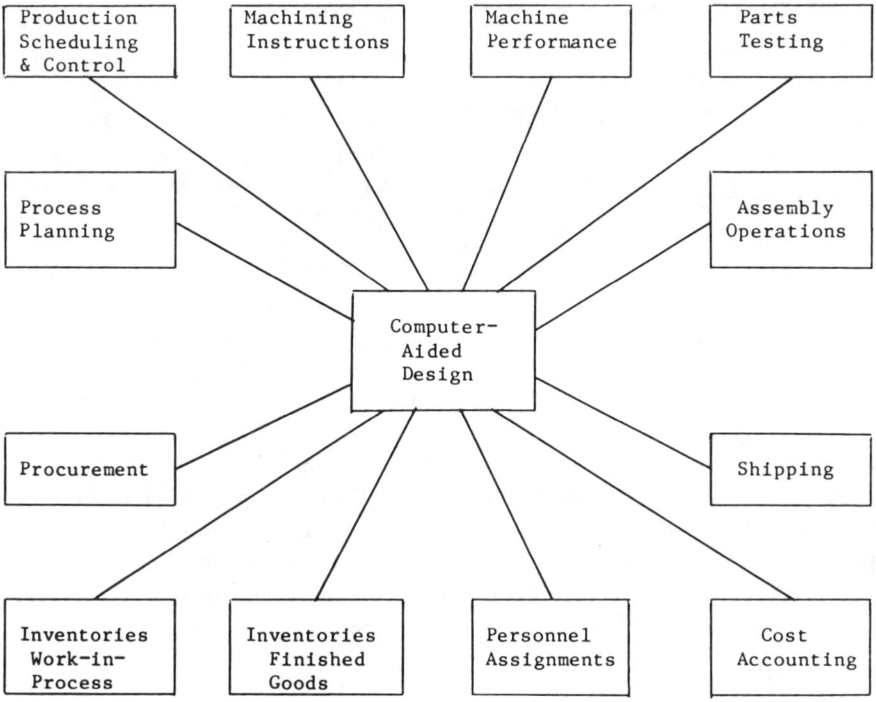

Figure 6–1. Potential Applications of Design Data Bases

around them. The key point to understand is that in the course of projecting the design shown on the screen, the computer is storing a detailed mathematical model of all of its features. Combining this information with specifications of the kinds of materials needed and the volume of such parts to be produced, along with expected waste and scrap rates, can generate procurement instructions. The definition of the dimensions and configurations of the part may be used to generate the sequence of machines to be used, the specific operating instructions for each, the tools required to perform such operations, the estimated time required to machine each piece, the dimensional criteria for testing the acceptability of the part, and the estimated unit cost of each operation including the wages of the operator. As indicated in Figure 6–1, various other kinds of performance evaluation and control information may also be generated.

But the preceding understates the potential benefits of such systems by tracing only one direction of information flows. In fact, all such flows may move in both directions. Engineers can use them to explore the relative costs of alternative designs. Manufacturing specialists can evaluate alternative processing sequences and machining instructions. Production controllers can adjust specific machine assignments to accord with delivery commitments and individual machine loadings. The estimated costs of producing specified products may be used to determine bids for contracts. And many other guides to policy decisions and to choices among operating practices can obviously be developed.

Programs have already been developed to apply each of the possibilities cited above. But few plants are actually utilizing many of them on a continuing rather than an experimental basis. Despite the clarity of the logic involved, the development of a functioning system requires confronting very large masses of details and many alternative possibilities at most stages of defining sequential decisions. As a result, serious questions have been raised about the factors affecting the transferability of some of these programs from one application to another. What is of primary interest here, however, is that such applications are growing in number, are encompassing an increasing array of managerial functions and are promising substantial advances in the effectiveness of resource utilization and, hence, in the determinants of future competitiveness.

6.5. Improving Management's Approach to Exploring CAM Potentials

Management Perceptions of CAM

The single most important requirement for successful exploration of CAM potentials seems to be the recognition within senior levels of management of the strategic importance of this essentially new dimension of manufacturing technology and also of the critical requirements for harnessing its powerful potentials. The former involves realization that CAM systems will be a rapidly increasing determinant of relative competitive strength, not unlike the role during recent decades of increasing research and development—another *general* form of technological progress.

Among the critical requirements for effectively exploiting CAM potentials, the following seem to rank highest:

1. commitment of increasing resources to long-term programs for developing improved and wider applications of this still-emerging technology;

2. acceptance of the need to evaluate individual CAM proposals within the context of expected continuing programs involving further applications which draw in part on the resources allocated to earlier projects;
3. awareness that such efforts call not only for new kinds of technical expertise, but also for growing understanding by management of the implications of resulting improvements in operational potentials for the modification of planning and control systems; and
4. willingness to consider possible changes in organizational structure, including the closer integration of design, manufacturing, distribution, and procurement with one another.

It is obvious that such far-reaching reorientations of management perspectives are unlikely to be effected rapidly. But the inertia of long-established habits of thought may be expected to diminish rapidly under the combined pressures of resource stringencies, limited markets, and intensified competition. At any rate, until managements become convinced that CAM systems offer major opportunities that are likely to be transformed into serious threats if neglected, little cumulative progress is likely to be achieved. Even successful "stand-alone" applications—so long as they are regarded as no different from past introductions of equipment with only locally restricted impacts—are unlikely to engender the momentum resulting from a clear recognition of broader potentials.

One of the major factors stimulating the rapid advances of computerization in Japanese industry was early recognition by many top managements of the tremendous potentials offered for strengthening productive efficiency as well as managerial planning and control. This led to an essentially top-down approach involving widespread recognition of senior management's commitment to progressively broader applications within an overall framework, which provided a continuous mapping of the missing blocks in the system along with a holistic rather than a localized view of the relative desirability of alternative next applications.

Such a top-down approach is almost the opposite of the essentially bottom-up approach found in many American companies. The latter tends to be more sporadic in coverage as a response to the changing pattern of pressures and initiatives generated by different operating units. Moreover, in the absence of a comprehensive plan for increasing computerization, the bottom-up approach tends to lose momentum, as each project's completion tends to be followed by new choices among various competing technological and non-technological proposals for allocating available capital. Even more serious, the bottom-up approach tends to face repeated difficulties in persuading each new sector of applications to accept its absorption into an integrated computerized system, instead of being assured of the ready cooperation engendered by awareness of top management's support for continuing extensions.[7]

Sources of CAM Proposals

More thorough exploration and development of CAM proposals would seem to require several deviations from arrangements that rely on having equipment acquisition recommendations generated by the managerial and technical specialists in narrow subsectors of operations. This would seem necessary in part because most, and often all, subsectors lack sufficient expertise in appraising CAM potentials convincingly and in part because personnel lacking confidence in their understanding of such CAM technology are likely to shy away from recommending it. Indeed, as was noted earlier, such personnel may often be biased against the introduction of innovations which threaten to undermine their technological security or to involve a need to share decision-making authority. But patiently awaiting the eventual burgeoning of interest in CAM by a random array of engineers and managers, which may not manifest itself at influential levels for several more years, may risk serious competitive advantages.

Accordingly, consideration might usefully be given to providing and stimulating the utilization of additional channels for generating CAM proposals. One of these might well be a manufacturing engineering group with demonstrated expertise in CAM applications whose responsibilities include the exploration of successive sectors of operations to identify attractive CAM potentials. This would support the formulation not only of stand-alone proposals for particular subsectors, but also of potential sequences of applications which are mutually reinforcing. Encouragement should also be given to the development of CAM proposals by other specialized line and staff groups (including engineering design, quality control, process planning, and materials management) whose activities interact with others and thus may suggest additional means of improving the effectiveness of joint operations.

Because of the broad potentials and implications of CAM, it may even be desirable for management to sponsor comprehensive efforts to alert all levels of managerial and technical staffs to the prospective benefits of utilizing it more fully. Resulting interest might then be reinforced by providing whatever training and development programs are likely to achieve the widespread familiarity necessary to multiply the potential sources of CAM application proposals and also to ensure the managerial responsiveness needed to encourage such innovative suggestions.

6.6. Improving Managerial Evaluations of CAM Proposals

Some General Vulnerabilities of Capital Budgeting Methods

It may be useful to begin by recalling that most of the capital budgeting methods used in evaluating equipment acquisition proposals are subject to serious vulnerabilities, even when applied to acquisitions not involving significant modifications in basic technologies. Among the determinants of such evaluations which may entail wide margins of error are the required estimates of *long-term* changes in product and factor prices, in output levels and product-mix, and even in actual final investment requirements—to say nothing of the discount rates applied to deferred net revenues.[3]

And the vulnerability of such *ex ante* estimates of the profitability of proposed acquisitions grows progressively with the extent of the plant personnel's unfamiliarity with the technologies embodied in the new facilities. This is due to the fact that the actual performance of new kinds of equipment varies widely with the effectiveness of technical and managerial adaptations to the potentials and limitations of the innovation, not only in the operation directly affected but also in the antecedent and subsequent operations with which coordination must be reestablished.[4] These latter difficulties in estimating the returns from innovations obviously apply with extra force to CAM systems, inasmuch as the technologies involved are quite different from the kinds of expertise available in most manufacturing plants, instead of merely requiring available technical personnel to supplement their past experience with some additional specialized seminars and workshops.

The primary concern of this report, however, is to suggest means of dealing more effectively with the *additional special challenges* to the evaluation of capital allocation proposals posed by CAM systems. To begin with, the basic coverage of CAM evaluations should obviously conform to the framework of the firm's customary capital budgeting model. This is necessary not only to facilitate comparisons with competing proposals, but also to ensure that CAM evaluations do not slight any of the estimated effects required of other proposals. Hence, CAM evaluations, too, must cover expected costs and revenues as well as net investment requirements over the expected effective working life of the proposed innovation.

In order to increase the applicability of such appraisals of CAM proposals, however, conventional approaches must be extended so as to:

1. penetrate more deeply into the bases for the estimates of inputs, outputs, and costs which are fed into the capital budgeting model;
2. include estimates of probable carryover effects on successively broader sectors of operations; and
3. encompass estimated effects over an array of successively longer periods.

Estimating Direct Costs and Benefits

Investment Outlays and Overhead Charges. In respect to the outlays made up to the point of achieving effective operations, the important differences tend to center around two categories. First, CAM systems have apparently taken longer to "debug" and have frequently required larger costs to modify and even to replace some of the original hardware. Although significant improvements seem to be emerging in this area as a result of improvements in equipment design, computer reliability, and instrument diagnostics, widespread awareness of the problems encountered in the past continues to encourage excessive estimates. Second, CAM systems have often required very much greater inputs of engineering, programming, planning, and maintenance personnel than anticipated. If such supporting outlays had been correctly estimated, and if they had been fully charged against initial applications, the diffusion of CAM systems might well have been even slower than has been the case. Thus, the basis chosen for allocating these costs may significantly alter new adoption decisions.

It is obvious, of course, that new kinds of expertise are necessary if CAM systems are to be operated effectively and also that such inputs are likely to be especially costly when plant staffs are just learning about specific CAM requirements and how to meet them. But it is also obvious that after such resources have been strengthened by on-the-job experience, they would be required only part-time by the initial application once it has begun to function effectively, thus freeing such specialists to support additional applications. One might contend, therefore, that learning how to plan, introduce, operate, and improve CAM systems may appropriately be regarded as a continuing part of strengthening a firm's competitiveness. In that perspective, the resources involved might be considered a strategic investment whose costs should be allocated as part of a general overhead, paralleling research and development or engineering staff functions, instead of being charged fully against the initial, or even the first few, applications.

Net investment would tend to decline, of course, for both general equipment and CAM installations according to whatever depreciation formulae are applied. But our preliminary field studies suggest that CAM system evaluations should consider the possibility that they may require more frequent and larger investments injections in order to take advantage of continuing advances in the technology and associated hardware.

Capacity and Output Adjustments. Most machine acquisitions tend to have clearly established production capabilities. These tend to approximate a maximum once effective functioning has been achieved and to decline gradually after some years. Moreover, capacity utilization rates likewise tend to decline as a result of changes in product design, precision requirements, and product-mix to which the given machines cannot be fully adapted.

CAM systems, however, may exhibit quite different adjustment patterns over time. As was noted earlier, continuing improvements in computers, programming, instrumentation, and maintenance frequently make possible progressive increases in the productive capacity of given systems. Moreover, the greater adaptability of such systems to changes in product characteristics and product-mix tends to ensure fuller utilization of capacity than can be maintained for specialized machinery. As a result, CAM system evaluations should consider the likelihood that they may offer substantially greater capacity and average output per dollar of net fixed investment than alternative machine acquisitions, especially in manufacturing industries producing relatively limited batches of a wide variety of products.

Direct Operating Costs. Direct labor costs per unit of output are likely to be reduced because of substantial decreases in man-hour requirements per unit. And this may be accentuated by lower wage rates associated with an accompanying decrease in average skill requirements. The resulting decline in unit wage costs would commonly be offset in part by a concomitant increase in indirect wage costs per unit, reflecting a somewhat expanded need for more and higher-priced maintenance and set-up labor. It should be noted in this connection, however, that such indirect labor requirements have been declining recently because of increases in system reliability, technical improvements in identifying and correcting malfunctions, and cumulative staff experience.

The potentially distinctive effects of CAM applications on unit material costs center around possible changes in input requirements and in the scrap rates resulting from processing. The latter would be expected to decline, of course, as a result of the increased consistency with which computer-controlled operations would satisfy defined product requirements. Material input requirements would tend to be held within closer tolerances in respect to dimensional or other properties for any production run and this might incur somewhat higher material input prices. But the greater flexibility of CAM systems would facilitate adapting such requirements if necessitated by changes in the supply, quality, or price of available materials. Together these capabilities are likely to yield at least modest savings in unit material costs as compared with alternative systems utilizing similar material inputs.

Cost Flexibility and Cost Trends. Increasing investments in CAM systems may decrease cost flexibility less than is commonly expected. [4, p. 141] Although capital charges are traditionally regarded as "fixed costs," various accounting practices are increasing their flexibility. One widely utilized method involves allocating capital charges on equipment at a fixed rate per machine-hour used; another involves allocating such charges at varying rates depending on capacity utilization rates in each period.

Similarly, although wage costs are commonly regarded as "variable costs," their flexibility has been declining markedly in many industries, especially those that have powerful trade unions. They have not only generated effective resistance to reductions in employment and wage rates during periods of declining output as well as pressures for increasing the penalties for lay-offs through higher unemployment insurance, but they have also progressively increased the relatively inflexible costs of a growing array of "fringe benefits," including pensions, medical coverage, vacations, and holidays.[5]

In addition, there are evidences for believing that capital inputs are becoming more economical than labor inputs relative to their contributions to output. The major reason for this is that continuing technological progress tends to enhance the productive contributions of capital equipment far more than those of labor. Thus increases in many capital costs tend to be partly or even wholly offset by reductions in labor requirements. It should also be noted that, although the prices of both of these input rise during periods of inflation, the prices of capital goods stop rising once they have been purchased, whereas wage rates tend to continue keeping pace with, or even out-running, inflation. Indeed, capital charges may even decline progressively over time under some depreciation formulae.

Net Returns and Other Effects. CAM installations tend to yield larger revenues because, as noted above, capacity tends to increase as a result of continuing improvements in technology and operations and also because average utilization rates tend to be higher as a result of greater adaptability to changes in demand which affect product designs and product-mix. Because such installations also tend to yield lower unit costs, they may be expected to provide larger net returns.

Attention should also be called to some additional potential advantages of CAM systems. Resulting increases in the effectiveness with which material flows are coordinated may help to reduce work-in-process inventories. The ability to adjust machines to altered tasks more rapidly tends to reduce equipment downtime. The closer integration of successive operations into flexible manufacturing systems may save floor space. Integrated CAM systems covering successive stages from CAD through sequential manufacturing and testing operations, and generating accompanying cost data, would help to reduce the cycle time both in preparing contract bids and also in delivering in response to new orders. Finally, it is worth noting again that one of the major benefits of CAM applications is that they provide the training and experience for engineers, programmers, maintenance staff, and operators which serve as the underpinnings of additional applications as well as of the informational bases for developing increasingly integrated planning and control.

In summary, a comprehensive assessment of CAM system effects tends to yield results that are often quite different from those to be expected on the basis of past experience with incremental improvements in customary types of equipment. Such differences may relate not only to the magnitudes and relative proportions of various categories of cost savings and to product quality, but also to the patterning of such benefits over extended periods.

Expanding the Traditional Coverage of Capital Budgeting Models

Expanding Functional Coverage. Unlike most equipment acquisitions, capital budgeting for CAM proposals must encompass operations and functions beyond the immediate points of application because of their tendency to facilitate, and even engender, interactions with other parts of the system. Accordingly, it seems desirable to have evaluations of prospective CAM applications during, say, the first three years after installation developed in three stages, as shown in Figure 6–2.

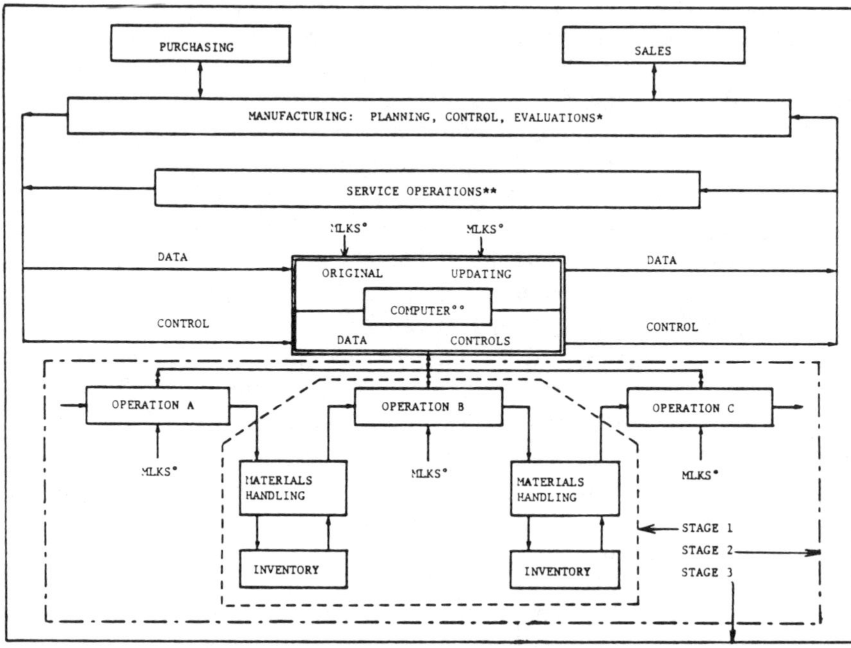

* Manufacturing Support
- Engineering & Design
- Production Methods
- Planning & Control
  - Production
  - Maintenance
  - Inventories
  - Quality
- Personnel
- Cost Accounting

** Service Operations
- Inventories
- Materials Handling
- Maintenance
- Heat and Power
- General Supplies

o Basic Inputs
- M-Materials
- L-Labor
- K-Capiital
- S-Salaried

oo Computer Support
- Data Management
- Programming
- Applications
  - Development
- Maintenance

Figure 6-2. Successive Stages of Coverage in Economic Evaluations of Applications of Computer-aided Manufacturing

Stage 1: Cover all effects on inputs, outputs, and costs that were reviewed above, but only within the sector of production operations which is directly affected.

Stage 2: Extend the coverage of Stage 1 to include prospective effects on the performance and costs of preceding and subsequent production operations as well as of associated service functions, such as materials handling, maintenance, and inventory management.

Stage 3: Extend Stage 2 further to also include prospective effects on production planning and control, quality improvement, personnel requirements, cost accounting, and other management planning, control, and performance evaluation functions.

The purpose of suggesting such a sequential development of estimates for the initial evaluation period is to encourage a systematic review of the progressively broader ramifications of CAM. These may not be fully realized, of course, in many cases, either because organizational arrangements encourage concentration only on the original sector affected, or because no one is responsible for developing such carryover contributions. But requiring that such broader potentials be considered may help to alert management to these larger realizable benefits as well as to the need for developing organizational means to promote their achievement.

Expanding the Time Period Covered. In order to encompass the distinctive potentials of CAM systems, it is also necessary to avoid the routine projections of revenues, costs, output, and investment beyond the first three years that are commonly made for equipment acquisition proposals. Instead, such longer-term adjustments should be examined afresh in order to take account of the special characteristics of CAM systems that were discussed above—including the possibilities of increasing capacity, higher average utilization rates, continuing increases in productivity relationships, and less rapid reductions in net fixed investment.

It would seem to follow, therefore, that the initial array of estimates for the first three years, as reviewed above, should be supplemented by a freshly developed array of parallel estimates for years four to six. In the case of more extensive CAM system proposals, even a third set of estimates covering an additional three to five years should be considered, as illustrated in Figure 6–3.

On Maximizing "Net Present Value." Attention also needs to be given to replacing the widespread emphasis on evaluating alternative capital projects on the basis of the relative "net present value" of their expected returns. This criterion seems particularly misleading in evaluations of major technological innovations. If estimated future returns are discounted at 20 percent annually, for example, all major projects which would take even three to four years to construct, "debug" and bring to high levels of capacity utilization would invite rejection in comparison with the recent yields from liquid and riskless investments in money markets. But such

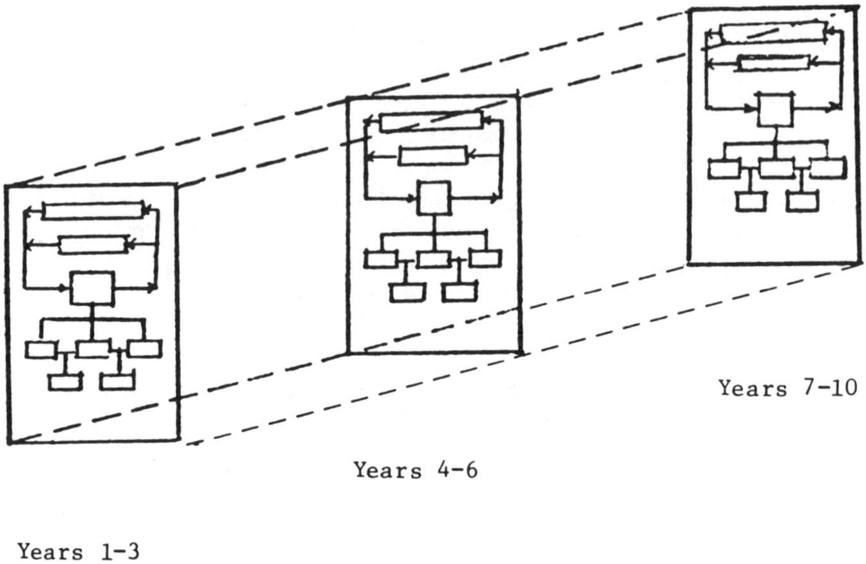

Figure 6-3. Sequential Capital Budgeting Evaluations

seemingly rational evaluation techniques suffer from a myopic point of view because they fail to consider the longer-term effects on competitiveness and profitability of the resulting successive rejections of each major advance in technology.

Consideration might accordingly be given to shifting the key criterion in capital budgeting evaluations from "maximizing net present value" to what I have called a "continuing horizons approach" [5, p. 24]. This involves choosing an array of capital projects so that when the overlapping time paths of net returns from each are aggregated, and the discounted net present value of this total is calculated as of successive three-to-five year periods, the results promise to safeguard acceptable profit levels over the long and intermediate as well as short term.

Because of the time required to develop and to achieve effective utilization of substantial CAM systems, few realistic evaluations are likely to offer discounted net present values which are competitive with the high interest rates available in money markets in recent years. This has accordingly tended to discourage more rapid and widespread adoptions. In doing so, however, it has thereby also helped to delay urgently needed major advances in the productivity and cost competitiveness of a substantial array of domestic manufacturing industries.

6.7. Some Problems of Implementation

Clarifying Equipment Acquisition Objectives and Prospective Benefits

Contrary to widely prevailing practice in capital budgeting, innovational proposals should be evaluated by comparison not with the costs, prices, output patterns, and competitiveness of current operations, but with prospective *trends* in each of these over the expected working life of the innovation. If such trends foreshadow declining rates of profitability from the continuation of existing operations, innovations may be considered justifiable not only if they offer higher profits, but even if they promise to limit prospective large reductions in future profitability.

In analyzing these trends, attention should be directed first beyond the firm to consider potential efforts by competitors to improve their market positions as well as to consider emerging adjustment patterns in input factor and in product markets. Resulting conclusions should then be coupled with the outcome of analyses of intra-firm trends in product capabilities, productive efficiency, and other determinants of future performance. These findings, together with an assessment of the resources available to the firm, constitute what has been called the "pre-decision environment," (Gold [3, pp. 142–144]).

Such estimates of needs and potentials, in turn, help to define the criteria to be used in determining the prospective benefits of CAM systems or other major technological innovations. To do so requires translating hoped-for profit adjustments into supporting improvements in costs, prices, and output. And these latter gains must then be translated into the alternative changes in various unit input requirements and associated factor prices as well as in product qualities which would yield the targeted results. Each of these successive stages of analysis is essential. For example, undertaking major innovations may yield disappointing results if current performance has been limited primarily by marketing inadequacies rather than by technological capabilities. Nor would there be much point in considering innovations that promise significant reductions in the unit cost of producing current products if market demand has shifted to higher quality or otherwise altered products.

An analytical framework that provides systematic coverage of the interactions that connect changes in the profitability of total investment and its direct determinants (which have been termed "the managerial control ratios") with changes in the underlying "structure of costs" and,

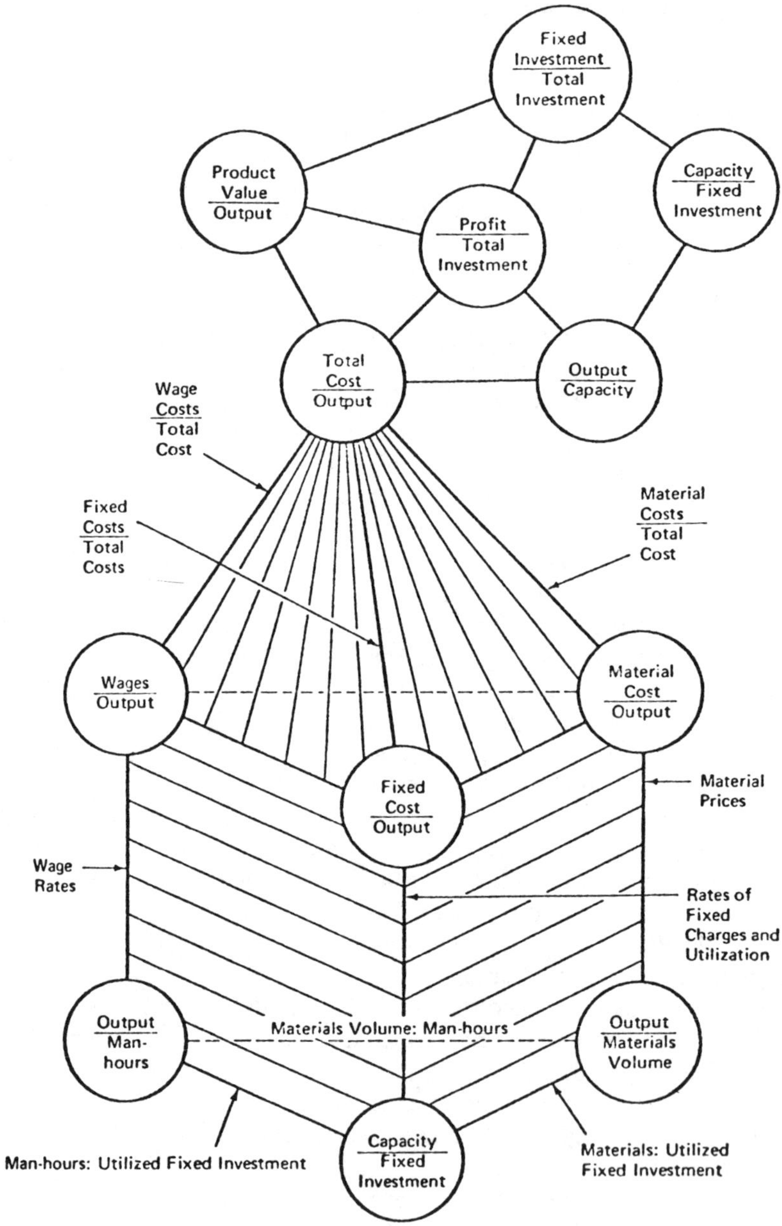

Figure 6-4. Productivity Network, Cost Structure, and Managerial Control Ratios

below that, with the "network of productivity relationships" is provided in Figure 6–4 (also presented in chapter 5).

This emphasizes that changes in output per man-hour constitute but one of the six interacting components of the network of productivity relationships and that a change in any one of these may engender adjustments in some or all of the others before the system has been effectively reintegrated. Hence, evaluation of a major technological innovation would first involve evaluating its effects on this network. The effects of these changes on various unit costs would obviously depend in turn on accompanying changes in factor prices. For example, associated changes in materials specifications often alter their prices, and wage rates tend to be responsive to shifts in the composition of skill requirements and to increases in output per man-hour. In order to determine resulting changes in total unit costs, the relative changes in each unit cost would then have to be weighted by its proportion of total costs. And finally, prospective changes in total unit costs would have to be integrated with the prospective effects of any innovation-induced changes in product quality on output levels and prices to estimate resulting changes in the determinants of profitability.[6]

In addition to ensuring that evaluations of prospective technological innovations cover the entire Profit-Cost-Productivity Analysis System, it is necessary that the "pre-decision environment" determinations of the specific physical input and physical output adjustments needed to improve competitive position be matched against the prospective physical contributions of the innovations being considered. And expected cost effects must similarly be compared with estimated cost adjustment needs.

Absorbing CAM Systems

CAM systems cover a wide range in terms of the complexity of the operations performed and, even more important, in terms of the array of other production activities and managerial functions on which they may impinge. This means that the resulting problems of effectively integrating such innovations into the structure and flow of plant operations may encompass a comparably broad spectrum.

The application of programmable controls to single machines poses no special problems. For example, programmable tube benders are used in the automobile industry to produce a wide array of exhaust pipe configurations more rapidly, with less time lost for readjustments and at lower costs than manually operated machines. But such encapsulated stand-alone applications are less likely to represent an entering wedge for developing expanded CAM systems than to blind managements and technical staff to the major differences between the limited contributions of traditional incremental improvements in individual machines and the powerful and expanding potentials of CAM systems.

A very large proportion of manufacturing activity involves production of smaller quantities of individual products or parts. The extent to which the economies of automated machine operations can be realized in such operations depends on the flexibility of the equipment in shifting from one sequence of tasks to another without long delays and large costs for modifying machine capabilities. Development of programmable controls has opened new horizons in this respect and thereby stimulated intensified efforts to utilize them, not only to increase the cost effectiveness of operations involving smaller outputs of a more variable product-mix, but also to try to broaden the flexibility of relatively highly dedicated systems.

Effective development and utilization of flexible manufacturing systems (FMS), however, requires substantial deviations from past approaches to the introduction of dedicated systems and even of batch production systems. Perhaps the most important of these is that the plant that is to use the system can no longer delegate the entire task of design, construction and testing to the machine builder, requiring the plant's staff to learn only to operate and maintain the system. On the contrary, the plant must develop sufficient expertise in its own staff to provide detailed guidance on design, instrumentation and controls as well as to specify criteria for performance testing, reliability, and ease of maintenance. Only on the basis of such comprehensive internal capability can management be assured both of the continuing adjustability of the system to changes in part designs, in quality specifications and even in product-mix, and also of safeguards against extended downtime while inexperienced personnel grope to deal with unexpected problems. Moreover, such involvement in the successive stages of developing an FMS might well reach beyond engineers to include some prospective foremen, maintenance personnel, and even operating labor, not only to help ensure comprehensive familiarity with the new system but also to facilitate its adaptations to specific operating conditions in the plant.

This latter point introduces a second set of important deviations from past experience with acquisitions of new equipment. In part, these derive from the fact that an FMS usually provides a substantial production capacity, thus posing special problems during the period of its introduction. For example, it is usually difficult and even impossible to test the completed system effectively prior to its installation in the plant because of its size and because of the need to integrate its inputs and outputs and servicing needs with the plant's physical arrangements and resources. This means that provision must somehow be made either to retain the production capabilities that the innovation is intended to replace until the latter functions reliably enough to take on the full replacement burden, or to provide for external sources of supply during the breaking-in period of the new equipment. In addition, the tendency for FMS capacity to rise over time is likely to introduce additional adjustment problems. If the FMS capacity is intended merely to replace the capacity of the prior production process eventually, there may well be a significant early period of utilization when it falls short of that target. On the other hand, if this target is met soon after application, it is quite likely that its capacity will continue to rise as a result of progressive improvements in its production capabilities as well as in its utilization—thus necessitating either under-utilization of these additions to capacity or readjustments in the preceding and subsequent stages of production.

Such revised approaches obviously become more necessary in respect to adoptions of still more complex CAM systems, such as might involve the integration of casting or forging with subsequent machine operations, or the integration of several parts machining lines with sub-assembly operations, or the still more far-reaching configurations underlying progress towards the "automatic factory," encompassing most or all of the components in Figure 6–1.

Some Organizational Repercussions

Serious efforts to harness the potentials of increasing applications of CAM systems would seem to require certain organizational developments. An initial requirement, as was noted earlier, would involve establishment of a new unit concerned with improving manufacturing technology with a special emphasis on CAM systems. Its tasks would include: keeping abreast of new developments in hardware, software and applications; developing new applications; formulating plans to ensure the mutual reinforcement of successive applications; and developing programs to increase the interest and knowledge of other technical and management personnel relating to CAM principles and potentials.

In time, increasing CAM capabilities would also have to be developed among the engineers, maintenance personnel, operating labor, and supervisors within each major manufacturing division.[7] This need arises from the inevitable limitations of having line operations supervised on a continuing basis by staff personnel, as well as from the likelihood that improvement efforts are likely to be intensified if driven by internal operating responsibilities.

A third organizational requirement seems to be the introduction of a new level of managerial responsibility to ensure effective coordination between the groups that interact at critical nodes in the system. For example, one of the most important of these involves the integration of manufacturing operations with the data base core generated by CAD. In the two cases in the present study which covered such interactions, achievements have so far fallen short of expectations. One of the important reasons seems to be that the transfer point is at the outer periphery of both the CAD and the CAM organizations, with no unified responsibility for ensuring the continuous mutual adaptations at this interface which are necessary. Unified responsibility may similarly be necessary to develop increasing coordination at some or all of the other nodes depicted in Figure 6–1.

Finally, there may well be an eventual need to provide some means of ensuring that progress in developing and utilizing the potentials of CAM systems is reviewed periodically and promoted systematically by some member of top management with responsibilities reaching beyond manufacturing alone. Because it is regarded as a key determinant both of market competitiveness and of the effective utilization of all company resources, such responsibilities are already lodged with senior corporate officers in some Japanese companies.

Evaluating CAM System Performance

In contrast to the considerable literature on pre-decision estimates of the effects of prospective technological innovations, there is an astonishing paucity of publications on evaluating the actual effects of such innovations after installation. The reason seems to be the widespread assumption that the purposes, methodologies, applications, and interpretations of such undertakings are so obvious as to offer no interesting problems. Our research suggests, however, that such efforts face quite substantial problems concerning the appropriate criteria for evaluations; how they should be timed; who should be responsible; and how results should be used.

Criteria of Evaluation. Most evaluations of major technological innovations, including CAM applications, tend to concentrate on financial results, especially on changes in outlays and costs relative to original expectations. But such findings tend to be inadequate and even misleading unless careful account is taken of all other associated changes, including: any changes in the qualities as well as quantities of inputs and outputs; any shifts in operating tasks to (or from) preceding or subsequent stages of production; any adjustments in below-quality output ratios; any changes in the mix of products processed and in the length of production runs; and any changes in the proportion of equipment down-time not attributable to decreased market demand. It is also important to recognize that many of these critical determinants of performance are likely not to be adequately reflected by existing cost accounting measures unless these have been thoroughly revised.

Understanding performance changes also requires analysis of the reasons for observed results. At the very least, this requires distinguishing among changes attributable to: the operating characteristics of the hardware; the planning and management of input and output flows; engineering modifications in production methods and product requirements; and labor capabilities and efforts. Inadequate probing of the specific causes of deviations from performance targets seems to encourage ascribing observed deficiencies all too readily to unpredictable or external factors, thus hindering identification of internal shortcomings.

It should also be recognized that experiences and insights during the processes of introducing and learning to utilize major innovations commonly result in modifying initial expectations concerning the specific tasks that can be performed most effectively as well as practical achievement potentials.

Timing of Evaluations. When should the results of major innovations be evaluated? Our studies suggest that most firms seem to rely on one appraisal within 6 to 12 months after the project's completion. Such early estimates often yield overly optimistic conclusions because generous allowances are made to offset actual shortcomings by assuming these to be attributable to temporary problems—such as excess maintenance, inadequate labor experience, or under-utilization due to incomplete integration into adjacent stages of production. Such one-shot appraisals may mislead managers by focussing on actual results achieved by the time when the appraisal is made instead of on trends in such performance measures. An analysis of such trends would be of far greater value by revealing whether performance was continuing to improve or not and by encouraging attention to the sources of additional gains. This would help to uncover any dubious claims of only temporary shortcomings, while also helping to focus attention on identifying additional sources of improvement and developing plans for harnessing them.

For example, in the case of many major innovations, and especially in the case of CAD/CAM applications, it is only after the innovation has achieved effective functioning and reasonably high levels of utilization that efforts are made to maximize realization of its fullest potentials by undertaking adaptive adjustments: in preceding and subsequent operations; in managerial planning and control processes; and even in product designs and operating methods. Accordingly, more effective appraisals would require evaluations every six months for at least three years (and even longer, if performance and potentials have not yet stabilized, as is likely to be true of complex CAD/CAM installations). These would serve not only to appraise successive changes in results, but also to provide the analytical basis for possible revisions of future performance targets.

Responsibility for Evaluations. One of the critical problems faced in appraising major innovations is the pressure for biased evaluations. In the case of very large projects, the tendency to seek out and to emphasize favorable aspects of results seems to be attributable to concern that negative judgments would reflect on the high-level officials responsible for approving such commitments and be resented by them. Such biases are often built into the evaluation process because allocation of such responsibilities to the officials deemed to have the relevent expertise often involves reliance on those who participated in making the project proposals.

Thus, technical evaluations are usually left to the specialized engineers and the investment and cost evaluations to the respective specialists who are likely to have been involved in preparing the original estimates. This is done partly because of the absence of qualified internal alternatives and partly to protect the confidentiality of findings. Moreover, those assigned to making such evaluations are often led to mute critical judgments lest these inhibit future cooperative relationships with the officials responsible for such projects.

In order to help minimize the influence of such biases on evaluations, it seems necessary to have them made under the direct supervision of the official responsible for increasing the contributions of manufacturing to the profitability of the plant through improving product quality and production efficiency while reducing average unit costs. Such evaluations would, of course, require contributions by engineering, production management, cost accounting, and finance. But it would also seem to require a blending of their respective specialized insights within the larger and longer-term perspectives of managerial efforts to improve market competitiveness and profitability.

This suggested need for special organizational arrangements for evaluating major innovations is especially important in the case of CAD/CAM applications. One reason is that, as has been noted earlier, this new technology tends to generate varied and far-reaching ramifications, thus requiring consideration of such multi-dimensional effects in attempting serious appraisals of results. An equally important reason is that such evaluative efforts can also serve as a valuable educational device, sensitizing to CAD/CAM potentials even those functional specialists who have not yet experienced major impacts from such developments.

Utilizing Evaluation Results. Oddly enough, *ex post* evaluations of innovations are apparently seldom used to identify the errors of pre-decision estimates as a basis for seeking to improve them. Neglect of such a feedback is attributed by some to the view that past decisions are regarded as "spilled milk," and by others to the view that each major innovational decision is unique and hence unlikely to provide useful insights into other decisions.

In the case of CAD/CAM applications, however, additional projects and extensions tend to represent a blending of unique elements with a very considerable admixture of the common elements characteristic of this technology and its capabilities. Hence, substantial benefits may result from using *ex post* findings of past installations to uncover the loci and primary causes of significant deviations from expectations as a basis for identifying those likely to be influential in later applications as well. Moreover, careful analysis of trends in the performance of any CAD/CAM project may help to reveal both the sources of constraints on further achievements and the means by which past constraints were eased or overcome. Finally, findings from past applications concerning the periods over which successive improvements have been achieved may help to ensure continued efforts to keep increasing performance levels instead of accepting the early ceilings on maximum capabilities associated with experiences involving other types of equipment innovations.

Incidentally, attention should be directed to the seemingly universal avoidance of post-installation estimates of the incremental contributions of major innovations to profitability. Efforts are often made to estimate reductions in some input requirements and, somewhat less frequently, in total unit costs. But this implied recognition of the difficulties in attempting to determine resulting effects on profitability, even on the basis of actual *ex post* data, raises even more serious doubts about the practical usefulness of continuing widespread reliance on *ex ante* estimates of such profitability effects as the basis for decisions involving the adoption or rejection of major innovations.[8]

6.8. Conclusions

CAM offers major potentials for improving the productivity and costs of a wide array of domestic manufacturing industries, and the effectiveness with which its capabilities are developed and utilized may well become a major determinant of future competitiveness.

The most important requirement for harnessing such powerful potentials are recognition within top management of the strategic importance of this new dimension of manufacturing technology and instituting a program to assure progressive realization of its benefits.

The critical elements of such an implementing program include:

1. commitment of increasing resources to continuing development of improved and wider applications of this still emerging technology;
2. acquisition of the new kinds of technical expertise required and provision of intensive training to ensure increasing understanding by managers as well as workers of the capabilities and operating characteristics of CAM;
3. modifying arrangements for generating technological improvement proposals as well as the criteria and estimation methods used in evaluating such proposals.
4. consideration of the need for possible changes in the existing organizational structure to encourage exploration of additional CAM applications, to facilitate integration of such applications in order to maximize resulting benefits, and to provide for the modification of existing management planning and control systems so as to utilize the additional capabilities offered by CAM systems.
5. provision for setting targets for such progress and also for periodic monitoring of results along with analyses of the reasons for any unexpected deviations from plans.

In order to gain the cooperation needed to achieve effective implementation of such a program, it may be necessary to: (1) persuade managers, technical staff, and the labor force of the critical role of CAM in maintaining the competitiveness and hence the survival of the plant; and (2) develop and publicize personnel policies designed to minimize the fears and resulting resistance of each of these groups, instead of regarding labor as the only source of such problems.

Viewed in broader perspective, increasing the rate of diffusion of CAM in domestic industries would seem to require:

1. more general awareness in industry and government of the need to accelerate exploration of CAM potentials in virtually all industries;
2. sharp expansion of the supply of engineers and manufacturing specialists who are knowledgeable about CAM capabilities and requirements;
3. increasing of the capability of CAM hardware and software systems to fit user needs more effectively and to ensure the increasing reliability and uptime of their products; and
4. immediate efforts to explore the prospective effects of increasing CAM applications on the employment levels and skill requirements of various industries in order to help develop constructive government, trade union, and management policies for dealing with resulting adjustments.

Notes

1. For example, see [2], [3], [4], [8], and [12].
2. A preliminary report was published in [10].
3. For a more detailed discussion, see [6]. For additional empirical evidence, see Skeddle [13, p. 561] as well as [8, Chapter 13].
4. Such problems are considered more fully in Gold *et al.* [12, Chapter 14].
5. For example, in the U.S. steel industry, such fringe benefits added 47 per cent to pay for hours actually worked by wage earners in 1976 as compared with an addition of only 18 per cent in 1957. (*Annual Statistical Report, American Iron and Steel Institute—1976* (Washington, D.C., 1977) p. 22.
6. For a more detailed discussion, see [9] or [8, Chapters 3, 5, 9, and 10].
7. It may be of interest in this connection to mention my observations of the process whereby computerization is applied to new sectors of operations in some Japanese steel mills. Instead of having the systems group alone study the operation and devise a CAM application for it, one or more of the operation's supervisors are sent off for intensive training in computers and systems analysis, while one or more specialists from the systems group are assigned to help manage the actual operations to be computerized for a comparable period of at least several weeks. When the two groups are brought together to jointly develop the CAM application, their cooperation is facilitated by each member's understanding of the interacting problems to be dealt with; and it is further motivated by the fact that the next supervisor might be chosen from *either* group. [7]
8. For further discussion of the problems of making and improving evaluations of technological innovations, see Gold *et al.* [12, Chapter 14].

References

1. A. Dogramaci (ed.), *Productivity Analysis: A Range of Perspectives* (Boston: Martinus Nijhoff, 1980).
2. S. Eilon, B. Gold and J. Soesan, *Applied Productivity Analysis for Industry* (Oxford: Pergamon Press, 1976). Russian Translation Moscow: *Ekonomist*, 1980.
3. B. Gold, *Foundations of Productivity Analysis* (Pittsburgh, PA: University of Pittsburgh, 1955).
4. ______,*Explorations in Managerial Economics: Productivity, Costs, Technology and Growth* (London: Macmillan, 1971; New York: Basic Books, 1971; Japanese Translation—Tokyo: *Chikura Shobo*, 1977)
5. ______ (ed.), *Technological Change: Economics, Management and Environment* (Oxford: Pergamon Press, 1975).
6. ______, "On the Shaky Foundations of Capital Budgeting," *California Management Review*, Winter (March) 1977. Reprinted in [11].
7. ______, "Factors Stimulating Technological Progress in Japanese Industries: The Case of Computerization in Steel," *Quarterly Review of Economics and Business*, Winter (December 1978). Reprinted in [6]. Spanish Translation in *Cienca Y Desarrolo* (Consejo National De Cienca Y Tecologia; Mexico, D.F.) November–December 1979.
8. ______, *Productivity, Technology and Capital: Economic Analysis, Management Strategies and Governmental Policies* (Lexington, MA: D.C. Heath—Lexington Books, 1979).
9. ______, "Improving Industrial Productivity and Technological Capabilities: Needs, Problems and Suggested Policies" in [1].
10. ______, "Revising Managerial Evaluations of Computer-Aided Manufacturing Systems," *Proceedings of the Autofact West Conference*, Vol. 1 (Dearborn: Society of Manufacturing Engineers, November 1980).
11. ______ (ed.), *Appraising and Stimulating Technological Advances in Industry, Omega: The International Journal of Management Science*, Special Issue—October 1980.
12. B. Gold, G. Rosegger, and M. G. Boylan, *Evaluating Technological Innovations: Methods, Expectations and Findings* (Lexington, MA: D.C. Heath—Lexington Books, 1980).
13. R. Skeddle, "Expected and Actual Results of a Major Technological Innovation: Float Glass" in [11].

7 PRODUCTIVITY ANALYSIS USING SUBJECTIVE OUTPUT MEASURES: A PERCEPTUAL MAPPING APPROACH FOR "KNOWLEDGE WORK" ORGANIZATIONS

Michael B. Packer

7.1. Introduction

The procedures available for analyzing productivity in "knowledge work" organizations appear to be poorly developed in theory and rarely adopted in practice.[1] One reason for this is the failure of productivity analysts to grapple successfully with the inherent nature of knowledge work activities.

The most obvious characteristic of knowledge work activities is that their immediate result often is largely intangible, reflecting in part the unstructured, creative aspects of knowledge work itself. Unlike other white-collar workers, knowledge workers such as basic research scientists, teachers, social workers, and senior managers must exercise substantial judgment and discretion in performing non-repetitive tasks. Thus, standard productivity measurement techniques based on pure counts of the number or physical quantity of output are useless for knowledge work organizations.

Another characteristic of knowledge work is the often substantial lag between the time the work begins and the time that results can be measured. Educational programs about preventive health measures, for instance, may lead to a better informed public now and better health years in the future. The ultimate *outcome* attributable to knowledge work (e.g., better health) may be far removed from the immediate *output* (e.g., knowledge about the value of physical examinations). As a result, it may be extremely difficult to match correctly this year's resource commitment (in manpower, equipment, etc.) with an uncertain benefit or outcome sometime in the future.

Organizations engaging in knowledge work also have difficulty even defining output. In certain cases, one objective may predominate (such as prevention of death in a hospital emergency room). Most knowledge work organizations, however, face numerous, conflicting goals. In addition, different "stakeholders" or constituencies (e.g., management, other employees, owners, or customers) will in general have different sets of goals for the organization. For example, electric utilities and environmentalists may have markedly different ideas about appropriate goals for an organization regulating nuclear power plants.

Since there may be several sets of goals for the organization depending upon one's point of view, clearly the concept of productivity itself cannot be given a single definition that is appropriate for all situations or all constituencies. In fact, productivity ("quantity of output divided by quantity of input") may be a less meaningful concept for knowledge work organizations than overall effectiveness, because without tangible products in these organizations, the definition of quantity of output is ambiguous.

Unfortunately, despite extensive research and much debate, academic scholars have yet to agree on a definition of organizational effectiveness. Kim Cameron's excellent review of the literature on this subject recounts the frustration researchers have felt attempting to create a sufficiently specific yet comprehensive definition of effectiveness.[2] Cameron traces this frustration to two fundamental problems. Organizational effectiveness is a mental construct created by the observer: it is an abstraction that can never be completely defined by citing particular measures or formulas. Furthermore, organizational effectiveness "is inherently subjective and is grounded in the values and preferences of various constituencies."[3]

As Cameron points out, this latter problem has several ramifications. First, different constituencies may not share the same values or use the same criteria for effectiveness. Second, values and criteria for effectiveness may change over time. For instance, the definition of equal opportunity that prevailed in the United States after the civil rights movement of the early 1960s differed dramatically from the meaning of the term a decade earlier. Third, it may be difficult for individuals to identify the criteria they use in evaluating organizational effectiveness. When asked, many people either omit criteria that, when prompted, they believe are important, or respond that a large number of criteria are about equal in importance. Finally, contradictory values and criteria often exist simultaneously in an organization. Managers may wish to foster entrepreneurial activity and yet be loath to relax strict financial controls and managerial discipline.

Cameron concludes that the four most common definitions of effectiveness—achieving a rational set of goals, developing human resources, succeeding in acquiring resources from the organization's environment to support growth, and streamlining the internal management processes in the organization—all fail to provide comprehensive definitions of organizational effectiveness.

The search for a single definition of organizational effectiveness thus appears to be a scholarly chase after a mirage. As Robert Quinn and John Rohrbaugh put it:

> Organizational effectiveness is a value-based judgment about the performance of an organization . . . (This) implies that a set of criteria exists upon which the value-based judgment of effectiveness is typically made. The criteria will be weighted very differently by different coalitions. These weightings will vary according to individual values, hierarchical position, type of unit, external or internal perspective, point in time, uncertainty in the environment, and numerous other factors. Organizational effectiveness, then, is whatever various coalitions judge it to be.[4]

7.2. Present Approaches for Measuring Knowledge Work Effectiveness

There are four basic approaches at the present time to measuring the effectiveness of knowledge work organizations. Because of the inherent nature of knowledge work activities, each approach has substantial drawbacks.

Intuitive

The intuitive ("gut feel") approach to effectiveness measurement relies upon purely subjective assessments of organizational performance ("They are doing a smashing job!"). While this avoids the trap of attempting to measure inherently intangible activities by completely objective means, it falls prey to bias, politics, ignorance, or confusion about organizational goals.

Single Indicator

The single indicator approach relies upon a solitary, easily quantifiable measure of performance. Typical of these indicators is profit. The principal drawback of single indicators is that organizational behavior can be skewed by attempts to improve only one aspect of performance to the detriment of others. For example, if a hospital were to measure its performance solely by the average length of patient stay, the logical response for a hard-pressed manager who wanted to improve his performance rating would be to dispatch his patients to the hereafter on the first day of their hospital stay.

Multiple Indicators

Using a set of several indicators simultaneously is an alternative approach. Thus a university might measure the amount of its research volume, the size of its student body, the magnitude of its deficit, and the average salary of its students five years after graduation. While this approach is often superior to the previous methods, it also suffers from many drawbacks. If subjective measures are used for some of the indicators, they may be unreliable (different people may give different answers). If surrogate measures are used (such as salaries of graduates as a surrogate for their success in business), they may not be valid substitutes for the items they are supposed to measure.[5] Moreover, there is no guarantee that the particular indicators in the set represent the criteria used by any given constituency.

Weighted Composite

The fourth approach utilizes a weighted composite of indicators. In an engineering group, for instance, a weighted sum of the number of technical presentations, the number of engineering design changes, and the number of projects completed on time might form a composite measure of performance. Many of these weighted aggregate systems still do not address many basic questions related to the intangible nature of most knowledge work (such as the quality of designs). In addition, the validity of systems based on indicators as highly intercorrelated as these is still in question.

No system of effectiveness measurement commonly in use today permits rigorous assessment of the performance of knowledge work organizations. Fortunately for the analyst, much work in other fields bears on this problem. In educational testing, psychological testing, consumer market research, and organizational development, researchers have been coping with the difficulties of measuring such intangibles as intelligence, mental health, consumer perceptions of products, and job satisfaction for many years.

Integrating techniques drawn from these fields permits the development of a more rigorous and useful methodology than those of popular approaches to productivity or effectiveness measurement.

7.3. An Integrated Approach to Measuring Effectiveness In Knowledge Work Organizations

Assumptions

Several assumptions underlie the approach to measuring organizational effectiveness that is described in the following pages. First, subjective assessments of effectiveness are both inevitable and desirable in knowledge work organizations. Since the knowledge work itself is largely intangible, no purely objective measures can describe organizational effectiveness. The use of subjective judgments is in any case firmly entrenched in the management of organizations because managers already make decisions on the basis of their subjective perceptions. Furthermore, there is nothing new or radical in the use of subjective judgments in reporting systems: even financial accounting data are based in large part on subjective judgment. However, because of managers' doubts about the reliability of subjective measures of effectiveness, special attention must be devoted in the analysis to detailed data about the reliability of various types of subjective assessments.

Second, the analysis scheme must be easy to interpret and must focus upon the variables instinctively used by managers in evaluating effectiveness. For example, in a basic research organization, managers rarely base their intuitive sense of the group's effectiveness on the number of papers they publish or the number of patents they obtain. Instead, to evaluate the organization properly, they need information about the quality of research projects, about their originality and their potential. Yet any information collected about these fairly abstract concepts must be reliable and meaningful if it is to help these managers make better-informed decisions.

Finally, any measurement approach must recognize that while common elements exist among all knowledge work organizations, no single set of measurement variables is universally applicable, and no single set of analytical techniques can serve to interpret data. The choice of variables and analytical techniques depends entirely on the nature of the organization and the purpose for which the information is being collected.

Methodology

In order to measure organizational effectiveness, one must ask various people connected with the organization about its activities. Yet when this is done, managers typically discard the results as unreliable. This raises an interesting quandary: managers need information about abstract concepts relating to organizational effectiveness (such as the quality of designs in engineering), but they recognize that simply asking people about these abstractions yields unreliable results. The reason for this lack of reliability stems not from the fact that people cannot agree on their assessments of organizations, but rather stems from two specific methodological problems.

First, questions about organizations often confuse two important and distinct issues: the extent to which an organization meets certain goals (e.g., high-quality research or quick payback projects) and the relative importance of these goals. One manager may rate a research project very highly in terms of its effectiveness because it is extremely innovative. Yet another might rate it low simply because it holds little short-term promise. The two managers may well agree on their underlying assessment of the project; what they disagree about is the relative importance of various goals for the organization. The analyst should conclude that any assessment of activities should be done separately from the assessment of the importance of those activities.

The other methodological problem concerns the typical vagueness of questions about organizational effectiveness. People respond less meaningfully to general questions about overall innovativeness of a project than to a list of detailed questions such as, "To what extent does this project show mathematical ingenuity in simplifying the governing equations of fluid flow?" However, if the list were long enough to cover everything we mean by "innovativeness" or "effectiveness," the resulting overabundance of information would be practically impossible to interpret.

The solution to this problem is to ask a series of detailed questions about organizational effectiveness, and then to aggregate the responses, forming composite measures of the abstract concepts managers care about but cannot explore directly. If this is done in a structured way, several benefits ensue. Grouping questions into composites improves the reliability of subjective evaluations of effectiveness by allowing random response effects to "cancel out." Furthermore, managers can more easily assess the relative importance of a small number of composite measures of concepts they care about than a bewildering host of specific indicators of organizational activity. Finally, composite measures open doors to a number of multivariate analysis techniques that can materially aid in the interpretation of data on effectiveness.

Analysis Procedure

Measuring the effectiveness of knowledge work organizations begins by determining the criteria of effectiveness used by various constituencies of the organization. Several techniques are available to accomplish this, ranging from informal interviews to structured group meetings using the nominal group technique.[6] Whatever the method, careful consideration of the suitability of various criteria and their mutual interactions is essential.[7] Constructing a hierarchy of criteria (in which broad criteria and more detailed criteria are tied in a tree-like framework) and formally testing these criteria for importance are not only crucial for the analysis procedure, but are also fruitful in helping members of the organization clarify their own sense of the criteria they use.

The next step is to identify a set of indicators for organizational effectiveness. Once a hierarchy of effectiveness criteria is established, this can be done fairly simply by matching organizational activities with the corresponding criteria of effectiveness they are intended to address. For instance, if quality of service is one criterion of effectiveness in an automobile repair shop, activities such as taking reservations for repair work and loaning substitute cars to customers might be activities intended to improve performance on this criterion. This list of activities is the basis for detailed indicators of effectiveness used in the analysis. These indicators should stress the extent to which each activity meets its corresponding criterion, and will usually require subjective assessments on the part of various constituencies of the organization (e.g., the average customer response on a survey inquiring about the quality of service). However, if meaningful, direct quantitative measures of performance are available, they should be incorporated in the analysis.

Because the criteria of effectiveness for most knowledge work organizations are typically quite diverse, the corresponding set of indicators will be equally varied. In general, at least nine areas will appear: pure efficiency or productivity, quality, human resource development, communication and information management, planning and goal setting, adaptability and flexibility, growth and competitive or financial success, group cohesion and morale, and stability or control.[8] The list of indicators must be complete in order to present a comprehensive picture of organizational effectiveness; thus some care should be taken in developing the list. Structured group meetings with various constituencies of the organization will again prove extremely helpful at this stage.

Data can then be collected for each indicator, using the subjective judgments of members of each constituency. Questionnaires with Likert or semantic differential scales can be used to quantify their subjective judgments.[9]

Once data about organizational effectiveness have been collected, the detailed indicators must be aggregated into composite measures that are meaningful to managers. Among several techniques available for this step, grouping the questions or detailed indicators simply by intuition is easiest. Many indicators will naturally fall into one or another of a small number of clusters (possibly along the lines of the nine areas mentioned above). While this procedure is easy for managers to assimilate, it does not take advantage of the power of formal quantitative clustering techniques now widely available.

Two formal clustering techniques are of particular interest in the analysis of organizational effectiveness: factor analysis and hierarchical clustering. Both techniques have been widely applied in a variety of fields, and standard computer packages for each can be found at most computer centers.[10] Both start from the matrix of correlations among the detailed indicators described above.

The major advantage of formal clustering techniques is that they describe the structure of clusters with greater precision than does the intuitive "gut" feeling that "these questions just go together." Measures of the extent to which any single cluster actually represents a single abstract concept of effectiveness such as quality or flexibility are calculated by these computer programs and can serve as a check on the reliability of the results. While the mathematical details of formal methods reduce the comprehensibility of the analysis procedure for many managers, a clear and simple explanation of the clustering process and the reasonably close correspondence of intuitive clusters to the formally derived clusters seems to mollify most managers.

A final check on the reliability of the clustering process and upon the appropriateness of the detailed indicators of effectiveness can be made by computing formal reliability coefficients based upon test theory.[11] These coefficients can be calculated from the correlations among the detailed indicators.

After the data are collected and the indicators aggregated into clusters, they can be displayed graphically on "perceptual maps," or graphs of the composite scores on each composite measure of effectiveness, averaged over all people in a particular group.[12]

At this point in the analysis, the extent to which the organization meets its various criteria of effectiveness has been determined. Before one can evaluate the overall effectiveness of the organization, however, one must assess the relative importance of these criteria. An intuitive method of performing this next step is to ask each constituency to assign subjective weights to the several composite measures of effectiveness created by the clustering process.

There are more formal methods of performing this weighting as well. Here the constituencies are simply asked to rate the overall effectiveness of the organization under several hypothetical scenarios or to rank several departments within the organization in terms of overall effectiveness. A multiple regression using the overall effectiveness scores as the dependent variable and the various composite scores as the independent variables reveals the weights implicitly assigned by these people to each composite measure. Overall effectiveness can then be evaluated using the several composite measures weighted by their regression coefficients.[13]

The relative importance of the criteria associated with each composite measure can be dramatically displayed on the perceptual maps derived earlier. A vector is plotted on the map, the slope of which corresponds to the ratio of weights assigned to each composite measure. The direction in which this vector points then defines the "ideal" mix of trade-offs among various facets of organizational effectiveness.

Advantages and Disadvantages

There are several advantages and disadvantages associated with this approach to evaluating the effectiveness of knowledge work organizations. The disadvantages fall into two categories: comprehensibility and feasibility. Since the formal techniques involve relatively sophisticated statistical analysis, managers may quickly reject the whole approach. Moreover, many people either resent having to answer questionnaires about organizations or are in no position to be doing so (e.g., patients in a hospital emergency room).

In contrast, there are at least six advantages to the approach. The system is relatively easy to maintain: one need only obtain new responses to the detailed indicators of effectiveness and then plot the resulting composite scores on the existing perceptual map. Second, the approach provides managers with excellent feedback by making explicit both the effectiveness criteria for the organization and the abstract concepts evident in their intuitive evaluations of performance. Situations in which stated goals do not correspond to actual ratings of overall effectiveness will be highlighted.

Third, if the procedure is repeated using the opinions of each constituency, the approach provides quantitative evidence about the extent to which perceptions of the organization are shared by these groups. Problems in communication quickly become evident in discrepancies between the perceptual maps drawn by each group. Another advantage to this approach is that the perceptual maps present in a simple, visual fashion the essential results of an analysis of organizational effectiveness. The technique is extremely useful for communication within the organization and with outside groups. Finally, the perceptual mapping approach measures the intangibles that managers instinctively think about—abstract concepts such as quality—and not just factors that happen to be "objectively" quantifiable. It is thus eminently suited for knowledge work organizations.

Illustration

The approach described above can be illustrated by a portion of a recent analysis of the effectiveness of retail branch banking.[14] The bank in this analysis maintains almost 200 offices and has approximately $3.4 billion in assets. It is committed to electronic banking and has invested heavily in automated teller machines (ATM). As a result of concerns about increasing competition for traditional banking customers, the bank instituted an "Ideal Branch" program in 1980. The program defines in detail required activities for each branch employee; sets standards for sales, transaction accuracy, and customer interaction, defines career paths, and provides a reward system for superior performance. However, bank managers were concerned whether the Ideal Branch program was indeed succeeding in improving performance.

Managers at both the branch and corporate levels were interviewed using the critical success factor technique to determine the goals and objectives of the bank.[15] Their responses, shown in Figure 7–1, fall into four distinct areas: branch operations, customer interaction, human resource development, and branch planning. Each of these broad goals is composed of more detailed sub-objectives. On the basis of these results, a list of forty-seven questions was developed to evaluate the effectiveness with which each branch of the bank meets its goals (Table 7–1). A questionnaire using seven point Likert scales was then distributed to the employees at four branches.[16]

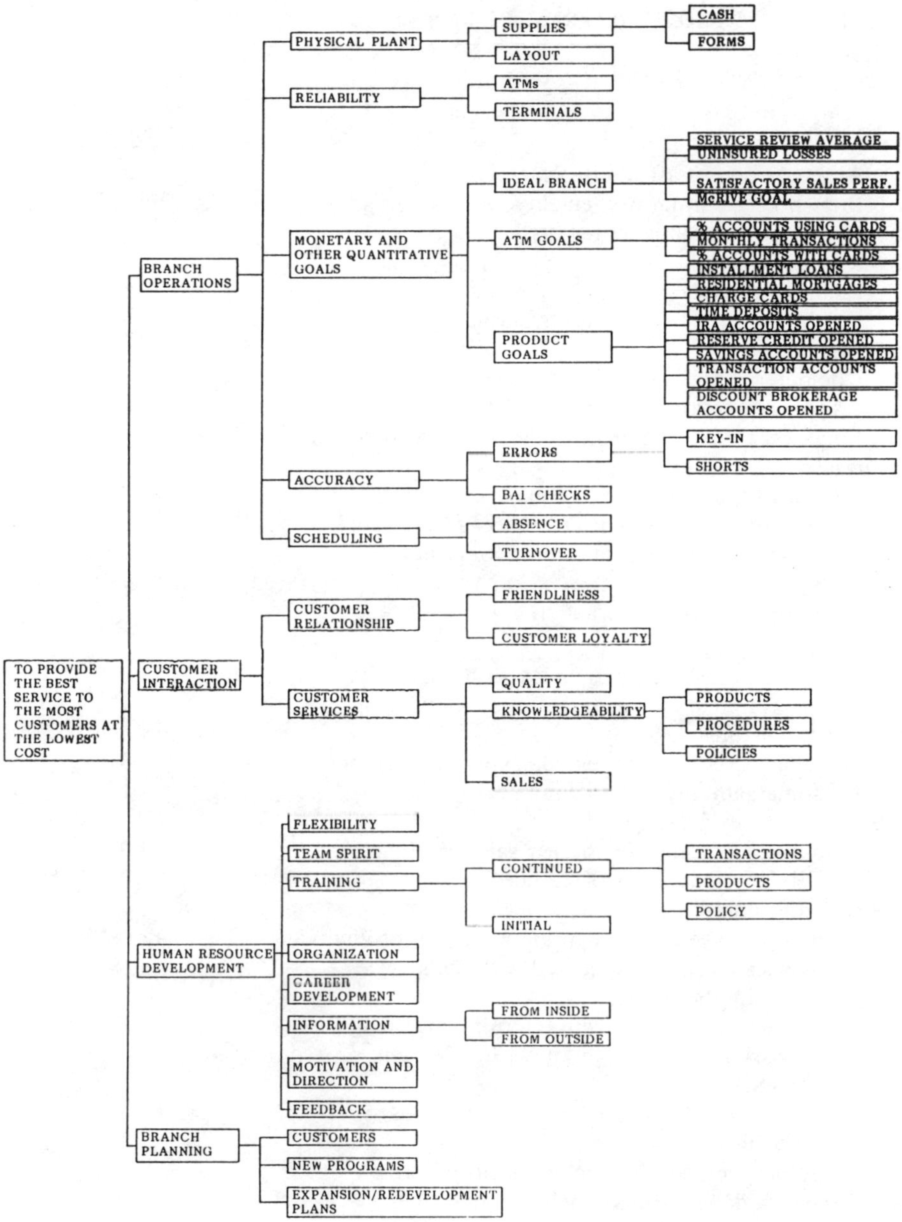

Figure 7-1. Goals and Objectives for Retail Branch Banking

Table 7-1. Detailed Indicators of Effectiveness

Area One: Branch Operations	
Scheduling	Hierarchical Cluster*
Absences do not affect efficiency.	8
Branch keeps hiring new employees.	none**
In general, branch is well-staffed.	2
Accuracy	
Employees rarely make key-in errors.	6
Employees rarely cause shorts/surpluses.	6
Reliability	
Computerized terminals help efficiency.	5
ATM malfunctions rarely affect efficiency.	6
Employees rarely slowed by equipment malfunctions.	2
Physical Plant	
Layout of the work area is convenient.	4
Employees have the right amount of forms/supplies.	6
Employees have the right amount of cash.	8
Area Two: Customer Interaction	
Customer Relationship	
Customers think branch employees are friendly.	8
Employees create a warm, personal relationship with customers.	1
We establish long-term relationships with customers.	8
Customers are loyal to this branch.	1
Employee Sales Effectiveness	
Employees are effective in their sales of services.	7
We sell large quantities of services.	7
Knowledgeability	
Employees have a thorough knowledge of products.	none**
Employees are well acquainted with the services offered by the branch.	5
Employees are familiar with the rules governing services.	5
Employees have thorough knowledge of bank procedures.	5
Quality of Service	
Employees know what is expected in standards and quality.	7
Customers respect the quality of our work.	1
The work done at the branch is high caliber.	8
Branch employees are well qualified/have right skills for their job.	8

Table 7-1 *(continued)*

Area Three: Human Resource Development	
Morale	
In general, my morale is high.	1
In general, branch morale is high.	1
Career Development	
Supervisors adequately assist in career planning.	6
Employees know the kind of career they want.	6
Team Spirit	
Employees feel part of a team.	2
We often work together as a team.	2
Employees seem to get along well with other.	2
Feedback	
Employees can tell whether they are doing a good job.	7
It's easy for supervisors to evaluate our work.	3
Employees know standards/quality expectations.	7
At this branch, it seems to matter if I do a good job.	3
Flexibility	
We are flexible enough to take on new tasks.	5
Our responses to emergencies are adequate.	2
Supervision	
Managers/supervisors are usually aware of problems in morale, personal matters.	1
Managers/supervisors are usually aware of operations problems.	1
Generally, office supervisors are well-organized.	3
Employees have a clear understanding of organizational goals.	8
Training	
Basic training received is sufficient.	7
Employees well-informed of policy changes.	4
Employees well-informed of transaction procedure changes.	4
Employees well-informed of changes in bank product lines.	4
Information	
It is easy to get help/advice from outside the branch.	1
It is easy to get help/advice from within the branch.	5

*The number refers to the cluster in which each question was grouped by the hierarchical clustering procedure.

**Some questions did not statistically group with any cluster.

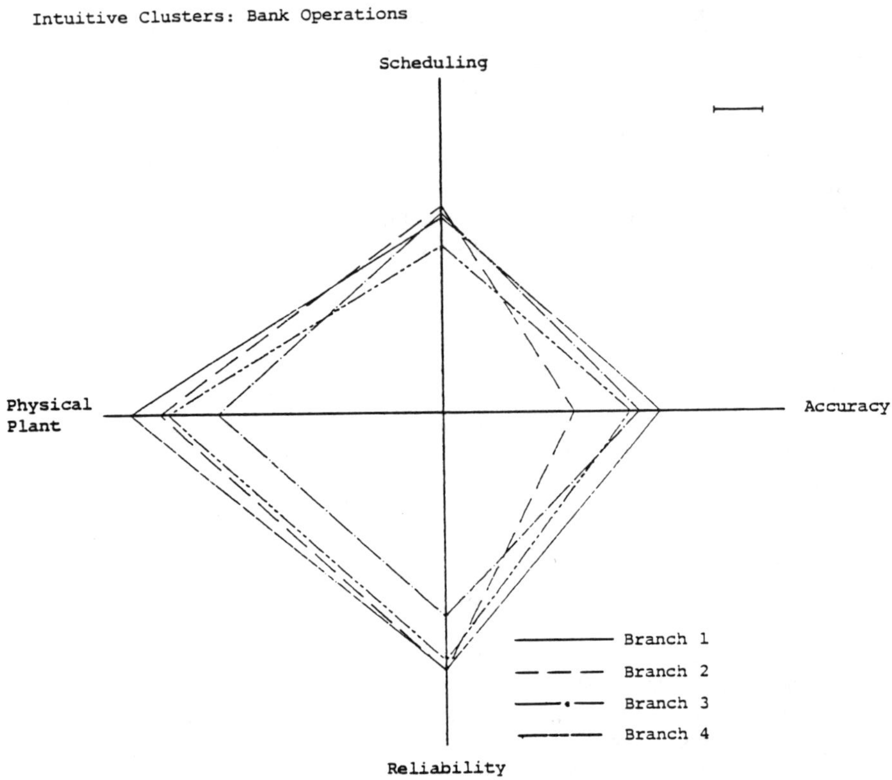

Figure 7-2. Perceptual Map of Clusters Formed by Goal Tree

The questions were clustered intuitively along the lines of the goals in Figure 7-1. A second clustering structure was created by formal hierarchical clustering techniques. The results are shown in "amoeba" type perceptual maps in Figures 7-2 and 7-3. In this type of map, the mean response for each composite measure is represented by the distance from the center of the map. One can label each statistically derived cluster by examining the nature of the indicators grouped in it. Thus the first cluster in Figure 7-3, for example, contains indicators relating to the level of morale at the branch and the overall branch atmosphere. While these labels distill the flavor of the indicators in each cluster, the grouping of indicators does not always make intuitive sense. It is perfectly reasonable to move certain indicators to other clusters or to omit them entirely to improve the

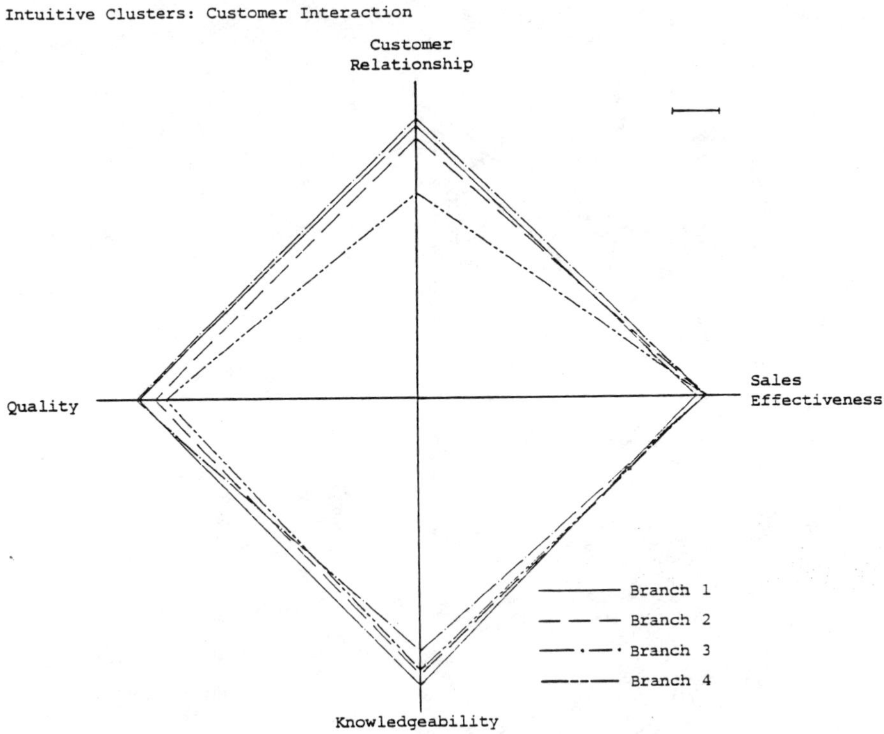

Figure 7-2 *(continued)*

Table 7-2. Reliability Coefficients

	Number of Questions in Cluster	*Reliability Coefficients* Cronbach's Alpha*	Beta*
1. Morale, branch atmosphere	8	0.923	0.772
2. Teamwork, cohesiveness	6	0.886	0.787
3. Supervision	3	0.876	0.847
4. Continued training, layout	3	0.825	0.748
5. Knowledgeability	6	0.855	0.690
6. Career development, operations	6	0.839	0.665
7. Sales effectiveness	5	0.829	0.722
8. Quality	7	0.806	0.551

*For definitions of reliability coefficients alpha and beta, see references listed in footnote 11.

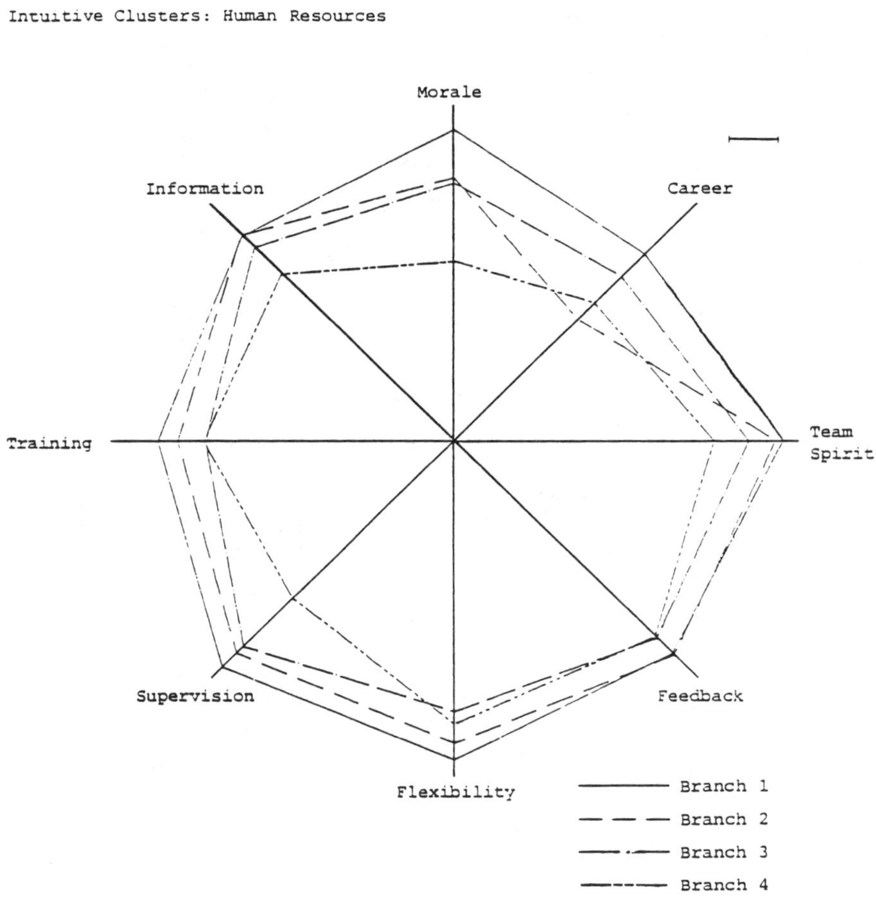

Figure 7-2 *(continued)*

interpretability of the results if this can be accomplished without sacrificing too much statistical validity.

These results show that Branches 1 and 2 are apparently more effective than Branches 3 and 4, whether statistically derived clusters or clusters derived from the hierarchy of effectiveness criteria in Figure 7-1 are examined. The managers found the latter representation more comprehensible, despite the lower statistical reliability of these clusters.

The largest differences in performance among the branches occur in the human resources area. The difficulties experienced by Branch 4 in morale

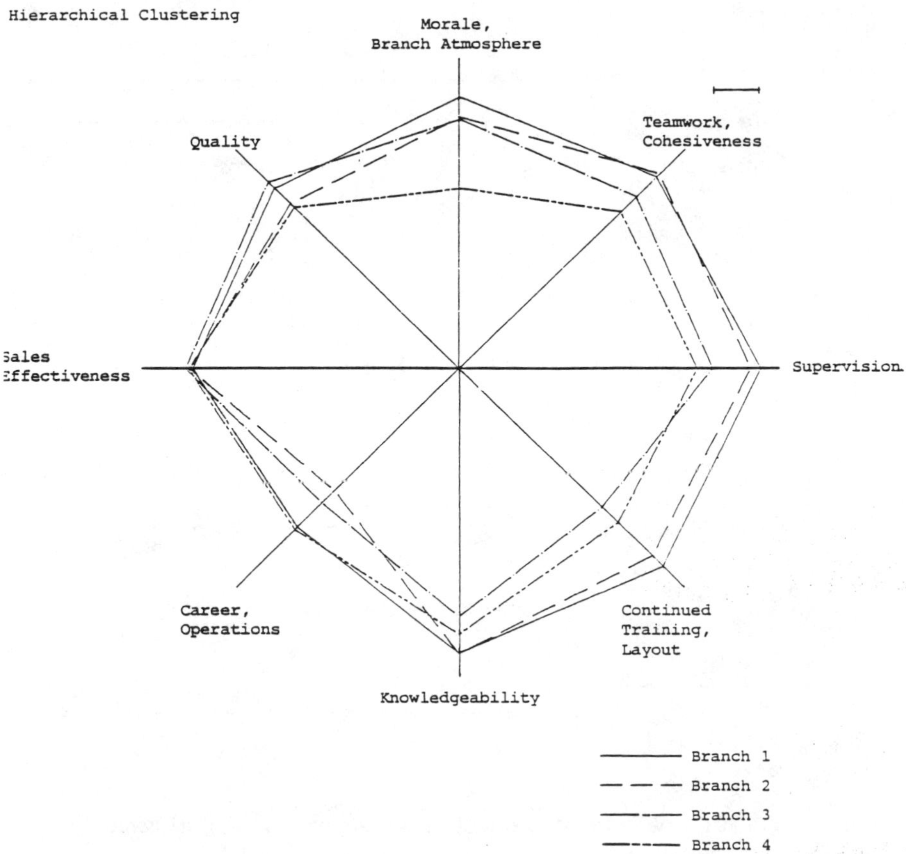

Figure 7-3. Perceptual Map of Clusters Formed by Statistical Analysis

and supervision highlight their particular need for more work in management processes such as team building and communication skills. The "Ideal Branch" program specifically targets the need for developing management process skills but thus far reinforces supervisors' behavior primarily by quantitative performance targets.

In order to assess the reliability of composite effectiveness measures formed by aggregating the indicators in each cluster, reliability coefficients were computed and are listed in Table 7–2.[17] In addition, the validity of the subjective assessments shown in the perceptual maps can be evaluated by comparing these data with more objective data collected as part of the Ideal

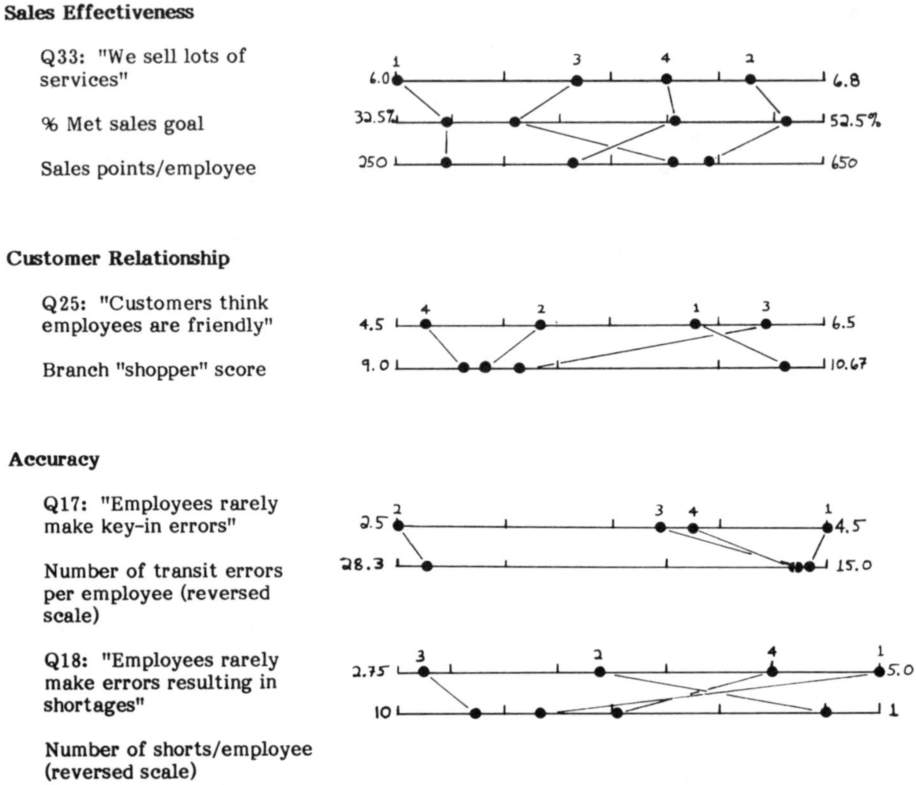

Figure 7-4. Comparison of Subjective Assessments of Performance with Objective Measures

Branch program. Figure 7–4 illustrates the general agreement between the two sets of data and thus tends to substantiate the validity of the perceptual mapping technique.

7.4. Conclusions

The analysis of effectiveness in knowledge work organizations has been hampered by the lack of techniques for measuring effectiveness in a reliable and meaningful fashion. Since the outputs of these organizations are to a great extent intangible, techniques that rely upon counting items of output (such as memoranda written or scholarly papers published) cannot capture the essence of knowledge work. Yet techniques that utilize subjective assessments have traditionally been implemented with little regard to the reliability of the results.

The approach described here, while still experimental, seems to avoid many of the difficulties that have plagued previous approaches to the problem by tying measurement to organizational goals, by clustering detailed subjective indicators of performance in a rational manner, and by explicitly assessing the reliability of the results. The use of quantitative analytical techniques complements nicely a structured approach to the development of subjective indicators of effectiveness and productivity.

Notes

1. The term *knowledge work* in this paper refers to non-repetitive, largely unstructured work that requires the exercise of substantial independent judgment and involves information processing as an essential component of work. It should be distinguished from repetitive tasks (e.g., many clerical or assembly-line jobs), from tasks which may require great skill but elatively little judgment, and from tasks which do not focus on information as an essential ingredient.

Summaries of the techniques for analyzing productivity in knowledge work organizations which are currently used are given in Ruch (1980), Schainblatt (1981), and Cameron (1981).

2. Cameron (1981).

3. *Ibid.*, p. 112.

4. Quinn and Rohrbaugh (1981).

5. There are several characteristics which a measure of productivity or effectiveness must possess if it is to be considered reliable and relevant. In order to be reliable, it should be *verifiable* (different people would arrive at the same answer), *valid* (measuring what it purports to measure and not some other construct), and *neutral* (covering the entire scope of the underlying concept and thus not being biased by omission). In order to be relevant, it should possess *feedback* value (ability to refine knowledge about historical or present activities), *predictive* value, and should be *timely* (available when needed for decision-making). For a more extensive discussion of the qualitative characteristics of productivity information, see Packer (forthcoming).

6. The nominal group technique is a structured group process designed to reduce counterproductive group behavior and to build consensus for decisionmaking. It has become extremely popular for the development of productivity indicators in white-collar (particularly clerical) organizations. In most cases, however, the indicators which are suggested by the group are "objective" measures which are not appropriate for knowledge work groups. For more details about the nominal group technique, see Delbecq (1975).

Another powerful technique for identifying criteria of effectiveness is critical success factor interviewing. See Rockart (1979).

7. The literature of statistical decision theory provides a great deal of important information about the specification of goals in an organization. For example, see Keeney and Raiffa (1976).

8. Quinn and Rohrbaugh (1981), pp. 122–140.

9. The design of unbiased questionnaires embodying the subjective indicators of output or effectiveness is a difficult yet crucial step in the approach. A good overview of the potential pitfalls of questionnaire design is given in Urban and Hauser (1980), Chapter 8.

10. A good description of clustering techniques at a non-technical level is given in Chapter 9 of Urban and Hauser (1980). Computer programs for factor analysis and hierarchical clustering are available in common statistical libraries such as the Statistical Analysis System (SAS). A microcomputer version of the programs necessary for implementing the approach to effectiveness measurement described in this paper is SYSTAT.

11. A summary of reliability theory can be found in Peter (1979). The essential idea is to estimate the fraction of variance in observed scores on a series of questions which is attributable to variation in the true underlying concepts and the fraction which is attributable to lack of reliability in the measurement instrument (the actual questions or indicators used).

12. Perceptual maps are explained from the perspective of consumer market research in Chapter 9 of Urban and Hauser (1980). An interorganizational comparison of effectiveness is analogous to a comparison of the attributes of consumer products as subjectively rated by consumers.

13. This weighting procedure (whether done intuitively or formally by regression) is only justifiable if the composite measures are independent. Otherwise, the intercorrelations of the composites would destroy the significance of the weights as measures of relative importance. While the original detailed indicators are usually highly intercorrelated, the clustering step maximizes the correlation of indicators within each cluster and some clustering processes also minimize the correlation among clusters. If principal components factor analysis is used, the composite measures are guaranteed by construction to be independent (although the interpretability of each composite measure may suffer as a result).

More disturbing is the problem of aggregating the values of different people as is done in calculating the weighting coefficients. This cannot be done in such a way that simultaneously satisfies all of the properties we would desire such aggregate weights to possess (e.g., if a group believes that organization A is more effective than B and that B is more effective than C, then the group will believe A to be more effective than C). In the present approach, this problem is mitigated by measuring the relative importance of criteria of effectiveness only with respect to a single constituency at a time. By definition, the members of a single constituency tend to share a common set of values. Thus discrepancies in the aggregate value structure of the group are unlikely to occur. Moreover, the errors which might occasionally arise in an aggregate set of weights are probably worth incurring for the sake of a technique more readily understandable than more formal mathematical techniques. See Keeney and Raiffa (1976), Chapter 10.

14. Lyle (1983). For another example, see Packer and Kahn (1983).

15. See footnote six for reference to the critical success factor technique.

16. The questionnaire used a seven-point scale for each indicator of effectiveness. Demographic questions and questions relating to other portions of the study were also included. The questions were presented in randomized order.

17. The reliability coefficients used in this illustration are calculated assuming that the detailed indicators are added with unit weights in the composites. See footnote 11.

References

Cameron, Kim [1981], "Construct Space and Subjectivity Problems in Organizational Effectiveness," *Public Productivity Review* 5:2, June: 105–121.

Delbecq, Andre L., Andrew H. Van de Ven, and David H. Gustafson [1975], *Group Techniques for Program Planning: A Guide to Nominal Group and Delphi Processes*, Glenview, IL: Scott Foresman and Company.

Keeney, Ralph L. and Howard Raiffa [1976], *Decision with Multiple Objectives: Preferences and Value Tradeoffs*, New York: John Wiley & Sons.

Lyle, Marilee A. [1983], *Perceptions of Bank Productivity*, (unpublished) S.B. thesis in Mechanical Engineering, Cambridge: Massachusetts Institute of Technology.

Packer, Michael B. [forthcoming], *Productivity Analysis in Public and Private Sector Organizations*, Englewood Cliffs, N.J.: Prentice Hall.

Packer, Michael B. and Zella L. Kahn [1983], "A Multi-firm Study of the Benefits of Computer-Aided Design Systems," *Proceedings*, National Computer Graphics Association Conference, Chicago, IL, June 26–30.

Peter, J. Paul [1979], "Reliability: A Review of Psychometric Basics and Recent Marketing Practices," *Journal of Marketing Research* 16: 6–17.

Quinn, Robert E. and John Rohrbaugh [1981], "A Competing Values Approach to Organizational Effectiveness," *Public Productivity Review* 5:2, June: 139.

Rockart, John F. [1979], "Chief Executives Define Their Own Data Needs," *Harvard Business Review* March–April: 81–93.

Ruch, William A. [1980], "Measuring Knowledge Worker Productivity," *Dimensions of Productivity Research*, J. D. Hogan and A. M. Craig, eds., Houston, TX: American Productivity Center, pp. 339–357.

Schainblatt, Alfred H. [1981], *Measuring the Productivity of Scientists and Engineers in R&D: A State of the Practice Review*, Washington, D.C.: The Urban Institute.

Urban, Glen L. and John R. Hauser [1980], *Design and Marketing of New Products*, Englewood Cliffs, N.J.: Prentice-Hall, Inc.

PART THREE

8 MEASURING EFFICIENCY IN PRODUCTION: WITH AN APPLICATION TO ELECTRIC UTILITIES

Rolf Färe, Shawna Grosskopf,
James Logan, and C.A. Knox Lovell

8.1. Introduction

Michael Farrell's (1957) pathbreaking investigation of the structure of efficiency in production has somewhat belatedly spurred a flurry of derivative research. Most of this research has focused on technical efficiency, although some studies have investigated technical, allocative (or price), and overall (or economic) efficiency. In addition, much of this research has followed Farrell by imposing rather severe restrictions on the structure of production technology. Finally, virtually all such studies ignore the implications of change or variation in efficiency for productivity growth or variation. In this paper we focus our attention on the technical component of overall efficiency. We relax Farrell's restrictive assumptions on the structure of production technology, and this enables us to examine the structure of technical efficiency by decomposing an overall measure of technical efficiency into its constituent parts. Finally, we mention briefly the connection between efficiency measurement and the measurement of productivity growth.

The paper unfolds as follows. In section 8.2 we introduce a production technology that is required to satisfy only a minimal set of axioms. In particular, it is not required to satisfy constant, or even nonincreasing, returns to scale, and it is not required to satisfy strong disposability of inputs. This technology is then contrasted with otherwise similar technologies that do satisfy one or more of these restrictions. In section 8.3 we use the basic technology, together with various restricted versions of the basic technology, to define a series of measures of technical efficiency. These measures measure purely technical efficiency in the sense of Farrell, weak technical efficiency, input congestion, scale efficiency, and overall technical efficiency. Additional measures are developed to identify the input or inputs responsible for congestion, and to identify the source of scale inefficiency as either increasing or decreasing returns to scale. In section 8.4 we develop a series of linear models of the basic and the restricted technologies. Based on these linear models, we formulate a series of linear programs whose solutions are the desired efficiency measures. In section 8.5 we apply this apparatus to a sample of 32 electric utility plants observed in their first full year of operation. We find an average rate of overall technical efficiency of roughly 90 percent, and we find substantial variation across plants in both the overall rate of technical efficiency and the importance of the various components of the overall rate. Finally, section 8.6 concludes with a summary and some suggestions for further research.

8.2. The Production Technology

A production technology transforming inputs $x \varepsilon R^n_+$ into net output $u \varepsilon R_+$ is modelled by a production function ϕ: $R^n_+ \rightarrow R_+$ or inversely by an input correspondence L: $R_+ \rightarrow L(u) \subseteq R^n_+$, where $\phi(x)$ denotes the maximum output obtainable from the input vector x and $L(u)$ denotes the set of all input vectors capable of producing at least output $u \varepsilon R_+$. The inverse relationship between ϕ and L is given by

$$L(u){:} = \{x{:}\ \phi(x) \geqq u\} \text{ and } \phi(x){:} = \max\{u{:}\ x \varepsilon L(u)\}. \quad (8-1)$$

The production function ϕ is assumed to satisfy the following axioms:

ϕ.1 $\phi(0) = 0$,
ϕ.2 $\phi(\lambda x) \geqq \phi(x)$, $\lambda \geqq 1$, and $\phi(\lambda x) > \phi(x)$ if $\phi(x) > 0$, $\lambda > 1$,
ϕ.3 ϕ is upper semi-continuous.

ϕ.2 imposes weak disposability of inputs on the technology. However ϕ is not assumed to satisfy either of two stronger versions of ϕ.2, namely strong disposability of inputs,

$\phi.2.S \quad \phi(x) \geqq \phi(y), x \geqq y,$

and constant returns to scale,

$CRS \quad \phi(\lambda x) = \lambda\phi(x), \lambda > 0.$

We note that Farrell (1957: 254–256) assumed both $\phi.2.S$ and CRS, while most subsequent writers have dropped CRS and retained $\phi.2.S$. By relaxing both of these assumptions we are able to study the structure of technical efficiency.

Although we do not enforce strong disposability of inputs ($\phi.2.S$), we frequently compare a weakly disposable technology satisfying $\{\phi.1 - \phi.3\}$ with a technology satisfying $\{\phi.1 - \phi.3\}$ together with strong disposability for a subset of inputs. For this purpose it is useful to introduce the notion of strong disposability for a particular input. Thus if ϕ satisfies $\{\phi.1 - \phi.3\}$ we say that input i is strongly disposable if

$$\phi.2S^i \quad \phi(x_1, \ldots, \lambda_i x_i, \ldots, x_n) \geqq \phi(x_1, \ldots, x_i, \ldots, x_n), \lambda_i \geqq 1$$

holds, or if output is not decreased when the ith input is increased. Of course ϕ satisfies $\phi.2.S$ if, and only if, it satisfies $\phi.2.S^i$ for all $i = 1, \ldots, n$.

The distinction between weak and strong disposability of inputs can be developed further by introducing three subsets of the input set $L(u)$. These subsets, the isoquant, the weak efficient subset, and the efficient subset, play a major role in our investigation of the structure of technical efficiency. They are defined by

$$IsoqL(u): \begin{cases} \{x: x \in L(u), \lambda x \notin L(u) \text{ for } \lambda < 1\}, u > 0, \\ \{0\}, u = 0. \end{cases} \quad (8\text{–}2)$$

$$WEffL(u): = \begin{cases} \{x: x \in L(u), y \overset{*}{<} x => y \notin L(u)\}, u > 0, \\ \{0\}, u = 0. \end{cases} \quad (8\text{–}3)^1$$

$$EffL(u): = \begin{cases} \{x: x \in L(u), y \leq x => y \notin L(u)\}, u > 0, \\ \{0\}, u = 0. \end{cases} \quad (8\text{–}4)^2$$

The distinctions among these three subsets of $L(u)$ are illustrated for a two-input technology in Figure 8–1. The input set $L(u)$ consists of the set of input vectors on or inside $ABCDF$. $Isoq\ L(u)$ consists of the set of input vectors on $ABCD$, $WEffL(u)$ consists of the set of input vectors on BCD, and $EffL(u)$ consists of the set of input vectors on BC. These distinctions

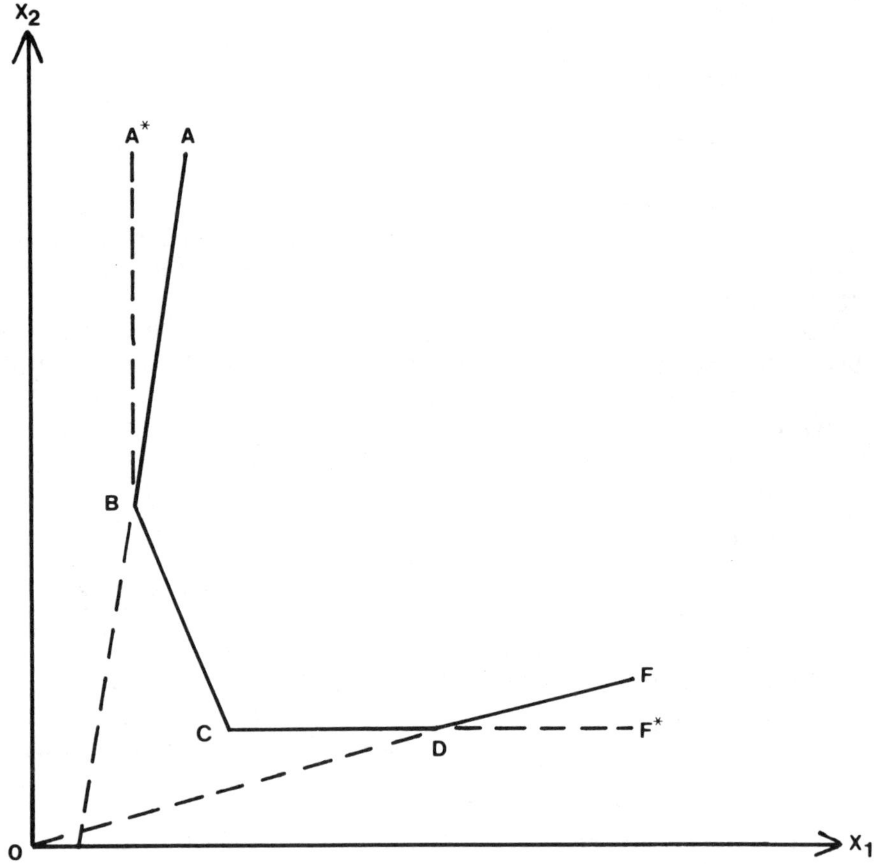

Figure 8-1. Distinctions among Three Subsets of $L(u)$ of Equations (8-2), (8-3) and (2-4).

arise whenever ϕ satisfies $\{\phi.1 - \phi.3\}$ but not $\phi.2.S$. The expanded input set bounded by A^*BCDF^* does satisfy $\phi.2.S$. If only x_2 is strongly disposable when ϕ satisfies $\{\phi.1 - \phi.3\}$ the input set $L(u)$ is then bounded by A^*BCDF. If only x_1 is strongly disposable when ϕ satisfies $\{\phi.1 - \phi.3\}$ the input set $L(u)$ is then bounded by $ABCDF^*$.

Although we do not enforce constant returns to scale (*CRS*) on the technology, we occasionally compare a technology satisfying only $\{\phi.1 - \phi.3\}$ with a technology satisfying $\{\phi.1 - \phi.3\}$ and either *CRS* or nonincreasing returns to scale. For this purpose it is useful to introduce an equivalent way of representing the technology, the graph of the technology, namely

$$GR: = \{(u,x): \phi(x) \geqq u, x \in R^n_+\} = \{(u,x): x \in L(u), u \in R_+\}. \quad (8\text{–}5)$$

Corresponding to GR is the smallest closed cone containing GR,

$$\overline{K(GR)}: = \overline{\{(u,x): (u,x) = (\lambda v, \lambda y), (v,y) \in GR, \lambda \geqq 0\}}, \quad (8\text{–}6)$$

and the star-closure of GR,

$$\overline{(GR)^*}: = \overline{\{(u,x): (u,x) = (\lambda v\ \lambda y), (v,y) \in GR, \lambda \in [0,1]\}}. \quad (8\text{–}7)$$

The graph of the technology GR, and the corresponding cone technology $\overline{K(GR)}$ and star-closure $\overline{(GR)^*}$ are illustrated in Figure 8–2. GR is the area bounded by the surface $OPCRB$ and the x-axis. The cone technology $\overline{K(GR)}$ generated by GR is the area bounded by the ray OA and the x-axis. The star-closure $\overline{(GR)^*}$ generated by GR is the area bounded by the surface $OQCRB$ and the x-axis. It is apparent from (8–6) and (8–7) and Figure 8–2, and easily proved, that $\overline{K(GR)}$ satisfies CRS while $\overline{(GR)^*}$ exhibits nonincreasing returns to scale.[3] A part of our investigation of the structure of technical efficiency is based on a distinction among GR, $\overline{K(GR)}$ and $\overline{(GR)^*}$, a distinction which arises if and only if ϕ does not satisfy CRS.[4] Finally, associated with $\overline{K(GR)}$ are an input correspondence $L^K(u)$ and a production function $\phi^K(x)$, and associated with $\overline{(GR)^*}$ are an input correspondence $L^*(u)$ and a production function $\phi^*(x)$.[5]

8.3. Measures of Technical Efficiency

We are now ready to introduce a series of output-based measures of technical efficiency defined on a technology satisfying $\{\phi.1 - \phi.3\}$ but not necessarily $\phi.2.S$ or CRS. We obtain $(n + 4)$ primary and $(n + 2)$ derived measures of technical efficiency, n being the number of inputs. The measures are labelled "output-based" because they show the amount by which output can be increased from given inputs through the elimination of each type of inefficiency.[6]

The first measure to be introduced is an output-based Farrell measure of technical efficiency. For this purpose we first define its effective domain

$$D(F_0): = \{(u,x): \exists\ \theta > 0 \text{ such that } x \in L(u/\theta)\}, \quad (8\text{–}8)$$

from which the Farrell measure is defined as

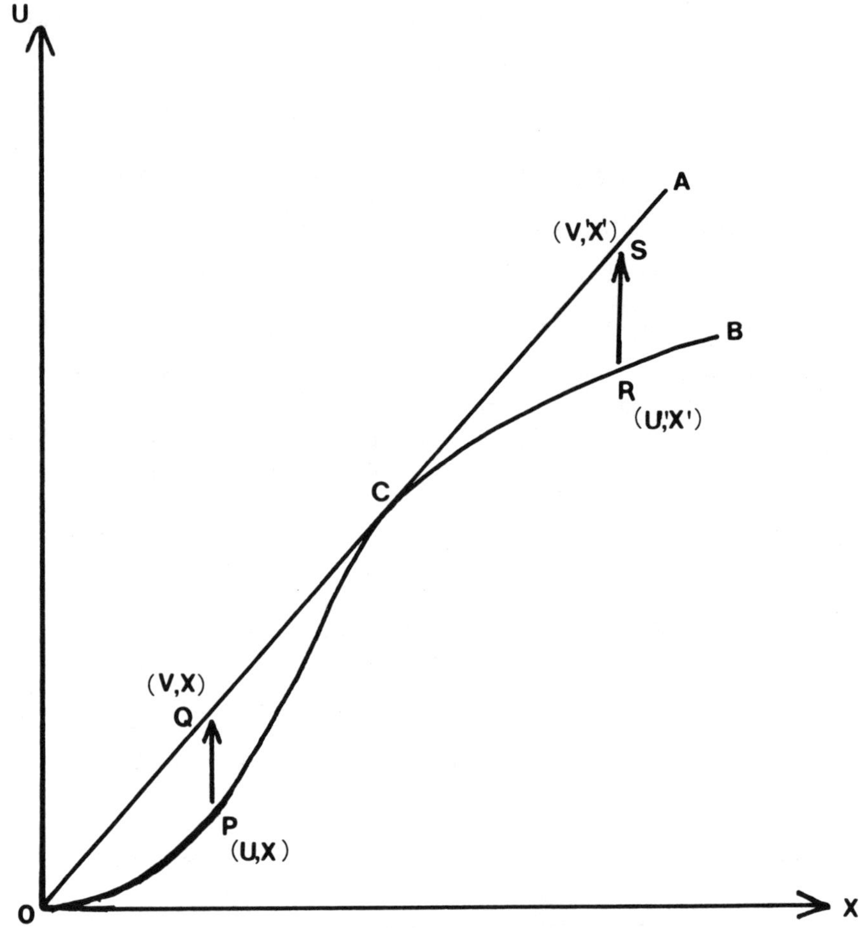

Figure 8-2. Graph of Technology of GR, and the Corresponding Cone Technology $\overline{K(GR)}$ and Star-closure $\overline{(GR)}^*$.

Definition (8–1):

The function F_0: $R_+ \times R_+^n \rightarrow R_+ \cup \{+\infty\}$ defined by

$$F_0(u,x) := \begin{cases} \min\{\theta : x \,\varepsilon\, L(u/\theta)\}, & (u,x) \,\varepsilon\, D(F_0), \\ +\infty, & (u,x) \,\varepsilon\, \text{Complement } D(F_0), \end{cases} \tag{8–9}$$

is called the Output-Based Farrell Measure of Technical Efficiency.

This measure gives the maximum amount by which output can be increased and still remain producible by the input vector x.[7] $F_0(u,x)$ satisfies the following properties:[8]

F_0.1 $0 < F_0(u,x) < +\infty$, $(u,x) \in D(F_0)$,

F_0.2 $F_0(\theta u,x) = \theta F_0(u,x)$, $\theta > 0$, $(u,x) \in D(F_0)$,

F_0.3 $L(u) = \{x: 0 < F_0(u,x) \leqq 1\}$, $u > 0$,

F_0.4 $Isoq\, L(u) = \{x: F_0(u,x) = 1\}$, $u > 0$.

Properties F_0.1 and F_0.2 are self-explanatory. F_0.3 states that F_0 provides a complete characterization of a technology satisfying $\{\phi.1 - \phi.3\}$, while F_0.4 states that $F_0(u,x) = 1$ if, and only if, $x \in IsoqL(u)$. Thus the output-based Farrell measure of technical efficiency uses the isoquant as its reference set for efficiency measurement.

The second measure of technical efficiency is defined on an effective domain

$$D(W_0) := \{(u,x): \exists\ \theta > 0 \text{ such that } (M(x) \cap L(u/\theta)) \neq \emptyset\}, \tag{8–10}$$

where $M(x) := \{y: 0 \leqq y \leqq x\}$. We can now define

Definition (8–2):

The function W_0: $R_+ X R^n_+ \to R_+ \cup \{+\infty\}$ defined by

$$W_0(u,x) := \begin{cases} \min \{\theta: (M(x) \cap L(u/\theta)) \infty \emptyset\}, (u,x) \in D(W_0), \\ +\infty, (u,x) \in \text{Complement } D(W_0), \end{cases} \tag{8–11}$$

is called the Output-Based Weak Measure of Technical Efficiency.

This measure gives the maximum amount by which output can be increased and still remain producible by an input vector no larger than x. $W_0(u,x)$ satisfies the following properties:[9]

W_0.1 $0 < W_0(u,x) < +\infty$, $u > 0$, $(u,x) \in D(W_0)$,

W_0.2 $W_0(\theta u,x) = \theta W_0(u,x)$, $\theta > 0$, $(u,x) \in D(W_0)$,

W_0.3 $L(u) \subseteq \{x: 0 < W_0(u,x) \leqq 1\}$ $u > 0$,

W_0.4 $WEffL(u) = \{x: x \in L(u), W_0(u,x) = 1\}$, $u > 0$.

Properties $W_0.1$ and $W_0.2$ are self-explanatory. Property $W_0.3$ states that the input set $L(u)$ is no larger than, and may be smaller than, the set of input vectors for which $0 < W_0(u,x) \leqq 1$.[10] Property $W_0.4$ states that if $x \in L(u)$ then $W_0(u,x) = 1$ if, and only if, $x \in WEffL(u)$. Thus the output-based weak measure of technical efficiency uses the weak efficient subset as its reference set for efficiency measurement.

Figure 8–3 illustrates $W_0(u,x)$ and its relationship to $F_0(u,x)$. The input vector $x \in L(u)$ located at point P belongs to *Isoq* $L(u)$. Hence no increase in output is possible without adjusting inputs. However if one allows for production using inputs not greater than x, i.e., $y \in M(x)$ where $M(x)$ is

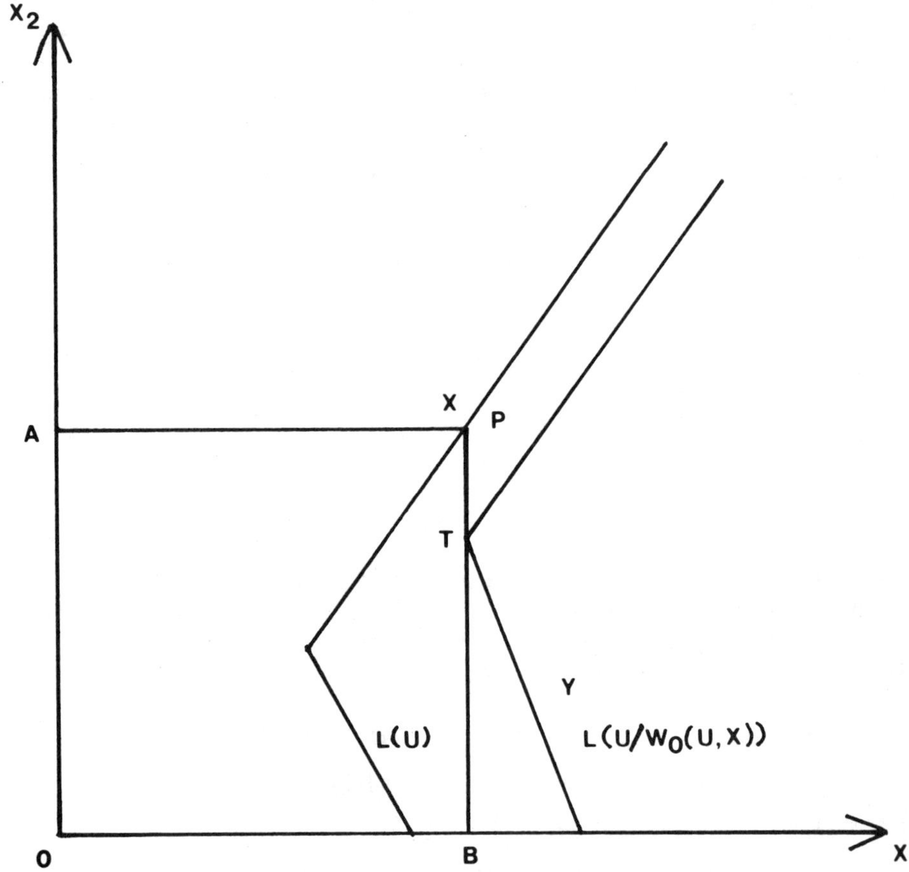

Figure 8-3. $W_0(u,x)$ and its Relation to $F_0(u,x)$

bounded by *PBOA*, then output can be increased to $(u/W_0(u,x))$, with production taking place at point *T*. Had the technology satisfied $\phi.2.S$ in addition to $\{\phi.1 - \phi.3\}$, then *Isoq* $L(u)$ would have been vertical from point *T*, including point *P*, and we would have had $W_0(u,x) = F_0(u,x)$. Conversely, the failure of $\phi.2.S$ implies that the *Isoq* $L(u)$ including point *P* excludes point *T*, giving $W_0(u,x) < F_0(u,x)$. This suggests[11]

Proposition (8-1):

Let ϕ satisfy $\{\phi.1 - \phi.3\}$. Then $W_0(u,x) \leqq F_0(u,x)$. Moreover, $W_0(u,x) = F_0(u,x)$ for all $(u,x) \in R_+ X R^n_+$ if, and only if, ϕ satisfies $\phi.2.S$ also.

Suppose next that ϕ satisfies $\{\phi.1 - \phi.3\}$ but not $\phi.2.S$, so that there exists (u,x) such that $W_0(u,x) < F_0(u,x)$. The difference between the two measures provides a measure of lost output due to a lack of strong disposability of inputs, commonly called input congestion.[12] We are thus led to the following definition of input congestion as a type of technical inefficiency:

Definition (8-3):

For $x \in L(u)$, $u > 0$, the Output-Based Congestion Measure is $C_0(u,x)$: $= W_0(u,x)/F_0(u,x)$.

The properties satisfied by $C_0(u,x)$ are derived from those of $W_0(u,x)$ and $F_0(u,x)$, and include

$C_0.1$ $\quad 0 < C_0(u,x) \leqq 1$,

$C_0.2$ $\quad C_0(u,x) = 1$ if, and only if, x does not congest u,

$C_0.3$ $\quad C_0(\theta u,x) = C_0(u,x), \theta > 0$.

Properties $C_0.1$ and $C_0.2$ are self-explanatory. The significance of property $C_0.3$ is that some input vectors may congest u while others may not. Thus in Figure 8–3 $C_0(u,x) < 1$ but $C_0(u,y) = 1$.

Returning to Figure 8–3, we know that there is input congestion at $x \in L(u)$ at point *P*. It is clear geometrically which of the two inputs is responsible. If x_1 is made disposable, so that in producing u all input combinations along *AP* could be used, output would not increase, and so x_1 is not congesting u. On the other hand, if x_2 is made disposable, so that in producing u all input combinations along *BP* could be used, output could be increased to $(u/W_0(u,x))$ by selecting the input vector located at point T along BP. Hence x_2 is the congesting input. What is needed is an analytical device for identifying the congesting input or inputs and measuring the resulting inefficiency associated with the congesting input or inputs. For this purpose we introduce the following single-input analogues to the output-based weak measure of technical efficiency.

Definition (8–4):

The functions W_0^i: $R_+ X R_+^n \rightarrow R_+ \cup \{+\infty\}$ defined by

$$W_0^i(u,x) := \begin{cases} \min\{\theta:(M(x\,|\,i) \cap L(u/\theta)) \neq \emptyset\}, & (u,x)\,\varepsilon\, D(W_0^i), \\ +\infty, & (u,x)\,\varepsilon\,\text{Complement}\, D(W_0^i), \end{cases} \tag{8–12}$$

$i = 1, \ldots, n$, are called the Output-Based Weak Measures of Technical Efficiency of Input i.

These measures are defined on effective domains

$$D(W_0^i) := \{(u,x): \cap\ \theta > 0 \text{ such that } (M(x\,|\,i) \cap L(u/\theta)) \neq \emptyset\}, \tag{8–13}$$

where $M(x\,|\,i) := \{y: 0 \leqq y_i \leqq x_i,\ y_j = x_j \text{ for } i, j = 1, \ldots, n\}$. The functions $W_0^i(u,x)$ satisfy properties similar to those of $W_0(u,x)$. In particular, if $W_0^i(u,x) = F_0(u,x)$ for all u,x), then the ith input is strongly disposable. This leads to

Definition (8–5)

for $x\,\varepsilon\, L(u)$, $u > 0$, the Output-Based ith Input Congestion Measure is $C_0^i(u,x) := W_0^i(u,x)/F_0(u,x)$.

If there is congestion at $x\,\varepsilon\, L(u)$, then $C_0^i(u,x)$ measures output loss caused by the ith input congesting technology. Clearly $C_0^i(u,x) = 1$ if, and only if, the ith input does not contribute to congestion.

We now turn to scale efficiency, or the extent to which the technology approaches operation at constant returns to scale. We begin by defining a weak efficiency measure, not on the original technology for which we already have $W_0(u,x)$, but on the CRS cone technology $\overline{K(GR)}$ generated by the original technology. The effective domain of this measure is

$$D(W_0^K) := \{(u,x): \exists\ \theta > 0 \text{ such that } (M(x) \cap L^K(u/\theta)) \neq \emptyset\}, \tag{8–14}$$

and we have

Definition (8–6):

The function $W_0^K\colon R_+ \, X \, R_+^n \to R_+ \cup \{+\infty\}$ defined by

$$W_0^K(u,x) := \begin{cases} \min\{\theta\colon (M(x) \cap L^K(u/\theta)) \neq \theta\}, (u,x) \,\varepsilon\, D(W_0^K), \\ +\infty, (u,x) \,\varepsilon\, \text{Complement } D(W_0^K), \end{cases} \qquad (8\text{–}15)$$

is called the Output-Based Weak Cone Measure of Technical Efficiency.

W_0^K satisfies properties similar to $\{W_0.1 - W_0.4\}$ and, by virtue of the *CRS* property of the cone technology, $W_0^K(u, \lambda x) = \lambda^{-1} W_0^K(u,x)$, $\lambda > 0$. $W_0^K(u,x)$ is illustrated in Figure 8–2. At point P, $(u,x) \,\varepsilon\, GR$ and so $x \,\varepsilon\, L(u)$. Had the technology exhibited *CRS* with point C remaining feasible, then input vector x could have produced larger output v so that $x \,\varepsilon\, L(v)$. This suggests that the distance QP measures output loss due to production that is not scale-efficient. This in turn suggests

Definition (8–7):

For $x \,\varepsilon\, L(u)$, $u > 0$, the Output-Based Scale Efficiency Measure is $S_0(u,x) := W_0^K(u,x)/W_0(u,x)$.

The properties satisfied by $S_0(u,x)$ are derived from those of $W_0^K(u,x)$ and $W_0(u,x)$ and from the fact that $W_0^K(u,x) = W_0(u,x)$ if, and only if, the technology exhibits *CRS*. These properties include

$S_0.1$ $\quad 0 < S_0(u,x) \leqq 1$,

$S_0.2$ $\quad S_0(u,x) = 1$ if, and only if, (u,x) is scale-efficient,

$S_0.3$ $\quad S_0(\theta u,x) = S_0(u,x)$, $\theta > 0$.

Suppose that $S_0(u,x) < 1$, so that (u,x) is scale-inefficient. We do not yet know whether scale inefficiency results from operation in a region of increasing returns to scale (as at point P in Figure 8–2) or from operation in a region of decreasing returns to scale (as at point R in Figure 8–2). What is required is an analytical device for attributing scale inefficiency to either increasing or decreasing returns to scale. Such an analytical device rests on the relationship of $\overline{(GR)^*}$ to $\overline{K(GR)}$. The first step is to introduce yet another weak measure of technical efficiency, this one on the nonincreasing returns to scale star technology $\overline{(GR)}^*$ generated by the original technology. The effective domain of this measure is

$$D(W_0^*) := \{(u,x) : \exists \; \theta > 0 \text{ such that } (M(x) \cap L^*(u/\theta)) \neq \emptyset\}. \tag{8-16}$$

Definition (8-8):

It follows that the function $W_0^*: R_+ X R_+^n \rightarrow R_+ \cup \{+\infty\}$ defined by

$$W_0^*(u,x) := \begin{cases} \min\{\theta : (M(x) \cap L^*(u/\theta)) \neq \emptyset\}, (u,x) \; \varepsilon \; D(W_0^*), \\ +\infty, (u,x) \; \varepsilon \text{ Complement } D(W_0^*), \end{cases}$$

is called the Output-Based Weak Star Measure of Technical Efficiency.

$W^*_0(u,x)$ satisfies properties similar to $\{W_0.1 - W_0.4\}$ of $W_0(u,x)$. More importantly, a comparison of $W_0^*(u,x)$ with $W_0^K(u,x)$ enables us to determine whether $S_0(u,x) < 1$ is due to increasing or decreasing returns to scale. Referring to Figure 8–2, for all points on OPC we have $W_0^K(u,x) = W^*_0(u,x) < 1$, while for all points on CRB we have $W_0^K(u,x) < W^*_0(u,x) = 1$. It follows that if $W_0(u,x) = W^*_0(u,x)$ as at point P, $S_0(u,x) < 1$ is due to increasing returns to scale while, if $W_0^K(u,x) < W^*_0(u,x)$ as at point R, $S_0(u,x) < 1$ is due to increasing returns to scale.

Collecting results from Definitions (8–1), (8–3), (8–6), and (8–7) we arrive at the following decomposition of the Output-Based Weak Cone Measure of Technical Efficiency:

$$W_0^K(u,x) = F_0(u,x) \cdot C_0(u,x) \cdot S_0(u,x). \tag{8-17}$$

Equation (8–17) describes the output-based decomposition of technical efficiency introduced by Farrell (1957), into (1) technical efficiency, (2) congestion and (3) scale efficiency, where (1) measures output loss arising from production in the interior of $L(u)$, (2) measures output loss due to congestion and (3) measures output loss due to deviations from CRS. We note that Farrell assumed that the technology satisfied $\phi.2.S$ and CRS. Therefore in his work, $C_0(u,x) = S_0(u,x) = 1$ for all (u,x), and so $W_0^k(u,x) = F_0(u,x)$.

In addition, if scale inefficiency exists we can compare $W_0^K(u,x)$ and $W^*_0(u,x)$ to determine whether $S_0(u,x) < 1$ is due to increasing or decreasing returns to scale. Finally, if input congestion exists we can use $C_0^i(u,x)$, $i = 1, \ldots, n$, to determine which inputs contribute, and to what degree, to $C_0(u,x) < 1$.

8.4. Calculating the Efficiency Measures

In this section we specify a series of linear programs that can be used to calculate each of the efficiency measures derived in section 8–3. We begin by specifying linear models of a technology satisfying $\{\phi.1 - \phi.3\}$, and with and without the additional restrictions of $\phi.2.S$, nonincreasing returns to scale, and *CRS*. We then formulate the linear programs based on these linear models of the technology to compute each of the efficiency measures. Included in this series of linear programs are those used to identify the input(*s*) creating congestion if it exists, and those used to determine whether increasing or decreasing returns to scale is the cause of scale inefficiency if it exists.

Following Shephard [1974], a linear technology satisfying $\{\phi.1 - \phi.3\}$ as well as $\phi.2.S$ and *CRS* is expressed as

$$L^S(u) = \{x: z \,\varepsilon\, R^k_t,\ zM \geqq u,\ zN \leqq x\}, \tag{8–18}$$

where z is a vector of intensity parameters and k is the number of observations. M and N represent output and input matrices, respectively. Since we restrict our attention to single-output technologies, M is a $k \times 1$ vector, with typical element m_i representing the observed output of the ith observation. N is a $k \times n$ matrix, n being the number of inputs, with typical element n_{ij} representing the observed usage of the jth input for the ith observation. Thus equation (8–18) constructs the input set $L^S(u)$ from the observed inputs and outputs. Since this input correspondence satisfies $\{\phi.1 - \phi.3\}$ as well as $\phi.2.S$ and *CRS*, it is the technology used to calculate $W_0^K(u,x)$.

In order to allow for congestion and scale inefficiency we need to modify the technology (8–18) so as to retain $\{\phi.1 - \phi.3\}$ without continuing to impose $\phi.2.S$ and *CRS*. The following technology achieves the desired modification.

$$L^W(u) = \{x: \sum_{i=1}^{k} z_i = 1,\ z \,\varepsilon\, R^k_+,\ zM \geqq u,\ zN - \delta x,\ \delta \,\varepsilon\, (0,1]\}, \tag{8–19}$$

where z,M,N,k,u, and x are defined as above. The scalar δ is included to allow for weak rather than strong disposability of inputs. Nonconstant returns to scale is allowed by adding the restriction $\Sigma z_i = 1$, without which the technology is a cone satisfying *CRS*. Since this input correspondence satisfies $\{\phi.1 - \phi.3\}$ but imposes neither $\phi.2.S$ nor *CRS*, it is the technology used to calculate $F_0(u,x)$, $W_0(u,x)$, $C_0(u,x)$, and in slightly modified form, the $W_0^i(u,x)$ and the $C_0^i(u,x)$. The technologies (8–18) and (8–19) are used jointly to calculate $S_0(u,x)$.

Finally, the technology $L^W(u)$ must be further modified in order to identify the source of scale inefficiency. A technology satisfying $\{\phi.1 - \phi.3\}$, $\phi.2.S$, and nonincreasing returns to scale rather than CRS, can be obtained from $L^W(u)$ as follows:

$$L^*(u) = \{x: \sum_{i=1}^{k} z_i \leqq 1,\ z \in R_+^k,\ zM \geqq u,\ zN = \delta x,\ \delta \in (0,1]\}. \tag{8-20}$$

This star technology satisfies nonincreasing returns to scale by virtue of the form of the constraint $\Sigma z_i \leqq 1$. It is used to calculate $W^*(u,x)$, which can be compared with $W_0^K(u,x)$ in order to identify the source of scale inefficiency as either increasing or decreasing returns to scale.

We now use these linear technologies as constraints in linear programs that are used to calculate the various efficiency measures. First, the overall efficiency measure $W_0^K(u,x)$ is calculated using the $L^S(u)$ technology and is the solution to the programming problem

$$\begin{aligned} &\text{minimize } \theta \\ &\text{subject to } zM \geqq u^0/\theta \\ &zN \leqq x^0 \\ &z \in R_+^k \end{aligned} \tag{8-21}$$

which can be transformed into the simpler linear program

$$\begin{aligned} &\text{maximize } \theta' \\ &\text{subject to } zM \geqq \theta' u^0 \\ &zN \leqq x^0 \\ &z \in R_+^k \end{aligned} \tag{8-22}$$

where $\theta' = 1/\theta$.

Next, the Farrell efficiency measure $F_0(u,x)$ is calculated using the $L^W(u)$ technology, and is the solution to the programming problem

$$\begin{aligned} &\text{minimize } \theta \\ &\text{subject to } zM \geqq u^0/\theta \\ &zN = \delta x^0 \\ &0 < \delta \leqq 1 \\ &\sum_{i=1}^{k} z_i = 1 \end{aligned} \tag{8-23}$$

$$z \, \varepsilon \, R^k_+$$

which can also be transformed into a simpler linear program by maximizing $\theta' = 1/\theta$ as above.

Next, the weak efficiency measure $W_0(u,x)$ is calculated using the $L^W(u)$ technology, and is the solution to the programming problem.

$$\begin{aligned} &\text{minimize } \theta \\ &\text{subject to } zM \geqq u^0/\theta \\ &zN \leqq x^0 \\ &\sum_{i=1}^{k} z_i = 1 \\ &z \, \varepsilon \, R^k_+ \end{aligned} \tag{8–24}$$

which can be converted into a simpler linear program by maximizing $\theta' = 1/\theta$ as above.

From (8–22) to (8–24) we obtain calculated values of $W^K_0(u,x)$, $F_0(u,x)$, and $W_0(u,x)$. From these we can derive calculated values of $C_0(u,x)$ and $S_0(u,x)$. The calculation of $W^*{}_0(u,x)$ is accomplished by modifying the linear program (8–24) by replacing the constraint $\Sigma z_i = 1$ with the constraint $\Sigma z_i \leqq 1$. The solution to this modified program is $W^*_0(u,x)$, which when compared with $W^K_0(u,x)$ identifies the source of scale inefficiency.

Identifying which inputs contribute to congestion requires a different modification of the linear program (8–25). We need to determine if inputs are strongly rather than weakly disposable, input by input, in order to calculate $W^i_0(u,x)$. To do so we reformulate (8–25) as

$$\begin{aligned} &\text{minimize } \theta \\ &\text{subject to } zM \geqq u^0/\theta \\ &zN_i \leqq x^0_i \\ &zN_j = \delta x^0_j \quad j \neq i \\ &0 < \delta \leqq 1 \\ &\sum_{i=1}^{k} z_i = 1 \\ &z \, \varepsilon \, R^k_+ \end{aligned} \tag{8–25}$$

the solution to which is $W^i_0(u,x)$. This program, which must be solved separately for each of n inputs, can be simplified by maximizing $\theta' = 1/\theta$ as above. From the $W_0^i(u,x)$ obtained as solutions to the linear programs (8–25) input-specific congestion measures $C_0^i(u,x)$ can be obtained.

8.5. An Application to Electric Utilities

In this section we illustrate the linear programming models developed in the previous Section using a sample of electric utilities. The sample consists of 32 coal-fired steam electric generating plants built between 1963 and 1973 and observed in their first full year of commercial operation. For each plant we specify one output (kilowatt hours of electricity generated) and three inputs (capital in megawatt capacity, fuel in btu's and labor in average annual employees). In addition, for each plant we have data on the number of boiler turbine generator units, the first full year of commercial operation, the FPC region, the output price and the earned rate of return. The plant data are reported in Table 8–1. These additional data prove useful in explaining the pattern of calculated efficiencies.

Plant technology is represented by the linear models given in (8–18) to (8–20) of the previous section, in which the M matrix is a 32×1 column vector of observed outputs and the N matrix is a 32×3 matrix of observed usage of capital, fuel, and labor. The linear programs (8–21) to (8–25) do not explicitly incorporate in their contraints either rate-of-return regulation or automatic fuel adjustment clauses. This omission should not adversely affect our results, however, since both of these regulatory constraints are widely believed to induce allocative inefficiency rather than technical inefficiency (see, for example, Atkinson and Halvorsen (1980)).

The outcomes of our linear programming experiments are summarized in Table 8–2. For each plant, this table reports calculated values of purely technical efficiency (F_0), congestion (C_0), scale efficiency (S_0), and overall efficiency (W_0^K). Also reported are input-specific sources of existing congestion (C_0^i, where i = capital, fuel, and labor), as well as the source of existing scale inefficiency (RTS). Eighteen of 32 plants are purely technically efficient ($F_0(u,x) = 1$), and the sample mean of the purely technical efficiency measure is 97.7 percent. Somewhat surprisingly, the 6 largest plants and 10 of the 11 largest plants (#1-#6, #8-#11) are purely technically efficient. However, due to congestion and scale inefficiency only 2 of 32 plants are overall technically efficient ($W_0^K(u,x) = 1$), and the sample mean of the overall technical efficiency measure declines to 90.2 percent. Congestion is not severe, with 18 of 32 plants showing only modest degrees of congestion. All three inputs cause congestion, although capital and fuel congestion are somewhat more pervasive, and somewhat more severe, than

Table 8-1. Data

Plant Number	Output in 10^6 Kilowatt Hours	Capital in Megawatt Capacity	Fuel in 10^{10} BTU's	Labor: Average Annual Employees	First Full Year of Commercial Operations	Federal Power Commission Region	Number of Boiler-Turbine Generator Units	Output Price: $\$/10^6$ Kilowatt Hours	Excess Earned Rate of Return
1	10561.1	2482.0	10270.2	316.0	1974	4	4	9130.0	−.01166
2	8170.2	1641.7	7922.2	182.0	1974	1	3	12979.9	.12081
3	6892.3	1632.6	6520.6	155.0	1972	2	2	7939.9	.15491
4	6849.6	1594.6	6445.7	207.0	1973	3	2	7360.3	.05530
5	6019.2	700.0	5226.1	100.0	1967	3	2	3752.5	.32923
6	5356.5	1140.5	5037.9	102.0	1967	3	2	4654.9	.27880
7	4919.3	1099.6	4670.3	162.0	1969	4	2	5690.2	.13058
8	4767.3	1319.4	4833.4	168.0	1969	4	2	6340.6	.26267
9	4226.0	633.6	4338.6	78.0	1965	8	3	3468.1	.17945
10	3905.1	727.6	3421.9	67.0	1966	1	2	5359.7	.30120
11	3822.1	482.0	3365.0	61.0	1965	1	2	5104.1	.33688
12	3789.1	771.8	3439.7	70.0	1972	3	2	7907.0	.04077
13	3521.8	817.2	3375.2	148.0	1972	2	1	11868.5	.01650
14	3512.7	598.4	3361.3	106.0	1965	3	2	4564.2	.41745
15	3394.1	623.1	3310.2	99.0	1971	4	1	6337.2	−.02452
16	2941.4	565.3	2768.7	82.0	1971	2	1	8600.4	−.03607
17	2739.8	410.9	2537.3	57.0	1967	3	1	4320.1	.28014
18	2292.6	382.5	2358.7	71.0	1974	6	1	9459.6	.02991
19	2258.2	330.0	2240.8	56.0	1966	4	1	4389.7	.53798
20	2174.4	531.1	2102.1	79.0	1971	2	1	7239.7	−.06240
21	2088.5	440.5	2035.3	68.0	1967	3	1	5770.8	.38379
22	2005.9	454.8	1815.3	120.0	1965	1	1	7545.7	.40942

(continued)

Table 8-1 *(continued)*

Plant Number	*Output in 10^6 Kilowatt Hours*	*Capital in Megawatt Capacity*	*Fuel in 10^{10} BTU's*	*Labor: Average Annual Employees*	*First Full Year of Commercial Operations*	*Federal Power Commission Region*	*Number of Boiler-Turbine Generator Units*	*Output Price: $\$/10^6$ Kilowatt Hours*	*Excess Earned Rate of Return*
23	1685.6	261.7	1578.9	55.0	1968	2	1	4907.7	.55166
24	1557.8	299.2	1507.7	81.0	1966	3	1	5867.7	.42653
25	1458.8	445.5	1533.3	75.0	1971	3	1	8913.5	−.15607
26	1365.6	355.5	1307.9	83.0	1973	2	1	10677.4	.24061
27	1316.3	217.6	1339.7	27.0	1969	7	1	4341.1	.06664
28	1172.7	206.6	1103.3	50.0	1965	3	1	5023.7	.46498
29	1168.8	212.8	1210.4	32.0	1971	5	1	5323.4	−.05311
30	1006.8	149.6	980.4	44.0	1966	3	1	5273.9	.53478
31	828.8	326.4	854.9	23.0	1972	7	1	9797.8	.00915
32	778.5	113.6	772.7	32.0	1966	8	1	6042.4	.40453

Source: U.S. Federal Power Commission, *Steam-Electric Plant Construction Cost and Annual Production Expenses*, Annual Supplements, 1965–1974, U.S. Government Printing Office, Washington, D.C.

Table 8-2. Calculated Efficiency Indexes By Plant

Plant #	F_0	C_0	S_0	W_0^K	$C_0^{Capital}$	C_0^{Fuel}	C_0^{Labor}	*RTS*
1	1.000	1.000	.893	.893	—	—	—	DRS
2	1.000	1.000	.895	.895	—	—	—	DRS
3	1.000	.960	.956	.917	.960	1.000	1.000	DRS
4	1.000	.962	.958	.923	1.000	.966	1.000	DRS
5	1.000	1.000	1.000	1.000	—	—	—	CRS
6	1.000	.923	1.000	.923	.925	1.000	1.000	CRS
7	.976	.940	.998	.915	.998	.940	.989	IRS
8	1.000	.858	.998	.856	.915	.861	1.000	IRS
9	1.000	.881	.978	.865	1.000	.897	.890	DRS
10	1.000	1.000	.991	.991	—	—	—	IRS
11	1.000	1.000	1.000	1.000	—	—	—	CRS
12	.989	.976	.990	.956	.976	.994	1.000	IRS
13	.967	.946	.990	.906	1.000	.948	.989	IRS
14	.920	.997	.989	.907	.998	.998	.997	IRS
15	.903	.997	.989	.890	.998	.998	.997	IRS
16	.939	.999	.983	.923	1.000	1.000	.999	IRS
17	.959	1.000	.972	.937	—	—	—	IRS
18	.866	.999	.976	.844	1.000	1.000	.999	IRS
19	.901	1.000	.976	.875	—	—	—	IRS
20	.944	.980	.971	.898	.981	.981	.998	IRS
21	.921	.999	.969	.891	.999	.999	1.000	IRS
22	1.000	1.000	.960	.960	—	—	—	IRS
23	.974	1.000	.952	.927	—	—	—	IRS
24	1.000	.944	.950	.897	.980	1.000	.944	IRS
25	.909	.956	.950	.826	.957	.956	.991	IRS
26	1.000	.966	.938	.907	1.000	.966	.981	IRS
27	1.000	1.000	.853	.853	—	—	—	IRS
28	1.000	1.000	.923	.923	—	—	—	IRS
29	.937	1.000	.894	.838	—	—	—	IRS
30	1.000	.983	.906	.891	1.000	1.000	.983	IRS
31	1.000	1.000	.842	.842	—	—	—	IRS
32	1.000	1.000	.875	.875	—	—	—	IRS
Sample Means	.977	.970	.956	.902	.987	.979	.993	—

Note: Not reported are calculated values of W_0 (used to compute C_0 and S_0), W_0^i (used to compute C_0^i), and W_0^* (used to infer *RTS*).

is labor congestion. If rate-of-return regulation and fuel adjustment clauses have any impact on our results, they probably show up in the form of capital and fuel congestion. Finally, scale inefficiency is both more widespread and more severe than is congestion and is the main contributor to the difference between overall efficiency W_0^K and its purely technical component F_0. As the last column of Table 8–2 indicates, the 4 largest plants are operating in a region of decreasing returns to scale, while the 21 smallest firms are operating in a region of increasing returns to scale. Only 3 plants operate at optimal scale ($S_0(u,x) = 1$).

In order to provide an overview of our results, Tables 8–3 to 8–9 report foregone output (expressed as a per cent of observed output) due to each of the inefficiencies, tabulated for various groupings of the plants in the sample. These tables are largely self-explanatory, and we offer only brief comments on them.[13] Table 8–3 shows that plants producing relatively large output lose a small percentage of output to purely technical inefficiency but lose a large percentage of output to congestion and scale inefficiency. Primarily because of scale inefficiency, the smallest and the largest plants have the lowest overall efficiency ratings. Table 8–4 tells largely the same story when plant size is measured by megawatt capacity. Table 8–5 shows that the number of boiler-turbine generator units in a plant is an important determinant of the purely technical component of efficiency, although the losses due to scale inefficiency largely offset the superior technical efficiency of the multi-unit plants. Table 8–6 shows that the oldest plants in the sample, those brought on line during 1965–1968, are substantially more efficient than are the more recently constructed plants. This merely reflects the well-known fact that it takes time to find and address inefficiencies, particularly those associated with deviations from optimal scale. Table 8–7 shows a wide variation in overall technical efficiency across FPC regions. This may be a reflection of regional variation in input prices, or it may be attributable to the highly skewed regional plant distribution in the sample. Finally, Tables 8–8 and 8–9 show no clear pattern of output loss due to inefficiency when plants are grouped by output price or earned rate of return.

8.6. Summary and Conclusions

In this paper we have accomplished three tasks. In section 8.3 we derived measures of overall technical efficiency and of its three components, purely technical efficiency, congestion, and scale efficiency. We also derived measures of input-specific congestion, and developed a measure to

Table 8-3. Output Loss In Output Size Groups

Output range (10^6 *kwh)*	*k*	*Average output in the group*	$\tilde{F}_0$	$\tilde{C}_0$	$\tilde{S}_0$	$\tilde{W}_0^K$	$\tilde{C}_0^{Capital}$	$\tilde{C}_0^{Fuel}$	$\tilde{C}_0^{Labor}$	*Plant #*
4,500–11,000	8	6,691.94	.226	3.937	5.344	9.573	2.192	2.474	.102	1-8
2,800–4,500	8	3,638.98	3.516	2.997	1.141	7.762	.368	2.456	.636	9-16
1,500–2,800	8	2,100.35	6.387	.840	3.379	10.881	.452	.263	.590	17-24
under 1,500	8	1,137.04	2.469	1.458	11.010	15.257	.721	1.267	.628	25-32
Total sample	32	3,392.08	2.250	2.998	4.387	9.766	1.311	2.026	.733	
Extremes (Plant #)			15.473 (18)	16.550 (8)	18.765 (31)	21.065 (25)	9.290 (8)	16.144 (8)	12.360 (9)	

Table 8-4. Output Loss In Capital Size Groups

Megawatt range	*k*	*Average megawatt in the group*	$\tilde{F}_0$	$\tilde{C}_0$	$\tilde{S}_0$	$\tilde{W}_0^K$	$\tilde{C}_0^{Capital}$	$\tilde{C}_0^{Fuel}$	$\tilde{C}_0^{Labor}$	*Plant #*
over 800	8	1465.95	.472	4.523	5.675	10.758	2.301	2.974	.184	1,2,3,4, 6,7,8,13
500-800	8	643.85	3.445	2.389	1.206	7.147	.498	1.883	1.837	5,9,10,12, 14,15,16, 20
329–500	8	412.71	5.796	.663	2.789	9.522	.375	.850	.233	11,17,18, 19,21,22, 25,26
Under 329	8	223.44	1.299	1.154	10.524	13.159	.334	.0	1.154	23,24,27, 28,29,30, 31,32
Total sample	32	686.49	2.250	2.998	4.387	9.766	1.311	2.026	.733	

Table 8-5. Output Loss In Boiler-Turbine-Generator-Units Groups

Boiler-turbine-generator units	k	Average output in the group	$\tilde{F}_0$	$\tilde{C}_0$	$\tilde{S}_0$	$\tilde{W}_0^K$	$\tilde{C}_0^{Capital}$	$\tilde{C}_0^{Fuel}$	$\tilde{C}_0^{Labor}$	Plant #
4	1	10,561.1	.0	.0	11.982	11.982	.0	.0	.0	1
3	2	6,198.1	.0	4.473	8.499	13.055	.0	3.915	4.213	2,9
2	10	4,983.32	.940	4.437	1.504	6.965	2.557	2.718	.131	3,4,5,6,7, 8,10,11, 12,14
1	19	1,881.89	5.520	1.365	4.736	11.876	.415	1.005	.583	13,15,16, 17,18,19, 20,21,22, 23,24,25, 26,27,28, 29,30,31, 32
Total sample	32	3,392.08	2.250	2.998	4.387	9.766	1.311	2.026	.733	

Table 8-6. Output Loss in First Year of Commercial Operation Groups

First year of full commercial operation	*k*	*Average output in the group*	$\tilde{F}_0$	$\tilde{C}_0$	$\tilde{S}_0$	$\tilde{W}_0^K$	$\tilde{C}_0^{Capital}$	$\tilde{C}_0^{Fuel}$	$\tilde{C}_0^{Labor}$	*Plant #*
1973–1974	5	5,847.82	1.213	1.098	9.135	11.489	.0	.989	.098	1,2,4, 18,26
1971–1972	9	2,907.67	4.095	2.698	3.498	10.563	1.891	1.269	.267	3,12,13, 15,16,20, 25,29,31
1969–1970	3	3,667.63	1.099	10.025	2.238	13.504	4.115	9.849	.497	7,8,27
1967–1968	5	3,577.92	1.908	2.510	1.193	5.698	2.439	.012	.0	5,6,17, 21,23
1965–1966	10	2,424.58	2.283	2.784	2.954	8.135	.160	2.030	2.651	9,10,11, 14,19,22, 24,28,30, 32
Total sample	32	3,392.08	2.250	2.998	4.387	9.766	1.311	2.026	.733	

Table 8-7. Output Loss in FPC Regions Groups

FPC Regions	k	Average output in the group	$\tilde{F}_0$	$\tilde{C}_0$	$\tilde{S}_0$	$\tilde{W}_0^K$	$\tilde{C}_0^{Capital}$	$\tilde{C}_0^{Fuel}$	$\tilde{C}_0^{Labor}$	Plant #
1	4	4,475.83	.0	.0	6.019	6.019	.0	.0	.0	2,10,11,22
2	6	3,096.77	2.612	3.141	3.465	9.442	1.772	1.525	.392	3,13,16, 20,23,26
3	11	3,231.95	2.222	2.813	2.439	7.594	1.783	.957	.376	4,5,6,12, 14,17,21, 24,25,28, 30
4	5	5,180	2.833	4.298	5.367	12.612	1.774	4.210	.251	1,7,8, 15,19
5	1	1,168.8	6.724	.0	11.857	19.332	.0	.0	.0	29
6	1	2.292.6	15.473	.100	2.459	18.483	.0	.0	.100	18
7	2	1,072.55	.0	.0	17.825	17.825	.0	.0	.0	27,31
8	2	2,502.25	.0	11.081	4.122	15.401	.0	9.696	10.437	9,32
Total sample	32	3,392.08	2.250	2.998	4.387	9.766	1.311	2.026	.733	

Table 8-8. Output Loss In Output Price Groups

$/10^6 kwh	*k*	*Average output in the group*	$\tilde{F}_0$	$\tilde{C}_0$	$\tilde{S}_0$	$\tilde{W}_0^K$	$\tilde{C}_0^{Capital}$	$\tilde{C}_0^{Fuel}$	$\tilde{C}_0^{Labor}$	*Plant #*
over 8,000	8	10,178.38	2.608	1.032	8.636	12.400	.211	.990	.270	1,2,13,16, 18,25,26, 31
6,000–8,000	8	7,089.11	1.748	4.876	3.141	9.895	2.845	3.532	.048	3,4,8,12, 15,20,22, 32
5,000–6,000	8	5,426.67	1.928	2.168	2.724	6.994	.223	1.609	.838	7,10,11, 21,24,28, 29,30
under 5,000	8	4,299.78	2,640	3,732	2.121	8.604	1.628	1.816	1.965	5,6,9, 14,17,19, 23,27
Total sample	32	6,748.49	2.250	2.998	4.387	9.766	1.311	2.026	.733	

Table 8-9. Output Loss In Earned Rate of Return Groups

Rate of return range	*k*	*Average earned rate of return*	$\tilde{F}_0$	$\tilde{C}_0$	$\tilde{S}_0$	$\tilde{W}_0^K$	$\tilde{C}_0^{Capital}$	$\tilde{C}_0^{Fuel}$	$\tilde{C}_0^{Labor}$	*Plant #*
over .4	8	.4729	4.282	.861	4.797	10.088	.278	.050	.861	14,19,22, 23,24,28 30,32
.2–.4	8	.3017	.985	4.278	.877	6.200	2.925	2.727	.088	5,6,8, 10,11,17, 21,26
.02–.2	9	.0973	1.347	3.957	5.207	10.649	1.015	2.765	1.506	2,3,4,7, 9,12,18,27
under .02	8	−.0398	3.952	1.250	7.008	12.405	.439	1.187	.268	1,13,15, 16,20,25, 29,31
Total sample	32	.2080	2.250	2.998	4.387	9.766	1.311	2.026	.733	

determine whether scale inefficiency is attributable to increasing or decreasing returns to scale. In section 8.4 we proposed a series of linear models of technology, and set up a series of linear programs whose solutions are the various efficiency measures developed in section 8.3. In section 8.5 we applied these models to a sample of electricity generating plants.

There are a number of ways in which this research might be extended. The first is to augment our list of measures of technical efficiency with a measure of allocative efficiency and a measure of overall economic efficiency. This would provide for an extension of the decomposition achieved in equation (8–17), and hence an extension of the original decomposition of Farrell (1957). Of course, the added allocative efficiency and economic efficiency measures would be price-dependent, with the set of relevant prices being determined by the objectives attributed to the plant's managers. One advantage of such an extension would be provided by the ability to test, albeit indirectly, for any distortionary effects of regulatory activities such as rate-of-return regulation and fuel adjustment clauses.

A second interesting extension is data-dependent. The availability of panel data would enable us to conduct these experiments over a period of years. This, in turn, would enable us to construct time series of each of the calculated efficiency measures. And this would enable us to extend traditional productivity growth models. Typically, these models measure the rate of growth of total factor productivity as a "residual," as the rate of growth of output minus the sum of the share-weighted rates of growth of inputs. These models assume, however implicitly, efficient production, and thus neglect the contribution of efficiency growth (or retardation) to output growth. The proposed extension involves modelling technology in such a way that efficiency growth is permitted to contribute to output growth. This might help reduce the importance of Solow's "measure of our ignorance" concerning the determinants of output growth. A promising step in this direction has recently been taken by Nishimizu and Page (1982).

Notes

1. $y \overset{*}{<} x$ means $y \leqq x$ and either $y_i < x_i$ or $y_i = x_i$ for $i = 1, \ldots, n$. In words, $y \overset{*}{<} x$ means $y_i < x_i$ in its positive components.

2. $y \leq x$ means $y \leqq x$ but $y \neq x$.

3. For proofs see Färe, Grosskopf, and Lovell (1985, Chapter 8).

4. The implications for efficiency measurement of the scale-related distinctions among GR, $\overline{(GR)}^*$ and $\overline{K(GR)}$ for a technology satisfying $\phi.1$, $\phi.2.S$, $\phi.3$ were noted by Afriat [1972].

5. It is possible that neither $\overline{K(GR)}$ nor $\overline{(GR)^*}$ is the graph of a technology, in which case neither $L^k(u)$, $\phi^K(x)$ nor $L^*(u)$, $\phi^*(x)$ can be defined. For example, if $\phi(x) = x^2$ then $\overline{K(GR)} = \overline{(GR)^*} = R^2_+$, from which input correspondences and production functions cannot be defined. The possibility of this phenomenon of forever-increasing returns to scale is remote, and we ignore it.

6. For a discussion of the distinction between input-based and output-based efficiency measures see Färe and Lovell (1978).

7. If $P(x)$: = $\{u: \phi(x) \geqq u\} = \{u: x \,\varepsilon\, L(u)\}$, then since ϕ is upper semi-continuous $P(x)$ is a compact set. Therefore since $x \,\varepsilon\, L(u) <=> u \,\varepsilon\, P(x)$, it follows that min $\{\theta: x \,\varepsilon\, L(u/\theta)\}$ = min $\{\theta: u/\theta \,\varepsilon\, P(x)\} = \max\{\lambda: \lambda u \,\varepsilon\, P(x)\}$ exists.

8. Proofs, which rest heavily on the second half of $\phi.2$ as explained in Al-Ayat and Färe (1979), can be found in Färe, Grosskopf, and Lovell (1985).

9. For proofs see Färe, Grosskopf, and Lovell (1985).

10. $W_0.3$ is an equality, making $W_0(u,x)$ a complete characterization of technology, if, and only if, $\phi.2.S$ holds, in which case *Isoq* $L(u)$ = *WEffL*(u) and $F_0(u,x) = W_0(u,x)$.

11. For proof see Färe, Grosskopf, and Lovell (1985).

12. See, for example, Färe and Svensson (1980).

13. In Tables 8–2 to 8–8 we use the notation

$$\tilde{F}_0: = \frac{\sum_{i=1}^{k} (u_i(F_0))_i - \sum_{i=1}^{k} u_i}{\sum_{i=1}^{k} u_i} \cdot 100,$$

and similarly for $\tilde{C}_0$, $\tilde{S}_0$, $\tilde{W}_0^K$, $\tilde{C}_0^i$ (i = capital, fuel, labor).

References

1. Afriat, S. [1972], "Efficiency Estimation of Production Functions," *International Economic Review*, 13:3 (October), 568–598.
2. Al-Ayat, R. and Färe, R. [1979], "On the Existence of Joint Production Functions," *Naval Research Logistics Quarterly*, 26:4 (December), 627–630.
3. Atkinson, S. and Halvorsen, R. [1980], "A Test of Relative and Absolute Price Efficiency in Regulated Utilities," *Review of Economics and Statistics*, 62:1 (February), 81–88.
4. Färe, R., Grosskopf, S., and Lovell, C. A. K. [1982], *The Measurement of Efficiency of Production.* Boston: Kluwer-Nijhoff Publishing.
5. Färe, R. and Lovell, C. A. K. [1978], "Measuring the Technical Efficiency of Production," *Journal of Economic Theory*, 19:1 (October), 150–62.
6. Färe, R. and Svensson, L. [1980], "Congestion of Production Factors," *Econometrica*, 48:7 (November), 1745–1753.
7. Farrell, M. J. [1957], "The Measurement of Productive Efficiency," *Journal of the Royal Statistical Society*, Series A, General, 120, Part 3, 253–281.
8. Nishimizu, M. and Page, J. M., Jr. [1982], "Total Factor Productivity Growth, Technological Progress, and Technical Efficiency Change: Dimensions of

Productivity Change in Yugoslavia, 1965–1978," *The Economic Journal*, 92: 368 (December), 920–936.

9. Shephard, R. W. [1974], *Indirect Production Functions*. Mathematical Systems in Economics, No. 10, Meisenheim Am Glad: Verlag Anton Hain.

9 ALTERNATIVES FOR PRODUCTIVITY-BASED PRICING IN PUBLIC UTILITY REGULATION—THE CASE OF TELECOMMUNICATIONS

M. Ali Chaudry and Ephraim F. Sudit

9.1. Introduction

Kendrick (1975) and Sudit (1979) proposed alternative models of indexed pricing of services, incorporating total factor productivity, and cost-saving incentives in the framework of rate of return regulation. Sinden (1980) discusses various models that might be used to determine how the productivity gains might be shared by the firm and the consumer once a rate adjustment formula based on productivity has been agreed upon. The purpose of this paper is to broaden these models by: (1) building efficiency and profit incentives directly into the allowed rate of return formulae to strengthen performance incentives; (2) advocating complete freedom for the regulated firm in pricing individual services, subject to an overall constraint in weighted average rate changes, to improve efficiency in pricing; (3) recommending the use of capital measures unadjusted for rates of utilization in computing total factor productivity to minimize allocative inefficiencies. Within this extended frame of reference, new total factor productivity data are presented to illustrate use of the proposed interim

The authors would like to thank Messrs. M. Burnside, L. F. Newens, P. B. Linhart, and H. K. Face for reading earlier drafts of this paper and providing valuable comments.

productivity-based rate adjustment clause. While the discussion in this paper is generally applicable to most regulated industries, the emphasis in our empirical analysis is on recent experience in the telecommunications industry with which the authors are directly familiar. It should be noted in this context that a large part of the telecommunications industry consisting of the local operating companies and interexchange network services of AT&T remains regulated after the recent reorganization of the industry. Consequently, our discussion below applies to the pricing of regulated telecommunications services in the post divestiture environment, as well as to the pricing of all other regulated public utility services.

Indexed pricing schemes and automatic rate adjustment clauses are not new. Lindsay (1977) and Schmidt (1980) provide good discussions of their history. Scott (1980) presents a comprehensive analysis of the effects of fuel cost adjustments for electric utilities. Productivity-based rate adjustment clauses have been proposed and/or implemented mostly, if not exclusively, in telecommunications. The New Jersey and Michigan Bell experiences under these clauses, as well as the Illinois Bell proposal are discussed in detail by Latimer (1974), Kendrick (1975), Sudit (1979), and Schmidt (1980).

Of course, the wider problems associated with a variety of inefficiencies inherent in rate of return regulation as it is practiced have been a subject of numerous studies. Among recent interesting contributions to analysis and discussion, to mention only a few, are Baron (1980*a*; 1980*b*) Sherman (1977, 1980), Vogelsang and Finsinger (1980), and Arzac and Edwards (1979). The relatively unique features of our recommendations to reduce inefficiencies in the existing system are that (1) they allow for nonoptimal strategic and asymmetric behavior on the part of all participants; (2) they take into account a dynamic, unstable, and inflationary environment; and (3) they consider transaction costs and alternative uses of regulatory resources.

In section 9.2 a simple behavioral model of rate of return regulation is proposed. The basic relationships between levels and changes in unit costs, rates and total factor productivity are presented in section 9.3. A broadened version of the "Comprehensive Interim Productivity-Based Rate Adjustment Clause" (CIPRAC) incorporating profit incentives is outlined in section 9.4. The built-in productivity incentives and the effects of alternative capital stock measurements on allocative efficiencies are discussed in detail in section 9.5. Section 9.6 deals with setting standards for unit costs and the underlying cost efficiency incentives. The likely effects of the rate of return incentives on the behavior of the regulated firm are assessed in section 9.7. Potential effects of the proposed adjustment clause on efficient pricing of individual services are discussed in section 9.8. Section 9.9 reviews the potential opportunities to improve the quality and effectiveness of regulation and management planning provided by the uncertainty-reducing features of CIPRAC. Key issues in determining productivity and cost standards are discussed in section 9.10. Section 9.11 provides a description of various automatic clauses for telephone companies, with special emphasis on the Michigan Bell CPI rate adjustment formula. In section 9.12, we present an empirical illustration (using industry average data) of how our proposed formula might be implemented. Some concluding remarks are presented in section 9.13.

9.2. Rate of Return Regulation: A Behavioral Model

In this section we propose a simple behavioral model which, in our view, describes reasonably well the essentials of rate of return regulation as it is currently practiced in the United States. We do not assume that regulatory agencies attempt to maximize social welfare functions, either global or partial. Nor do we hypothesize that regulators set well-defined multi-criteria objective functions with prespecified trade-offs. Likewise, regulated firms are not assumed necessarily to maximize profits, minimize costs, or even operate on technically efficient frontiers. Finally, we allow for the possibilities of imperfect information, asymmetry of information and strategic behavior on the part of regulators and firms alike.

Consider a regulatory commission which sets the rates $\mathbf{P} = (P_1, P_2, \ldots P_j \ldots P_m)$ for m services so as to reflect the basic interests of customers of those services, as well as the interests of the shareholders, bondholders, and employees of the regulated firms. Under rate of return regulation the task of the regulator can be stated as follows:

$$\text{Set } P = (P_1, P_2, \ldots P_j \ldots P_m) \tag{9–1}$$

subject to:

$$Z \leq r = \left\{\frac{\sum_{j=1}^{m} P_j Y_j - \sum_{i=1}^{n} W_i X_i}{K}\right\} \leq S \tag{9–1a}$$

where Y_j is the quantity of the jth service, X_i and W_i are respectively the quantity and price of the ith input, K is the stock of capital, r is the actual rate of return, and S is the maximum allowed rate of return. Z is a "minimum" cost of capital below which the return to investors, as compared with alternative opportunities at comparable degrees of risk, will be eroded.

The regulatory agency periodically sets new rates, **P**, within the rate of return constraint. The regulated firm may initiate rate proceedings if it perceives r to fall below Z in (9–1a). The commission will consider the request to increase rates to protect the interests of investors and employees and to preserve the economic viability of the firm. It sets a maximum allowed rate of return, S, to protect the customers from excessively high monopoly prices and, presumably, society from monopoly welfare losses. By keeping S and thereby **P** as low as possible, without endangering the provision of services or their quality, the regulatory agency could be viewed as moving in the direction of maximizing consumers' surplus subject to operational constraints.[1]

Among the latter, preservation of quality of service is important. For example, one key quality parameter may be the reliability of service, which means that production capacity would be sufficient to meet the anticipated demand. Since it is possible to increase profitability or to keep rates low at the expense of service quality, safeguarding minimal quality standards is designed to protect the interests of the consumers.

In theory, the commission sets and leaves the determination of rates to the discretion of the regulated company. In practice, the freedom of the firm to set rates for specific services is subject to regulatory review and is often constrained by subsidiary objectives of the regulators intended, to protect interests of specific customer groups and to ensure that quality of service is maintained. Input prices and quantity requirements are also subject to regulatory review, with the commission empowered to disallow costs which are deemed by it excessive or unjustified, thereby affecting S and **P**.

9.3. Costs, Rates, and Productivity

To establish the relationship between changes in unit costs, rates, and productivity over time we rearrange the rate of return expression in (9–1a):

$$\sum_{j=1}^{m} P_j Y_j = \sum_{i=1}^{n} W_i X_i + (Z + \pi)K \tag{9–2}$$

where $\pi = r - Z$ is the above-normal rate of return on capital. Differentiating (9–2) with respect to time we obtain:

$$\sum_{j=1}^{m} \dot{P}_j Y_j + \sum_{j=1}^{m} P_j \dot{Y}_j = \sum_{i=1}^{n} \dot{W}_i X_i + \sum_{i=1}^{n} W_i \dot{X}_i + \dot{Z}K + \dot{K}Z + \dot{\pi}K + \dot{K}\pi \tag{9–3}$$

where " $\dot{}$ " denotes the first derivative with respect to time. Rearranging (9–3) and dividing both sides of the equation by total revenue,

$\sum_{j=1}^{m} P_j Y_j$, we get:

$$\sum_{j=1}^{m} \frac{\dot{P}_j}{P_j} \beta_j = \sum_{i=1}^{n} \frac{\dot{W}_i}{W_i} \alpha_i + \frac{\dot{Z}}{Z} \alpha_K - \frac{T\dot{F}P}{TFP} + \frac{\dot{\pi}}{\pi} \gamma_K + \frac{\dot{K}}{K} \gamma_K \tag{9–4}$$

where

$$\beta_j = \frac{P_j Y_j}{\sum_{j=1}^{m} P_j Y_j}; \quad \alpha_i = \frac{W_i X_i}{\sum_{i=1}^{n} P_j Y_j}; \quad \text{and } \alpha_K = \frac{ZK}{\sum_{j=1}^{m} P_j Y_j}$$

are respectively the shares of revenues generated by the *j*th output, total factor costs incurred by th *i*th input and total costs incurred by capital out of total revenues.

$$\gamma_K = \frac{\pi K}{\sum_{j=1}^{m} P_j Y_j}$$

is the share of above-normal profits out of total revenue.

$$\frac{T\dot{F}P}{TFP} = \sum_{j=1}^{m} \frac{\dot{Y}_j}{Y_j} \beta_j - \sum_{i=1}^{n} \frac{\dot{X}_i}{X_i} \alpha_i - \frac{\dot{K}}{K} \alpha_K - \frac{\dot{K}}{K} \gamma_K$$

is the percent change in Total Factor Productivity (TFP), stated as the difference between the weighted percent changes in outputs and inputs. The weights applied to the percent changes in outputs and inputs in the productivity formula are their respective revenue shares, as defined above. This expression of TFP change corresponds to a Divisia (1926) index and is consistent with productivity derivations by Solow (1957) and Jorgenson and Griliches (1967). The use of revenue shares instead of cost shares is designed to preserve path independence of the Divisia TFP index in the case of nonconstant returns to scale in production (see Hulten (1973) and Nadiri and Schankerman (1980)). Rearranging (9–4) we obtain a statement of distribution of productivity gains:

$$\frac{\dot{\text{TFP}}}{\text{TFP}} = \sum_{i=1}^{n} \frac{\dot{W}_i}{W_i} \alpha_i + \frac{\dot{Z}}{Z} \alpha_K + \frac{\dot{\pi}}{\pi} K - \sum_{j=1}^{m} \frac{\dot{P}_j}{P_j} \beta_j. \tag{9–5}$$

Productivity gains, $[\dot{\text{TFP}}/\text{TFP}]$, represent a source of funds that could potentially be used to invest in productivity-enhancing equipment and processes; to offset increases in other costs $[\Sigma_{i=1}^{n} \alpha_i \dot{W}_i/W_i]$; to keep employee compensation rates at competitive levels; and to pay shareholders and bondholders $(\alpha_K \dot{Z}/Z)$ in order to stay competitive in financial markets.

The residual funds, if positive, can also be passed on as reduction in rates $[-\Sigma_{j=1}^{m} \dot{P}_j/P_j \beta_j]$ to benefit consumers, and, possibly, allowed to flow through to increase above normal profits of shareholders $(+K\dot{\pi}/\pi)$. If the requirements of labor and outside suppliers outpace productivity gains, largely as a result of high levels of inflation, rates for consumers will have to rise unless current profits are found to be too high. In the absence of any productivity gains $[\dot{\text{TFP}}/\text{TFP} = 0]$, inflation will produce a zero-sum gain for increased compensation among employees, bondholders, shareholders, customers, and suppliers.

To better understand the cost-productivity relationship in (9-4) let us assume what will be traditionally conceived as perfect regulation: The commission *always* sets the maximum allowed rate of return, S, precisely equal to the cost of capital Z. The regulated company manages to obtain an actual rate of return exactly equal to the allowed one. Consequently, $r = Z = S$ and $\pi = 0$. $\pi = 0$ implies $\gamma_K = 0$. The expression in (9–4) reduces to:

$$\sum_{j=1}^{m} \frac{\dot{P}_j}{P_j} \beta_j = \sum_{i=1}^{n} \frac{\dot{W}_i}{W_i} \alpha_i + \frac{\dot{Z}}{Z} \alpha_K - \frac{\dot{\text{TFP}}}{\text{TFP}} \tag{9–6}$$

According to (9–6), the regulator will let the weighted sum of the percent changes in rates equal the difference between the sum of the weighted changes in input prices and changes in total factor productivity (with the levels and changes in the actual rate of return of the firm held equal to the corresponding levels and changes in the cost of capital of the firm and changes in input prices and productivity reported by the regulated firm and audited by the commission).

Under the present system of regulation rates are allowed to change periodically following hearings and proceedings. In between regulatory proceedings, rates remain unchanged (i.e., $\Sigma_{j=1}^{m} \dot{P}_j/P_j\, \beta_j = 0$).

Consequently, in the absence of regulatory action, the system will be in "steady state" only so long as productivity advances fully offset increases in input prices; otherwise, the constraint in (9–1a) will be violated and regulatory intervention to either increase or decrease rates will be called for.

It is clear from the cost-productivity relationships in (9–4) and (9–5) that in inflationary times when productivity advances lag significantly behind increases in input prices the frequency of rate proceedings will rise. In between regulatory rate decisions, the system will be in a state of disequilibrium. The effects of continuous regulatory lags over long periods of continuously high inflation are a matter of some controversy. Baumol (1970) viewed regulatory lags as providing efficiency incentives by motivating regulated firms to increase productivity in order to minimize the erosion of earnings between regulatory proceedings. But in reality, the "make-whole mentality" prevents such gains from being realized because there is a tendency to keep costs up just before going into a rate case. Thus the regulatory lag provides only a short-term incentive, if any. In addition, with exogenous uncontrollable inflationary increases in input prices exceeding productivity gains by a factor of two or three, the potential rewards to reasonable improvements in the rate of productivity growth are likely to be perceived as minimal. Thus in the absence of some interim relief, planned investment programs may have to be delayed or existing programs may have to be discontinued.

In any case, with inflation outpacing productivity gains by a substantial order of magnitude, the frequency of regulatory hearings, and the associated transaction costs for all parties involved, rise significantly. Furthermore, other inefficiencies stemming from the "make-whole mentality" inherent in rate of return regulation may intensify. Consequently, the need to supplement the present regulatory system with interim productivity-based rate adjustment clauses appears more acute than ever.

9.4. A Comprehensive Interim Productivity-Based Rate Adjustment Clause

Based on the productivity-cost relationship discussed in section 9.3, we propose in this section a Comprehensive Interim Productivity-Based Rate

Adjustment Clause (CIPRAC) which incorporates: (1) built-in productivity incentives; (2) built-in input cost-saving incentives; and (3) built-in profit incentives. Using the productivity-cost relationship in (9–6) we propose the following interim rate adjustment clause:

$$\left[\sum_{j=1}^{m} \frac{\dot{P}_j}{P_j} \beta_j\right]^{A} = \sum_{i=1}^{n} \left[\frac{\dot{W}_i}{W_i}\right]^{\text{Std}} \alpha_i + \left[\frac{\dot{Z}}{Z}\right]^{\text{Std}} \alpha_K - \left[\frac{\text{T\dot{F}P}}{\text{TFP}}\right]^{\text{Std}} \tag{9–7}$$

subject to:

$$Z \leq r \leq S + \delta\left[\frac{\text{T\dot{F}P}}{\text{TFP}} - \left(\frac{\text{T\dot{F}P}}{\text{TFP}}\right)^{\text{Std.}}\right] + \mu\left[\left(\frac{\dot{W}}{W}\right)^{\text{Std.}} - \frac{\dot{W}}{W}\right] \tag{9–7a}$$

where

$$0 \leq \delta \leq 1; \text{ and } 0 \leq \mu \leq 1.$$

$[\dot{W}/W]^{\text{Std.}}$ is the standard for the change in unit price of the ith input; $[\dot{Z}/Z]^{\text{Std.}}$ is the standard for the change in the opportunity cost of capital; and $[\text{T\dot{F}P/TFP}]^{\text{Std.}}$ is the standard set for productivity growth. $[\Sigma_{j=1}^{m}\ \beta_j\dot{P}_j/P_j]^{\text{A}}$ is the weighted sum of rate changes allowed by the adjustment clause. The superscript "Std." denotes a standard set by the commission, and the supercript "A" denotes the adjustment allowed by the clause in (9–7), δ and μ are profit-related incentive parameters pertaining to productivity and costs.

The constraint in (9–7a) provides a way for making adjustments to the current level of the allowed rate of return (S). The adjustments could depend on the cost and productivity performance of the firm, relative to the respective standards. The cost standards and productivity standards, as well as the incentive parameters δ and μ are set by the regulators who would take quality and reliability of service into account in setting and periodically reviewing these standards and parameters. In order to avoid volatility in the rate of return adjustments, it is intended that the actual T$\dot{\text{F}}$P/TFP performance be measured by a three-year moving average and be compared with a [T$\dot{\text{F}}$P/TFP] standard which should be based on a five-year average growth rate of TFP, (or using some other method such as sum-of-the years digits) with some "stretch" for a built-in incentive. These and other practical considerations are discussed further in section 9.10. The allowed rate of return, S, is set by the commission in the course of conventional rate of return proceedings. In the interim periods between rate proceedings, rates are adjusted periodically, say, on quarterly or annual basis according to the formula in (9–7). If and when, despite the interim adjustments, the rate of return constraint is violated, either the regulator or the firm may initiate full-fledged hearings. More specific hearings, narrower in scope, may be initiated by either party to review the level of one or more of the standards or incentive parameters. Thus, in inflationary times, an interim adjustment clause is likely to reduce significantly the frequency and often the scope of regulatory proceedings, thereby reducing regulatory transaction costs. Furthermore, beyond the savings in transaction costs, CIPRAC, the comprehensive adjustment clause in (9–7), incorporates important built-in productivity, cost and profit incentives, to be discussed in detail below. The use of CIPRAC does not require any across-the-board price changes and does not involve the Commission in determining the rate structure. The firm should be allowed to set individual rates subject to the proviso that no cross-subsidy is involved. This concept, in conjunction with the built-in productivity incentives, will be shown below to have important implications with respect to pricing efficiency.

9.5. Productivity Incentives

Standards for target productivity performance $[T\dot{F}P/TFP]^{Std.}$ are set and monitored by the commission. These standards will be determined through formal regulatory proceedings and will be based on historical trends in productivity performance by the regulated firm, productivity growth records in the industry and related industries, cyclical factors, and special circumstances expected to confront the company. Sinden (1980) suggested using a "threshold formula" in which a fixed TFP "threshold" is implied. For purposes of CIPRAC we propose a flexible "threshold"—our $T\dot{F}P/TFP$ standard—which would be sensitive to the changing circumstances of the firm. If the actual productivity improvement by the company exceeds the standard, it will be allowed to convert a portion of it to higher earnings via the rate adjustment in (9–7) and subject to the constraint in (9–7a). Hence, the built-in incentive to increase productivity.

However, the CIPRAC formula in (9–7) is a two-way adjustment clause. Consequently, if factual productivity growth realized by the company falls below standard (a five-year moving average), the company would be "penalized" by lower earnings via application of the higher productivity standard in the rate adjustment formula. If the shortfall is of sufficient magnitude to cause the actual rate of return r to fall below the cost of capital, the firm may request regulatory action to increase rates. However, in the course of justifying its request for rate increases beyond the periodic increases mandated by the formula the firm will have to explain in detail its "deficient" productivity performance. If, however, poor productivity performance persists, the constraint in (9–7a) would suggest an adjustment in the allowed rate of return, unless the firm is able to keep its input price increases sufficiently below the standard.

It is important to underscore that it is recommended that the capital stock measure used in CIPRAC for the computation of total factor productivity not be adjusted for capacity utilization. This provides a built-in disincentive for unproductive overbuilding or "gold plating" of plant which would depress actual productivity performance by inflating the growth in its capital input without generating corresponding increases in output. Moreover, for the very same reasons, the incorporation of unutilized capital in TFP measures is likely to attenuate or counteract Averch-Johnson type of incentive to overcapitalize. This is particularly important in view of the fact that our rate adjustment clause allows for the possibility that the allowed rate of return will be adjusted above the cost of capital level to provide profit incentives as defined in (9–7a).

9.6. Built-In Cost Efficiency Incentives

Cost efficiency incentives are incorporated into the CIPRAC formula in (9–7) by making the allowed rate changes $[\Sigma_{j=1}^{m} \beta_j \dot{P}_j/P_j]^{A}$ a function of standard changes in input prices $[\dot{W}_i/W_i]^{\text{Std.}}$ rather than the actual changes $[\dot{W}_i/W_i]$ for $i = 1, \ldots, n$. The standards for changes in wages, fringe benefits and prices of materials, rents, and services purchased from outside suppliers can be determined by using exogenous market references for the same or comparable inputs. If the regulated firm succeeds in economizing on input prices by keeping their increases below the corresponding increases in the market reference standards of these inputs it will be rewarded by being allowed to "keep" a portion of these savings as increased earnings via (9–7) and (9–7a). By the same procedure, the firm will be penalized earningwise for a failure to keep input prices it pays at or below market levels. Hence, the incentive to economize on input costs.

In conventional regulatory proceedings, cost control is exercised through cost audits by the regulators. In practice, cost information is asymmetric and commission staffs often lack the resources and time to acquire information adequate for effective examination and audit of the reliability and reasonableness of company figures. Thus, built-in cost incentives, of the type proposed in (9–7) are likely to be an important supplementary instrument in promoting effective cost management. Better cost control should improve overall economic efficiency by reducing waste in the utilization of resources by the firm.

The determination of the standard for cost of capital changes $[\dot{Z}/Z]^{\text{Std.}}$ in (9–7) requires some elaboration. The procedures commonly employed by commissions to determine the cost of capital for the regulated firm are described by Robichek (1980). The regulator usually seeks expert testimony on the cost of equity and weights the cost of equity and embedded debt by the respective *actual* share of total book value of equity and debt funds in total obligations. Sherman (1977) has shown that this procedure may motivate strategic behavior on the part of the firm by providing it with the incentive to manipulate its equity component if it anticipates that the allowed rate of return S will be set at a margin above its perceived cost of capital Z, as usually would be the case following the procedure in (9–7a). To attenuate this problem, we recommend that, in setting $Z^{\text{Std.}}$ and $[\dot{Z}/Z]^{\text{Std.}}$ the commissions follow the practice outlined in Baron (1980) and Nichols (1955). Cost of capital standards should be set on the basis of a comparable earnings on debt and equity. Since the determination of the standard cost of capital will depend on exogenous factors only, the process will attenuate incentives for strategic behavior.

9.7. Built-In Rate of Return Incentives

The problems arising from the lack of effective built-in profit incentives in the rate of return mechanism are aptly summarized by Sherman (1980, p. 11): "Even if management of this regulated firm is faithful to the shareholders' interest in profit, there is still a problem of efficiency under rate-of-return regulation: Whereas the ordinary firm seeks only profit, the rate-of-return regulated firm has two goals. One goal is to earn profit and the other is to be allowed to keep it." The built-in rate of return incentives in (9–7a) are designed to allow the regulated company to keep a portion of the above normal profits it earned by productivity and cost performances which exceed exogenous standards for these areas and to lose those resulting from performance that falls short of these standards.

The incentive coefficients, δ and μ used to reflect the relative importance of the incentives in the rate of return constraint, are determined by the regulator subject to presentations and arguments of all parties to the regulatory process. All parties to the regulatory process can ask at any time for a hearing to review and/or change the levels of the incentive coefficients.

The agreed-upon levels of these parameters in conjunction with the productivity and other standards involved in the process will determine the strength of the respective incentives. The impact of these incentives on the upper limit of the constraint (9–7a) is *not* cumulative (as is apparent from the formula). In other words, the performance rewards or penalties will change the ceiling for r only for the adjustment period in question. For the next adjustment period the "base level" of the upper limit in (9–7a) will be the nonincentive portion S, the allowed rate of return determined during the preceding full-fledged rate-of-return proceedings plus the incentive terms for next period only. This will avert any perpetuation of rewards or penalties, which would be unfair and could seriously interfere with the maintenance of effective efficiency, cost, and quality incentives.[2]

In order to motivate management to respond to the profit incentive, it may be desirable to supplement CIPRAC with a profit sharing plan, depending upon the specific circumstances of the firm. The "surplus" profits that the regulated firm is allowed to keep as a reward for above-standard performance,

$$\delta K\left[\left(\frac{\dot{\text{TFP}}}{\text{TFP}}\right)-\left(\frac{\dot{\text{TFP}}}{\text{TFP}}\right)^{\text{Std.}}\right]+\mu K\left[\left(\frac{\dot{W}_i}{W_i}\right)^{\text{Std.}}-\left(\frac{\dot{W}_i}{W_i}\right)\right]$$

could be distributed in such a way as to help maintain and to further improve good performance.

Clearly, the incentive parameters, δ and μ should be set by the commission at levels that will assure that a significant portion of the gains realized by above-standard performance will be passed as benefits to consumers (e.g., in terms of lower rate increases than those that would have been called for in the absence of above-standard performance). Only a portion of those gains should be retained by the firm. As is now the case, the regulator of course will continue to monitor quality of service and provide appropriate incentives to maintain or improve quality and reliability. It is possible to improve productivity performance at the expense of service standards and the continued monitoring of service quality should serve to avoid this possibility.

9.8. Pricing Efficiency

The lack of incentives for efficient pricing of services in the framework of conventional rate-of-return regulation, has been extensively discussed in the literature (see, for example, Baron (1980a, 1980b) and Sherman (1977,

1980) among others). Such incentives are not adequately treated in the rate adjustment clauses which have been proposed or tried so far, because these clauses imply that the allowed rate adjustments would be implemented uniformly across the board for all services. While the solution to the RHS of CIPRAC in (9–7) yields an overall percentage rate adjustment, it is not intended as a prescription for a uniform rate change for all services. In the framework of CIPRAC, we propose that the regulated company should be given freedom to set rates for specific services in an efficient manner so long as the weighted rum of the rate increase does not exceed the percent change, $[\Sigma_{j=1}^{m}\ \beta_j \dot{P}_j/P_j]^{A}$, allowed by the adjustment formula in (9–7). While the practice will not necessarily guarantee equilibrium at Ramsey efficient prices, the built-in productivity incentives in (9–7) will motivate movement toward elasticity-oriented and more efficient pricing. (We are concerned here with the relative demand elasticities for the specific regulated services. The prices of nonregulated services will be, of course, determined competitively).

One way to improve actual TFP performance is to set the rates for specific services to be inversely related to their respective price elasticities of demand. The lower the relative elasticity, the higher the relative price of one service with respect to another. This type of pricing, if pursued, will increase the rate of growth in total output and productivity generated by a given rate of growth in total inputs. The resulting improvement in actual TFP performance will, via the interim adjustment formulae in (9–7) and (9–7a), benefit the company by increasing its earnings. Hence, the combined effect of built-in productivity and profit incentives is likely, other things being equal, to motivate movement in the direction of welfare efficient pricing. These price changes could, of course, be made subject to commission review within a specified period. This will ensure that the commission is still retaining a measure of control over specific prices.

9.9. Uncertainties and Efficiency in Planning and Control

One very important beneficial by-product of CIPRAC is the likely reduction in revenue requirements and earnings uncertainties brought about by its implementation. Rate adjustments could become considerably more predictable under the proposed rate adjustment clause than in its absence. The very complexity of conventional rate of return proceedings is suspected of having at times the potential ability to magnify uncertainties concerning the timing, size, and nature of prospective rate relief outcomes. Regulatory action as a source of risk and the relative risks borne by investors and consumers are reviewed by Sherman (1980). CIPRAC is likely to increase the predictability of earnings to the extent that underlying trends in total factor productivity and unit costs relative to standards lend themselves to more accurate forecasting than the anticipation of the timing, magnitude, and composition of the parameters of regulatory decisions in conventional rate proceedings.

The consequent reduction in earnings uncertainty that is likely to be induced by providing productivity-indexed rate adjustment clauses could have a number of positive effects. Cost of capital could be lowered due to a lower perception of earnings uncertainty. Lower levels of Z in (9–7) and (9–7a) can thus result in increased flows of benefits to consumers and/or investors. At the same time, managements of regulated firms are likely to face lesser uncertainties concerning revenue requirements. This could possibly facilitate better and longer-range investment planning. Also, improved ability to predict rate changes may enhance the accuracy of service demand forecasts, thereby providing the opportunity to improve reliability planning. Finally, regulatory commissions, through reduction in the frequency of rate cases and improved ability to predict the timing of hearings, may be able to increase the scope and depth of their periodic auditing and control functions. More resources can be devoted to study cost and productivity patterns of regulated firms to acquire more data and greater expertise in setting corresponding performance standards.

9.10. Key Issues in Choosing Productivity and Cost Standards

In this section we address some of the outstanding issues dealing with the choice of productivity and cost standards, either external or internal to the regulated firm.

Productivity is generally measured annually and it is well known that productivity can fluctuate widely from year to year. If data can be generated at more frequent intervals (e.g., quarterly or monthly) the fluctuations are likely to be even wider. If adjustment clauses are to achieve one of their primary objectives—namely, the avoidance of abrupt rate changes—it is desirable to use an average rate of productivity growth rather than the ever-changing annual values. An average over a five-year period would have the advantage that it would span a typical business cycle and would therefore be more stable over time. As new annual data become available average growth for the most recent five years should be computed and the formula value updated. The updated value should be incorporated after an annual review of the basic data in the clause. The annual review would generally be a brief proceeding in order to put the new parameters on the official record.

The relative stability of the productivity standard would tend to reduce the uncertainty inherent in the use of widely fluctuating year-over-year values and it would give the utility added lead time in planning its investment program based on the revenue potential of the anticipated rate increase. The use of seven- or nine-year sum-of-the-years digits weighting is likely to reduce the uncertainty even further.

A period much longer than five years would yield a more stable average growth rate, but it would be relatively insensitive to the most recent experience and might weaken the incentive to improve productivity on an ongoing basis. The choice of the length of the period over which averages have to be computed might also be affected by the special circumstances of the regulated firm which might warrant a shorter or a slightly longer period for averaging. The TFP moving average may be a simple arithmatic average or some form of weighted average rising in appropriate distributed lag structure such as the sum-of-the-years digits, Pascal, or some other distribution which would give desired weights to various periods.

As for whose productivity growth should be used in the formula, we argue that the firm's own historical five-year moving average productivity growth record should be used as a standard. However, a case can also be made for using an external standard based on related industry aggregates. While the latter alternative is quite appealing on theoretical grounds (see Baron (1980) for a discussion of the attractiveness of exogenous standards), the choice of the entity whose productivity should be plugged into the formula is no easy task. If, in a specific case where the necessary data are not available readily and adequate external TFP standards can be found, it would be advantageous to use the external standards.

The following menu contains the available productivity measures that might be considered as candidates.

Company level	TFP
Telephone communications	Output per hour only
Telephone & Telegraph Industry	TFP
Communications (SIC48)	TFP

Given the state of the art and the data most utilities are required to develop for regulatory audits and reviews, it is possible for the company to set up a measurement system for total factor productivity. Such a measure would be most appropriate because it would reflect the specific situation of the company.

However, there are at least three other measures that might be relevant in the case of telephone companies. The BLS publishes output per hour for telephone communications, which the New Jersey Plan had used. But the output per hour measure suffers from the basic flaw that it is a partial measure and that it is affected by the changing input mix. Thus it fails to reflect the contribution of capital and other factors underlying the productivity performance of the firm.

Kendrick and Grossman (1980) have estimated TFP for the communications sector as a whole, which includes radio and television broadcasting. Fraumeni and Jorgensen (1980) have estimated TFP for the telephone and telegraph subsector. The TFP measure for total communications is highly aggregated and would be affected by the inclusion of radio and TV broadcasting. Therefore, like other industry-wide measures, it does not adequately reflect the specific economic conditions affecting the firm because of its geographic location or other specific factors over which the regulated firm generally has no control. The telephone and telegraph subsectoral measure would also be subject to similar criticisms.

If an entity other than the firm involved is chosen, it is very important that economic ties between the firm and the standard entity be such that both are affected by the economic cycle to the same degree and that linkages between the two are strong. The basic difficulty is that such a match is very hard to find and defend in regulatory proceedings. It is sometimes argued that the standard must be based on something published by the government. However, there is no guarantee that the measures published by the government are any more appropriate or reliable than measures produced by the regulated firm under direct supervision of a professional economist. Frequently, the quality of the data available to the firm is far better and more detailed than what government agencies have on an aggregated basis.

It therefore seems more reasonable for the commission to require that a productivity study be done by the company to meet professional standards than to spend valuable resources and time in hearings on arguing about why the external standard chosen is a good proxy for the firm's productivity. As for the incentive component in the productivity standard, it might be desirable to start with the firm's own productivity estimate and add a certain fraction, which can be determined on the basis of a comparison with the industry in which the firm operates, with proper allowances for the special circumstances of the firm. It is noteworthy that the firm will be "penalized" under the CIPRAC regime for attempting to lower productivity performance so as to reduce future internal standards. The penalty arises from the fact that TFP enters CIPRAC as a general efficiency measure for determination of adjustments to the allowed rate of return applicable to the next period in (9–7a), as well as a standard in (9–7).

We have emphasized in this paper that total factor productivity, and not partial productivity measures, should be used in the adjustment formulae. There have been instances where, for lack of good data, the use of an output per hour measure for the industry was suggested instead, which would only be applied to the labor costs. However, labor costs are only a part of the total picture which includes capital, materials and services, and indirect business taxes. All these costs must be covered if the firm is to earn its allowed rate of return. Therefore, in determining an overall adjustment in prices, the formula must be based on a productivity measure that takes into account all factor inputs.

This brings us to the distinction between the well-known value-added measure of TFP and the total productivity measure which is based on gross output and all inputs including capital, labor, and materials and services purchased. It should be noted that most TFP measures for various sectors of the economy and selected industries are of the value-added variety and therefore cannot be used directly without some adjustments. This is another reason why it is better to concentrate on getting the firms to do a good job of measuring productivity than to apply arbitrary standards or measures.

With regard to the establishment of standards for input costs, we suggest that instead of using the firm's own input price indexes, one should use some external composite proxies for various input prices. For example, some of the candidates for such proxies would be:

PGNP—Measures implicit price changes in all prices in the economy and can be affected by changes in the mix of GNP.

PIFIXNR—Measures changes in prices of nonresidential fixed investment goods in the economy (including structures and producers' durables).

PIPDE—Measures changes in prices of producers' durable equipment.

PINRC—Measures changes in prices of nonresidential construction.

HOURLY EARNINGS—Measures changes in the hourly earnings of all workers in the relevant industry.

CPI—Measures changes in consumer prices (includes volatile mortgage interest rates, among other items in the basket of goods that certain urban workers buy, and includes very little of what business firms generally buy).

Clearly no single index, if used alone, would bear any direct relationship to the actual cost experience of the firm being regulated. Ideally, external standards for input prices should be set for *each* individual input rather than a composite of inputs. For the purposes of CIPRAC each standard should be weighted by its respective *actual* cost share for the firm in the test year. In well-managed companies, several input price standards are ordinarily determined with reference to or at least checked against external market indicators for purposes of setting purchasing guidelines. From a practical viewpoint, however, use of composites may nevertheless be necessary to reduce the transaction costs associated with the computation of a large number of detailed indexes. Because some reliance on external input price standards is necessary in order to preserve the cost incentives built into CIPRAC, it would be desirable to use three cost standards as follows: (1) Use changes in industry hourly earnings (based on total compensation) as a standard for inflation in labor costs; (2) use changes in prices of fixed nonresidential investment goods as a standard for the cost of plant and equipment, with proper allowances for the capital mix; and (3) use changes in the implicit GNP deflator for purchased materials and services. Certain input costs may still be treated separately if exceptional circumstances warrant such treatment, as might be the case with, for example, energy costs.

9.11. Adjustment Clauses in Telecommunications: Historical Perspective and Current Practice

There have been three attempts in the telecommunications sector to apply some form of automatic adjustment clause in the United States and one in Canada. At the present time there is only one clause in effect, namely, the one in Michigan. In this section we briefly review the U.S. experiments with a special emphasis on the Michigan plan.[3]

First, we briefly describe the New Jersey Bell Plan and the Illinois proposal which were discussed in detail in Schmidt (1980), Kendrick (1975), Latimer (1974), and Lindsay (1977). We then proceed with a detailed discussion of the Michigan Plan which is the only one currently in effect.

In December 1972, the New Jersey Board of Public Utilities Commissioners proposed an automatic rate adjustment clause, which after hearings was approved in December 1973. The plan would allow New Jersey Bell to raise prices to recover cost changes in the following four categories: wages and salaries; taxes (excluding income taxes); depreciation; and all other expenses, subject to the maximum allowed rate of return. The allowed return had been determined in a 1972 rate case. A productivity adjustment of 4 percent based on the BLS measure of *output per hour* for Telephone Communications was proposed in connection with increases in wages and salaries only. The plan, however, was challenged by the New Jersey state attorney general in 1975. Even though the New Jersey Supreme Court ruled in favor of the board, the plan was abandoned by the board in an order issued on September 15, 1975, because the Supreme Court had required that all rate increases authorized under the plan be subject to a hearing.

It is interesting to note that the board after examining the record recognized that the use of a 4 percent labor productivity growth in the Telephone Communications industry as a whole "would not be appropriate for New Jersey Bell, because it was based on national averages over a long period during relatively stable economic conditions and does not appear feasible in today's volatile economy."

In March 1974, Illinois Bell proposed another type of comprehensive revenue adjustment clause to the Illinois Commerce Commission. While the New Jersey plan was in effect for a short time and subsequently rescinded by the commission, the Illinois proposal was never sanctioned. The innovative features of the Illinois proposal include a total factor productivity based efficiency incentive and unit cost incentives. Kendrick (1975) provides a detailed analysis of this proposal. Both the New Jersey plan and the Illinois proposal constituted improvements over conventional regulation, but both had arbitrary elements and a number of other deficiencies discussed in Sudit (1979).

In 1979, the Michigan Public Service Commission staff proposed that Michigan Bell be allowed to adjust its rates according to the following formula based on increases in the CPI and a productivity standard chosen by the commission.

$$\text{\% Rate Adjustment} = .9\,[\text{\% Change in the CPI} - \text{4\% TFP Standard}] \qquad (9\text{–}8)$$

This formula is now in effect and will be reviewed by the commission in 1983 when the commission will decide whether the plan will continue beyond the initial three-year trial period.

Prior to the adoption of the plan, Michigan Bell had entered a plea for a reopener process, requesting rate relief to cover the following three specific types of cost increase: (1) wage increases for nonmanagement employees; (2) wage increases for management employees; and (3) estimated increases in depreciation that were to result from new depreciation rates effective

January 1, 1980. The commission staff proposed an automatic adjustment clause as an alternative to the reopening procedure. It stipulated that 45 percent of the increase in the CPI over the last 12 months be allowed as an automatic rate adjustment. As this proposal did not explicitly include a productivity offset, it implied that in inflationary times the firm would have higher productivity and that it would have lower productivity in periods of lower inflation rates. The commission decided that this proposal was inappropriate for Michigan Bell.

The Michigan attorney general came in with another proposal, which provided the framework for the plan which was eventually adopted. The commission agreed with the attorney general in that it would be in the public interest to implement a CPI-based rate adjustment plan. The plan calls for determining annual percentage changes in the CPI, reducing this percentage by a 4 percent offset for the productivity increases, and multiplying the resulting number by .9, representing an additional offset to balance the reduction of regulatory lag. It should be noted that the attorney general had picked 4 percent as a productivity offset on the basis of Michigan Bell's projection of TFP gain in 1979 alone.

However, the 4 percent offset was considered by the commission to be appropriate, despite Michigan Bell's exception recommending a 1.71 percent offset, which was the average annual productivity growth for the period 1973–1977. The commission also rejected the 2 percent offset proposed by the administrative law judge.

The commission explained its choice of 4 percent on the ground that it was based on the company's estimates of its own productivity growth in 1978, 1979, and 1980. This estimate was considered to be more reliable than the choice of 1973–1977 actual productivity growth which the company proposed.

With regard to the additional 10 percent offset for reduction of regulatory lag, the commission found that, while the CPI plan does not eliminate regulatory lag, it would reduce the lag-time and thus increase the firm's opportunity to earn its authorized rate of return and provide a more even cash flow. This offset was found to eliminate the need for a reduction in the company's return on common equity as proposed by the General Services Administration (GSA), and therefore the commission rejected the GSA proposal.

In response to company's request that it be made clear that this CPI Rate Adjustment Plan applies only to the company's "intrastate revenue," the commission found that this was in the public interest and agreed. The CPI Plan adjustments would apply to intrastate rates in effect as of the date of the final order in this case and to new service offerings that might be established during the next few years. This would include all tariffed items with the exception of contract portions of Dimension and two-tier offerings already entered into as of the date of the order.

With regard to when changed conditions would warrant an alteration of the company's revenues on a basis other than by the CPI Rate Adjustment Plan, the staff proposed that request for rate changes would be entertained only where the company sustains the heavy burden of proof necessary to show by a strong preponderance of evidence that it will suffer significant detriment, which will interfere with its ability to serve the public due to significant changes occurring in state or federal laws or because of court decisions for state or federal regulatory decisions which apply to the company. The commission found the staff proposal reasonable and in the public interest and therefore adopted it.

The commission set the following calendar for the plan: Hearings would open in June 1980 for the determination of the changes in the CPI from December 1978 to December 1979. The resulting change in rates, either up or down, due to the change in CPI could become effective in October 1980. The pattern of June determination and October effective dates shall continue thereafter.

The commission also found that the plan should operate for a period of three years with the last adjustment occurring in October 1982. Subsequent to October 1982, but no later than April 1983, the company must report to the commission upon performance of the CPI Rate Adjustment Plan and request alteration, cessation, or continuation. The staff would participate in these proceedings and make recommendations. All interested parties would be allowed to participate in these proceedings which were to be conducted as a contested case. No annual CPI Rate Adjustment Plan adjustment would occur in October 1983 or subsequently unless specifically authorized by the commission.

As called for by the plan, a brief hearing was held in June 1980 to determine the percentage change in the CPI from December 1978 to December 1979 (13.3 percent), which translated to a 8.4 percent increase in Michigan Bell rates, effective in October 1980. The process was repeated in June 1981 with the hearing lasting a total of 45 minutes and involving 45 pages of testimony. The CPI increase of 12.4 percent from December 1979 to December 1980 was put on the record and a 7.56 percent rate increase was authorized to go into effect in October 1981.

The Michigan plan has the following desirable properties. First, it is based on a TFP standard instead of some partial measure of productivity. The TFP standard, although too high in light of the recent average total factor productivity growth Michigan Bell had achieved between 1973 and

1977, was nevertheless set to provide an incentive for the company to do as well or better than the standard. Secondly, the plan is fairly simple to understand and implement, because it requires just three numbers, two of which have been fixed by the commission for a period of three years. The only parameter that requires annual review is the change in the CPI, which is readily verifiable and is not subject to revision once published by the BLS. Perhaps the CPI was chosen for ease of verification and perhaps because it is an official index and external to the company.

9.12. Simulation Results

In this section, we provide an illustration of how CIPRAC might be implemented. For lack of data for a specific regulatory jurisdiction, we have used the 1980 average data for the Telephone and Telegraph industry. Unfortunately, however, this does not indicate how the productivity incentive would have worked for any firms in the industry. It merely shows what data are needed for CIPRAC.

For the purposes of the CIPRAC simulation in Table 9–1 the standards for the increases in labor and materials input prices are respectively the changes in labor compensation rates for the Telephone and Telegraph industry (8.2 percent), and changes in the GNP deflator (9.0 percent) (Table 9–1, row b). The standard minimum cost of capital input increase (9.0 percent) was computed on the basis of the increase in implicit deflator for nonresidential fixed investment (row c). The cost shares (row a) are the average industry shares for 1980. The weighted cost components in row d are added to yield the CIPRAC allowed percentage increase in average input prices (8.3 percent in row e). The productivity standard (3.3 percent in row f) in this example was based on the average TFP growth for 1975–1980 in the Telephone and Telegraph industry as estimated by Chaudry (1981). Consequently, according to (9–7), the CIPRAC rate adjustment for the industry would have been 5.0 percent.

The CIPRAC results in Table 9–1 include the adjustment in the allowed rate of return (row h), assuming that the productivity and cost parameter are set by the commission respectively at $\delta = .05$ and $\mu = .05$. For this purpose we propose that the TFP performance to be compared with the standard based on the average percentage change in TFP in the last three years. This should be done to avoid the volatility of year to year changes in TFP brought about by the fluctuating economic conditions beyond the control of the firm. The cost performance, however, should refer to the current years. For purposes of computing the constraint in (9–4a) the

Table 9-1. CIPRAC Simulation Results for Telephone & Telegraph Industry—1980

		Percent Changes in Input Costs				
		Labor	Materials	Capital	Total	
(a)	Cost shares	.37	.15	.48		
(b)	Inputs price standards	8.2	9.0	—		
(c)	Capital input cost standard			9.0		
(d)	Weighted cost standard	3.0	1.4	4.3		
(e)	Total weighted standard	—	—	—	8.3	
(f)	Productivity standard	—	—	—	—	3.3
(g)	CIPRAC allowed % rate adjustment	—	—	—	—	5.0
(h)	Adjustment to allowed ROR = .05(3.1 − 3.3) + .05(8.3 − 7.2) = −.01 + .06 = .05					

Sources: U.S. Department of Commerce, Bureau of Economic Analysis. (GNP and Private Fixed Non-residential investment deflators.)

U.S. Department of Labor, Bureau of Labor Statistics (average hourly earnings in the Telephone and Telegraph industry).

M. A. Chaudry, "Productivity and Technological Change in the Telecommunications Industry," unpublished working paper (1981).

actual cost increases of the company should be compared with the weighted average of the individual external cost standards discussed at the end of section 9.10. The relative weights, of course, should be the actual input cost shares for the firm.

Based on the average industry results, CIPRAC would permit the allowed rate of return to be adjusted upward by .05 (row h). It is important to note that we have used the industry productivity standard merely to illustrate how CIPRAC may be implemented using readily available data. However, we recommend against using industry aggregates or arbitrary productivity standards for any specific company, without regard to the company's circumstances, especially when company-specific data are readily available. We have argued in this paper that a five-year average of the company's own total factor productivity growth with a small "stretch" be used as a standard. Similarly, the external cost standards should also be chosen with great care.

9.13. Concluding Remarks

The Comprehensive Interim Productivity-Based Rate Adjustment Clause (CIPRAC) proposed in this paper incorporates built-in productivity and cost incentives into the price adjustment formula as well as into the rate of return constraint. It thus strengthens all major performance incentives by rewarding the regulated firm not only by expediting rate relief via the price adjustment formula but also by providing prospects for performance-contingent above-normal profits via the rate of return adjustments. The productivity-based incentive used in conjunction with capital measures *un*adjusted for utilization tend to attenuate Averch-Johnson over-capitalization motivations. Freedom for regulated firms to price individual services within the constraint of the overall average price adjustment allowed provides incentives, within the CIPRAC framework for movement in the direction of Ramsey efficient pricing. Like other adjustment clauses, CIPRAC is also likely to reduce earnings uncertainties, thereby potentially improving long-term planning on the part of management and possibly reducing the cost of capital for the firm. The reduction in frequency and the associated transaction costs of full-fledged hearings could free commission staffs for other oversight functions, thus making regulation more effective while substantially reducing the cost of regulation.

We contend that CIPRAC is preferable to other productivity-based adjustment clauses on theoretical as well as on practical grounds. Its most attractive feature, compared with alternative adjustment schemes, is that it incorporates a more powerful and more mutually consistent set of efficiency and cost incentives which are likely to motivate the company toward greater cost efficiency, pricing efficiency, and allocative efficiency with minimal, if any, sacrifices in quality of service. A simulation of CIPRAC for 1980 price adjustments for the telephone and telegraph industry illustrates the ready availability of the informational inputs required by CIPRAC and the relative ease of its implementation.

For a specific firm, the application of CIPRAC (9–7) would require (1) five-year moving average growth in total factor productivity to be used as a standard (with a possible "stretch" added to provide an incentive to improve productivity); (2) external cost standards discussed in section 9.10 above; (3) firm's own input cost shares in the year under review; and, for use in the rate of return constraint (9–7a); (4) a three-year moving average of TFP growth; and (5) firm's input price changes. An index of the firm's actual costs can be constructed as a weighted sum of the firm's individual input price deflators, with the weights reflecting the relative importance of each unit in the year under review. These data are readily available in the productivity study data base, which contains the history of prices both for output and inputs. Thus if the company's productivity study is a part of the record, all the necessary price information is also available to the commission.

It should be emphasized that the basic CIPRAC formula (9–7) requires the use of a weighted average of external cost standards (to preserve incentives) with weights reflecting the regulated firm's own input mix. The productivity standard, however, is derived from the firm's own experience. But we suggest that this standard should also be broadened by adding a "stretch" factor, which the commission could determine depending on its view of the firm's circumstances.

Notes

1. It is noteworthy that any evaluation of the economic efficiency of public utility regulation is clouded by the fact that most regulatory commissions require the use of historical book values for the measurement of capital for setting the allowed rate of return.

2. To promote efficient allocation of resources by the firm, capital should be measured in repriced constant dollars and rates of return measures adjusted accordingly. This will require reform in regulatory practices. Nonetheless, even under current regulatory proceedings relying mainly on book costs, implementation of CIPRAC is likely to reduce waste and spur productivity gains.

3. For a review of the history of sporadic applications of productivity-based pricing in actual public utility regulatory proceedings in the United States, see Trebing (1981, pp. 385–394) and Schmidt (1980).

References

Arzac, E. R. and F. R. Edwards [1979], "Efficiency in Regulated and Unregulated Firms: An Iconoclastic View of the Averch-Johnson Thesis," in M. Crew *Problems in Public Utility Economics and Regulation*," Lexington MA, D.C. Heath—Lexington Books.

Backman, J. and Kirsten, J. B. [1974], "Comprehensive Adjustment Clause for Telephone Companies," *Public Utilities Fortnightly*, November 28, pp. 21–26.

Baron, D. P. [1980a], "Regulatory Strategies Under Asymmetric Information," working paper, Northwestern University, Evanston ILL.

Baron, D. P. and R. A. Taggart Jr. [1980b], "Regulatory Pricing Procedures and Economic Incentives," in M. Crew (ed.), *"Issues in Public Utility Pricing and Regulation,"* Lexington MA, C.D. Heath—Lexington Books.

Baumol, W. J. [1970], "Reasonable Rules of Rate Regulation: Plausible Policies for an Imperfect World," P. W. MacAvoy (ed.), *The Crisis of the Regulatory Commissions*, New York, W.W. Norton.

Chaudry, M. A. [1981], "Productivity and Technical Change in the Telecommunications Industry," unpublished working paper, AT&T Co.

Divisia F. [1926], *L'indice Monetaire et al Theorie de la Monnaie*, Societé Anonyme du Recueil Sirey, Paris.

Edwards, F. R. [1977], "Managerial Objectives in Regulated Industries: Expense-Preference Behavior in Banking," *Journal of Political Economy*, February.

Fraumeni, B. M. and Jorgenson, D. W. [1980], "The Role of Capital in U.S. Economic Growth, 1947–1976," in G. M. von Furstenberg (ed.), *Capital Efficiency and Growth*, Ballinger Publishing Company, Cambridge, MA.

Hulten, C. R. [1973], "Divisia Index Numbers," *Econometricia* 41.

Jorgenson, D. and Griliches, Z. [1967], "The Explanation of Productivity Change," *Review of Economic Studies*.

Kaufman, A. [1970], Automatic Adjustment Clauses, Naruc. Mimeo.

______ [1974], Automatic Adjustment Clauses Revisited, Naruc. Mimeo.

Kendrick, J. W. [1975], "Efficiency Incentives and Cost Factors in Public Utility Automatic Revenue Adjustment Clauses," *Bell Journal of Economics* Spring.

Kendrick, J. W. and Grossman, E. S. [1980], *Productivity in the United States, Trends and Cycles*, The Johns Hopkins University Press, Baltimore, MD.

Latimer, M. A. [1974], "The Cost and Efficiency Revenue Adjustment Clause," *Public Utility Fortnightly*, August.

Lindsay, W. W. [1977], "Automatic Adjustment Clauses as a Means for Improving Regulation," in J. L. O'Donnell, *Adapting Regulation to Shortages, Curtailment and Inflation*, Michigan State University Press.

Michigan Public Service Commission [1980], "In the Matter of the Application of Michigan Bell Telephone Co. for Authority to Revise Its Schedule of Rates and Charges, Opinion and Order," April 1, Case No. U-6002.

Nadiri, M. I. and M. A. Schankerman [1981], "Technical Change, Returns to Scale and the Productivity Slowdown," *American Economic Review* May.

Nichols, E. [1955], *Ruling Principles of Utility Regulation: Rate of Return*, Washington, D.C.: Public Utility Reports.

Ram-Mohan, S., Salve, V. and Whinston, A. [1977], "An Automatic Price Adjustment Formulae for a Regulated Firm," *Applied Economics* 9, pp. 243–252.

Re [1975], "In the Matter of Schedules Filed by the New Jersey Bell Telephone Company Increasing Basic Exchange Rates, Message Toll Rates and Charges," Docket No. 747-522, September 18.

Renshaw, E. F. [1978], "A Note on Cost and Efficiency Revenue Adjustment Clauses," *Public Utilities Fortnightly*, January 5, pp. 37–78.

Robichek, A. A. [1978], "Regulation and Modern Finance Theory," *Journal of Finance,* June.

Robinson, F. S. [1980], "Total Factor Productivity Studies as a Rate Case Tool," *Public Utilities Fortnightly*, March 13, pp. 19–24.

Schmidt, M. [1980], *Automatic Adjustment Clauses: Theory and Application*, MSU Public Utility Studies, Michigan State University Press.

Scott, F. A. [1980], "Fuel Adjustment Clauses and Profit Risk," in M. Crew (ed.), *Issues in Public Utility Pricing and Regulation*, Lexington MA, D.C. Heath—Lexington Books.

Sherman, R. [1977], "Financial Aspects of the Regulated Firm," *Southern Economic Journal*, October.

Sherman, R. [1980], "Hope Against Hope" in M. Crew (ed.), *Issues in Public Utility Pricing and Regulation*, Lexington MA, D.C. Heath—Lexington Books.

Sinden, F. [1980], "Inflation Adjustment Formulas and Efficiency Incentives," a paper presented at the Twelvth Annual Conference of the Institute of Public Utilities, Williamsburg, Virginia, Dec. 1–3.

Solow, R. W. [1957], "Technical Change and the Aggregate Production Function," *Review of Economics and Statistics* 39.

Sudit, E. F. [1979], "Automatic Rate Adjustments Based on Total Factor Productivity Performance in Public Utility Regulation," in M. Crew (ed.), *Problems in Public Utility Economics and Regulation*, Lexington MA, D.C. Heath—Lexington Books.

Trebing, H. M. [1981], "Motivations and Barriers to Superior Performance under Public Utility Regulation," in Cowing T. G. and Stevenson E. R. (eds.), *Productivity Measurement in Regulated Industries*, Academic Press.

Vogelsang I. and Finsinger J. [1979], "A Regulatory Adjustment Process for Optimal Pricing by Multiproduct Monopoly Firms," *Bell Journal of Economics* Spring.

Author Index

Ashley, Richard, 65
Afriat, S., 212,213
Al-Ayat, R., 213
Arzac, E. R., 216,239
Atkinson, S., 213
Auerbach, Alan J., 9,33

Backman, J., 239
Baird, R. N., 130,131
Balk, B. M., 64,65
Baron, D.P., 225,226,239,240
Barro, Robert J., 64,65
Baumol, W. J., 221,240
Berndt, Ernst R., 65
Blejer, Mario L., 64,65
Boylan, M. G., 130,131,160
Bradford, David F., 9,33

Cameron, Kim, 179,181
Chaudry, M. A., 236,240
Chirinko, R., 29,33
Clark, Peter, 29,33,64,65,77
Clements, Kenneth W., 64,65
Cordes, Joseph J., 16,33
Craig, C. E., 8,10
Cukierman, Alex, 64–66

Davies, Sally M., 33,35,45,46
Delbecq, Andre L., 179,181
Deloitte, 32,33
Denison, Edward F., 30,34,64–66,130,131
Dicks-Mireaux, Louis, 31,34,43,44
Divisia, F. 219,240
Dogramaci, A., 130,131,160

Edwards, F. R., 216,239,240
Eilon, S., 125–127,130,131,159,160
Eisner, Robert, 29,33
Elwertowski, Thomas C., 64,67
Erdilek, A., 130,131
Esenwein, Gregg A., 16,34

Fare, R., 212,213
Farrell, M. J., 185,212,213
Feldstein, Martin F., 16,29,31,34,44
Fellner, William, 66
Finsinger, J., 216,241
Fischer, Stanley, 64,66
Foster, Edward M., 64,66
Fraumeni, Barbara M., 15,34,38,131,230, 240
Friedman, Milton, 66
Fullerton, Don, 8,9,31,33–35,47

Glesjer, Herbert, 66
Gold, Bela, 111, 125–127,130,131,140,159, 160,144,149
Gollop, F. M., 130,131
Gordon, Robert J., 56,64,66
Gravelle, Jane G., 9,16,31,34
Griliches, Z., 219,240
Grosskopf, S., 212,213
Grossman, E. S., 230,240
Gustafson, David H., 181

Hall, Robert E., 9,16,34,38
Halvorsen, R., 213
Harberger, Arnold C., 8,34
Harper, Michael J., 30,35,50,64,67
Haskins, 32,33
Hauser, John R., 180,181
Henderson, Yodnzyeki H., 9,34,47
Hercowitz, Zvi, 64,66
Hogan, J. D., 131
Holland, Daniel M., 34,38
Hudson, Edward A., 65,66
Hulten, Charles R., 8,9,15,16,17,30,33–35, 37,39,45,46,220,240

Jaffee, Dwight, 66
Jorgenson, Dale W., 9,15,16,30,31,33–35, 38,45,46.65,66,130–32,219,230,240

Kahn, Zella L., 180,181
Kaufman, A., 240
Keeney, Ralph L., 180,181
Kendrick, J. W., 86,130,132,215,216,230, 232,233,240
King, Mervyn A., 9,31,35
Kirsten, J. B., 239
Kleiman, E., 66
Kraus, J., 10/8
Kunze, Kent, 30,35,50,64,67

Latimer, M. A., 216,232,240
Leiderman, L., 65
Lindsay, W. W., 216,232,240
Logan, James, 185
Logue, Dennis E., 64,66
Lovell, C. A. Knox, 185,212,213
Lucas, Robert E., 66
Lyle, Marilee A., 180,181

Marquez, Jaime, 66
McKee, Michael J., 66
Modigliani, Franco, 31,35,66
Myers, Stewart C., 34,38

Nadiri, M. I., 220,240
Nguyen, P., 64,65
Nichols, E., 225,240
Nishimizu, M., 212,213
Norsworthy, J. R., 30,35,50,64,67, 130,132

Okun, Arthur M., 64,67

Packer, Michael B., 161,180,181
Page, J. M., Jr., 212,213
Parks, Richard W., 64,67
Pechman, Joseph A., 35,40
Peter, Paul J., 180,181
Poterba, James, 31,34,44

Quinn, Robert E., 179–181

Raiffa, Howard, 180,181
Ram-Mohan, S., 240
Rasche, Robert H., 67
Renshaw, E. F., 240
Robertson, James W., 8,33–35,45,46
Robichek, A. A., 225,241
Robinson, F. S., 241
Rockart, John F., 179,181
Rohrbaugh, John, 179–181
Rosegger, G., 131,160
Ruch, William A., 179,181

Salve, V., 240
Schainblatt, Alfred H., 181,179
Schankerman, M. A., 220,240
Schmidt, M., 216,232,241
Schwab, Robert M., 15,19,21,31,35,40,42
Scott, F. A., 216,241
Sells, 32,33
Sheffrin, Stephen M., 16,33
Shephard, R. W., 197,214
Sherman, R., 225–227,241
Shiller, Robert, 31,35
Shoven, John B., 8,35
Sinden, F., 223,241
Skeddle, R., 160
Soesan, J., 125–127,130,131,159,160
Solow, R. W., 219,241
Stiglitz, Joseph E., 35
Sudit, E. F., 215,216, 233, 241
Sullivan, Martin A., 9,16,35,45–47
Summers, Lawrence H., 16,31,34,35
Svensson, L., 213

Taggart, R. A., Jr., 240
Tatom, John A., 67
Trebing, H. M., 241

Urban Glen L., 180,181

Vaccara, B., 132
Van de Ven, Andrew H., 181
Vining, D., 64,66,67
Vogelsang, I., 216,241

Wachtel, P., 66
Willett, T. D., 64,66
Whinston, A., 240
Wood, O., 65
Wykoff, Frank C., 9,15,17,30,35,37,39

Subject Index

accelerated methods of depreciation and tax rate, 13,17
after tax rate of return, 9,19,43
aggregate effective tax rates, 16
aggregation levels, 119
allocative efficiency, 185
Asset Cost Recovery System, 22

balance sheet accounting, 81
banking, retail branch, 170
before tax rate of return, 9

capacity estimates, 113
capacity and output adjustments, 143
capital budgeting methods—vulnerability, 141
capital formation, 5,30
capital inputs, 89,93,112
capital transactions matrix, 37
commercial aircraft, 56
computer aided design, 135,137
computer aided manufacturing, 133–158
cone measure of technical efficiency, 195
cone technology, 189,194
congestion measure of inputs, 186,193,194
congestion measures of outputs, 193
constant returns to scale, 188
corporate planning, 105
cost of capital and tax rate, 8–17
cost flexibility and cost trends, 144
cost productivity relation, 220
cost standards, 228,232
counter cyclical tax policy, 21
critique of industry averages, 110–114
critique of output measures, 113
Cronbach's alpha, 175

demand for capital, 25
direct operating costs, 143
Divisia index, 219

economic depreciation, 9–10,15
Economic Recovery Tax Act, 6
effective tax rate, 8,12,17,20,23,26,40–47
efficiency loss from inflation, 57–61
efficiency measure versus productivity, 185
electric motors, 54–55,69–71
electric utilities, study of, 200–212
energy and capital formation, 62–63
energy prices and productivity growth, 61–63, 127
errors in price measurement, 55–56
estimating direct costs and benefits, 142
evaluation of equipment acquisitions, 135, 149
expanding functional coverage, 145

factor analysis, 168
Farrell measure of technical efficiency, output based, 189,190
financial measures, 81,82
flexible manufacturing systems, 152
flow of funds approach and tax rates, 8–9
flow of services concept, 93

hierarchical clustering, 168

incentives—
  productivity improvement, 223
  cost efficiency,224
  rate of return, 225
income augmenting factors, 82–89
income absorbing factors, 82–89
inflation and taxes, 7,19,24
inflation and productivity, 49–64,99–100
innovativeness—measurement issues, 166
input congestion, 186,193,194
investment tax credit, 11,17,19

knowledgework
  definition, 161
  characteristics, 161

labor inputs, 94,95
labor productivity, 49–53,82
linkages between causes and effects of productivity changes, 116–119

machinery manufacturing plant, 120–124
management perceptions of CAM, 138
managerial objectives, 114–115
marginal effective tax rates, 6,9
materials input, 95,112
measurement error in real output, 54–57

net income and productivity analysis model (NIPA) 81–106
net present value, 147
nominal group technique, 167

organizational implications of CAM
output based weak cone measure of technical efficiency, 196
output based weak measure of technical efficiency, 191

output based weak star measure of technical efficiency, 196
output measures, 52–55,90,93,116
output measures (subjective), 161

perceptual maps, 168,174
planning horizon, 147
price deflator for private nonfarm business output, 52
pricing efficiency, 226–227
pricing of services, 215
production technology, mathematical model of 186–189
productivity based pricing, 215–239
productivity slowdown, 5,49–52
productivity versus effectiveness, 162

rate of return regulation, 217–218
reliability coefficients, 175
reliability of surrogate measures
responsibility for evaluations, 156
return on capital, 218
returns to scale, 185–186

scale efficiency, 186,195,199
significance of industry averages, 110–112
sources of CAM proposals, 140
steel mill study, 124–128
strong disposability of inputs, 187,188,193
subjective measures of output 161–179

Tax Acts of 1981 and 1982, 22–25
Tax Equity and Fiscal Responsibility Act, 6
tax policy, corporate, 5–30
tax rates, 8,23,24
tax rates, marginal effective, 6
technical efficiency, 185,189–196
time periods to study (for CAM), 147
total factor productivity, 215,219,229

weak disposability of inputs, 186,187
weighted composite of indicators, 164